CONTEMPORARY ANTHROPOLOGY

A series published with the Society for the Anthropology of Religion

Donald Seeman and Tulasi Srinivas, Series Editors

Published by Palgrave Macmillan:

Body / Meaning / Healing
By Thomas J. Csordas

The Weight of the Past: Living with History in Mahajanga,
Madagascar
By Michael Lambek

After the Rescue: Jewish Identity and Community
in Contemporary Denmark
By Andrew Buckser

Empowering the Past, Confronting the Future
By Andrew Strathern and Pamela J. Stewart

Islam Obscured: The Rhetoric of Anthropological Representation
By Daniel Martin Varisco

Islam, Memory, and Morality in Yemen:
Ruling Families in Transition
By Gabrielle Vom Bruck

A Peaceful Jihad: Negotiating Identity and Modernity in
Muslim Java
By Ronald Lukens-Bull

The Road to Clarity: Seventh-Day Adventism in Madagascar
By Eva Keller

Yoruba in Diaspora: An African Church in London
By Hermione Harris

Islamic Narrative and Authority in Southeast Asia:
From the 16th to the 21st Century
By Thomas Gibson

The Anthropology of Protestantism

Faith and Crisis among Scottish Fishermen

Joseph Webster

THE ANTHROPOLOGY OF PROTESTANISM
Copyright © Joseph Webster, 2013.

All rights reserved.

First published in hardcover in 2013 by PALGRAVE MACMILLAN® in the United States—a division of St. Martin's Press LLC, 175 Fifth Avenue, New York, NY 10010.

Where this book is distributed in the UK, Europe and the rest of the world, this is by Palgrave Macmillan, a division of Macmillan Publishers Limited, registered in England, company number 785998, of Houndmills, Basingstoke, Hampshire RG21 6XS.

Palgrave Macmillan is the global academic imprint of the above companies and has companies and representatives throughout the world.

Palgrave® and Macmillan® are registered trademarks in the United States, the United Kingdom, Europe and other countries.

ISBN: 978–1–137–52729–5

The Library of Congress has cataloged the hardcover edition as follows:

Webster, Joseph, 1985–
    The anthropology of Protestantism : faith and crisis among Scottish fishermen / Joseph Webster.
        p. cm.—(Contemporary anthropology of religion)
        ISBN 978–1–137–33653–8 (alk. paper)
        1. Anthropology of religion—Scotland. 2. Protestantism—Scotland. 3. Fishers—Scotland—Religion. 4. Fishers—Scotland—Social conditions. 5. Scotland—Religious life and customs. I. Title.

GN585.G8W44 2013
306.6—dc23   2012051226

A catalogue record of the book is available from the British Library.

Design by Newgen Knowledge Works (P) Ltd., Chennai, India.

First PALGRAVE MACMILLAN paperback edition: July 2015

10 9 8 7 6 5 4 3 2 1

For Judith

Again, the kingdom of heaven is like unto a net, that was cast into the sea, and gathered of every kind: Which, when it was full, they drew to shore, and sat down, and gathered the good into vessels, but cast the bad away. So shall it be at the end of the world: the angels shall come forth, and sever the wicked from among the just, And shall cast them into the furnace of fire: there shall be wailing and gnashing of teeth.

(Matthew 13:47–50)

Contents

Part III   Signs

Figures

Abbreviations

AoG	Assemblies of God
CB	Closed Brethren
CofS	Church of Scotland
EB	Exclusive Brethren
FPCU	Free Presbyterian Church of Ulster
OB	Open Brethren

A Note on the Text

I have made liberal use of single quotation marks throughout the book. These have been used in two different but related ways. First, they mark out local Christian terminology as distinct from the technical language of anthropology. Words such as 'witness' and 'testimony' normally appear in single quotations, as do phrases such as 'born-again' and 'the last of the last days.' Such punctuation is not meant to mock—what Csordas refers to as a 'tongue-in-textual-cheek' (1994: xii)—but is instead used to create some sense of analytical differentiation (as opposed to privilege) between local folk theology and my own argumentation. Words common to anthropology, such as sacrifice and enchantment, are not framed by single quotations. Second, single quotations are also used when directly quoting informants within a paragraph, or when indirectly reproducing local sentiments ('you're never too old for the gospel!,' 'feasting upon the Word,' and so on) that emerge from a commonly held Christian lexicon. Double quotations are only ever used when presenting quotes within quotes.

Acknowledgments

At every stage of planning, fieldwork, and writing, this book would not have been possible without the help of many different people. I am indebted to the College of Humanities and Social Sciences at the University of Edinburgh and to Downing College, Cambridge, for generously funding my research. I am also greatly indebted to Dimitri Tsintjilonis and Michael Rosie for their support and advice and to Michael for first asking 'Have you ever been to Gardenstown?' Thank you to Fenella Cannell and Maya Mayblin for their critical feedback, much of which has been used to make this a more rounded text. Thanks also go to Alexander Robertson and all those at the University of Edinburgh anthropology 'writing up' group who gave much valuable feedback, and to Laurel Kendall and one anonymous reviewer who commented so insightfully on a full draft of the manuscript.

I also need to thank John for his constant encouragement, support, and critical feedback. Thanks also go to Jane, for her encouragement, support, and exacting standards of proofreading, and to Catherine for her superb proofreading. Special thanks go to Judith for her endless sense of fun, when I was, too often, no fun at all.

Most obviously, however, thanks are due to all those in Gamrie who extended to me so much kindness and hospitality over my 15-month stay in their village. Particular thanks go to the Christian leaders in Gamrie without whose help this project would never have happened: DM, NH, GB, BJ, SH, and G. Special thanks also go to K., my landlady, who treated me with exceptional Christian kindness. Thanks also to the many people across all six churches who took me into their homes and extended to me such warm hospitality over dozens of meals and hundreds of cups of tea. It was at these times that many people shared with me their Christian experiences and it was from their willingness to do so that the real substance of this ethnography has emerged. GC; J. and M.; A. and M.; G. and M.; D. and M.; and many, many others were especially kind to me in this respect.

Heartfelt thanks go to MJ, who, despite being almost 70 years my elder, became my closest friend during my time in the village.

Looking beyond Gamrie, MC and all those at the Fishermen's Mission were very good to me during my time in Fraserburgh. Thanks also to the crews of the *Flourish* and the *Celestial Dawn* for allowing me to work alongside them, and to Z. and G. for risking having me aboard while they labored at sea.

In thanking all these people, use of initials rather than names is, unfortunately, as close as I have been permitted to come in revealing the true identities of those to whom I owe this debt of gratitude. Pseudonyms have been used throughout the main text as a more humane substitute.

Lastly, let me offer a word of apology. As with past research I have undertaken on conservative Protestant communities in Scotland, I am aware that there will be some in Gamrie, who, having shared their lives with me, will receive this book and not like what they read. I have tried hard to give a sympathetic account but am anxious that some will deem I have failed.

Prologue

This book is about 'religion.' More specifically, it is a book about Christianity, Protestantism, and a staunchly conservative blend of millennialist Brethrenism and Presbyterianism. This book is also about 'the north.' Again, more specifically, it is a book about the north Atlantic, northern Europe, Britain, northeast Scotland, the Aberdeenshire coast, and the fishing village of Gamrie. As anthropology, its theoretical and methodological approach is ethnographic and comparative. By describing something very particular—why spraying a box of fish with red dye is indicative of the imminent apocalypse—it speaks into much 'bigger' social scientific debates about religious radicalism, materiality, environment, economy, language, and the symbolic. Taken together, these debates—occurring within the ostensibly 'secular' context of contemporary Scotland—call into question certain assumptions about the decline of religion in modern industrial societies. This approach is possible because Gamrie presently stands at something of a 'unique moment,' between a history of demographic, economic, and religious security, and a future of dramatic change. Such a realization allows this book to be read simultaneously as about a single fishing village and the global processes of environmental governance, political union, venture capitalism, and religious conversion.

As an exercise in history, this book is also about how the past relates to the present and how the present relates to the future. While time is linear in this millennialist worldview, it is not always forward facing. Not only the past, but so too the future, cast long shadows over the present. The little Brethren halls in Gamrie generally had as their only decoration simple hand-painted banners displaying words of scripture. One had chosen the apocalyptic warning in Matthew's gospel as their text: 'THEREFORE BE YE ALSO READY.' Another text, taken from First Corinthians, simply read 'TILL HE COME,' a reference to the command instantiating the practice of taking communion to 'proclaim the Lord's death until he comes.' If it is this sense of 'being ready' that allows not just (past) history, but all of time, to be 'read backwards' (Harding 2000) from the point of a future event (the Second Coming), the reverse is also true, that is, the past is folded upon the present. The presentism of global, national, regional, and local events (preaching the gospel, fishing for prawns, and searching for signs of the times) are thus made sense of with reference to the dispensationalist certainties of past *and* future, the details of which have been clearly recorded, so my friends reminded me, in 'The Word of God.'

Another duality lies at the center of Gamrie's religious experience— not the temporality of past and future, but the spatiality of churches on land and boats at sea. These again exist not as binary oppositions but in a relationship of co-constitution. Where the sea provided a livelihood, boats existed as a second home for many, and for some was their first and only place of residence, making it difficult to over-emphasize the importance of these small 'floating villages' within Gamrie sociality and ontology. Because the return to dry land was a return to worship, Gamrie's obsession with churches and 'meeting halls' will also become apparent.

Insofar as this book is an explication of an indigenous ontology and its enchanting effects upon the world, it is necessarily also a book about theology. 'Beliefs' about scripture, preaching, conversion, baptism, communion, and eschatology all feature in the pages that follow. These beliefs are discussed not primarily as doctrinal propositions (although their propositional content is vital [cf. Keller 2005]) but as ways-of-being-in-the-world. Beliefs, then, are a kind of activity—they *do* things in the world and with the world, becoming a kind of sociality. In believing that the European Union is the Antichrist, a person will make certain changes, for example, to the ways that they fish, preach, read the newspapers, or vote. This book traces those actions and inflections, locally and globally.

An analysis of theological-belief-as-social-activity is part of the comparative project of anthropology. How do practitioners of different faiths live and work and worship differently in different parts of the world? How are their lives similar? This takes us to the core of the anthropology of religion, and to debates surrounding the subfield of the anthropology of Christianity. When studying a community of Scottish Protestant fishermen, is our ethnographic subject/object 'religion,' 'Christianity,' or both (Hann 2007)? Can we speak with confidence about what global Christianities have in common while also remaining sensitive to how they differ from each other and from other forms of human experience we deem 'religious'? The comparative scope of this book concentrates on Christianity within European and north Atlantic contexts, while also attending to the global south. By comparing the religious lives and livelihoods of Scottish Protestant fishermen to Catholic peasant-farmers in Spain (Christian 1972) or Portugal (Pina-Cabral 1986), or by distinguishing Scots-Brethren eschatology from American Baptist dispensationalism (Harding 2000; Crapanzano 2000), it is this project of comparison that I am pursuing.

Some have suggested that this classical anthropological quest is not so very different from the quest of Christianity (Asad 1993, 2003; Robbins 2003; Sahlins 1996). Might we speak profitably of the 'Christianity of anthropology' (Cannell 2005) in similar terms to the anthropology of Christianity? The parallels are conspicuous. Christianity produces theologians; anthropology produces theorists. Christianity is built upon the gospels and epistles; anthropology upon the writings of Boas, Malinowski, Radcliffe-Brown, and others. Missionaries go into the 'mission field' and keep journals; ethnographers go into 'the field' and keep 'fieldnotes.' Christians are confessional; anthropologists are reflexive. Christians preach; anthropologists lecture. Christians follow the Ten Commandments; anthropologists follow ethical codes of practice. Christians testify, anthropologists advocate. Christians evangelize; anthropologists may aim for 'outreach.' Both share a zeal for 'the encounter'—to make first contact with, and dwell among, the other. Both are highly logocentric, relentlessly driven on by the need to read, write, speak, study, interrogate, translate, transcribe, classify, record, report, and know.

If the residually Christian 'form' and 'function' of anthropology needs to be borne in mind when reading this ethnography, so does my own positionality as a Christian anthropologist studying Christians. While I address this issue in the introduction, it seems helpful here to reflect upon why such a state of affairs is deemed an 'issue' at all. Having presented my work on conservative Christians in Scotland fairly frequently over the last few years, I very often find in seminars that the first question I am asked is, 'Are you a Christian?' My replying in the positive usually creates a brief moment of awkward silence that is then filled by further words of clarification (sometimes requested, sometimes freely offered) about what type of Christian I am, generally explained in terms of my Anglican upbringing and my membership, as an adult, of the Free Church of Scotland. Such conversations are striking in closely resembling the ways friends in Gamrie interrogated me about my religious beliefs upon arriving in their village. At issue was the state of my soul; the anthro-theological need to peer in, to locate, to position. The solution, both for my anthropological colleagues and Christian informants was for me to 'give my testimony,' that is, a reflexive 'confession' of my faith. Insofar as anthropology can be seen as a kind of Christianity, such parallel witnessing may be of little surprise.

These issues of 'positionality' seem further heightened when the anthropologist is not only a Christian studying Christians, but studying Christians *at home*. Is such a project anthropology, analogy, or apology? Such incestuous fieldwork makes the standard processes of ethnographic 'othering' more difficult to track. Who is writing about whom? And to what end? To force a different kind of confession? To bring about a new kind of conversion? My friends and informants in Gamrie do indeed hope that those who read this book will experience born-again 'saving faith in Christ' through the 'words of witness' recorded within its pages. These hopes might seem intellectually awkward, illiberal, dangerous, repugnant, or immoral from the liberal and pluralist perspectives of anthropology, despite where the absolutist evangelistic quest of my friends is somewhat deflected by my own relativizing acts of ethnographic comparison.

Even when comparison is written (and read) carefully, with sensitivity to the local, with an eye for difference, and with the modesty to keep comparative comments toward the smaller end of the scale, it remains important to state that Scotland, despite being part of Britain, is not England. Nor is Britain, despite being part of the north Atlantic, North America (where many of the 'strangest' forms of Protestantism—from televangelists to serpent handlers—are to be found). The danger is that, in discussing what many readers will recognize as Christian 'fundamentalism,' the words and lives of those people who make up this book will be sanitized by virtue of being exoticised. While the anthropology of religion has no monopoly over this problem, the (strangely familiar) feeling of absolute otherness continues to haunt ethnographies of Christianity, doubled, perhaps, when undertaken at home. In discussing dissertations with our tutor, a strong consensus emerged that an earlier project of mine on Scottish Sabbatarianism was utterly other ('*so, so weird!*') where projects sharing this broad theme of religion (UFO worshippers preparing for alien invasions or Transhumanist efforts to achieve eternal youth via new technology) were comparatively mundane. Where African Christians who reject the Bible as a medium for divine presence by comparing its pages to toilet paper (Engelke 2007) attract this 'othering,' it is likely that Scottish Christians who reject the climate change agenda as a demonic counterfeit salvationist religion (Webster 2013) have a similar fate in store.

My hope is that, during the course of reading, this reaction will seem unwarranted. In describing and explaining the indigenous cosmology of Gamrie Christianity, this book is an attempt to answer the question, '*What does the world have to be for this to be so?*' and in answering this, it seeks to make sense of an enchanted ontology that is local and universal, material and spiritual, immanent and transcendent, and rooted in the here and hereafter.

Introduction

Gamrie, Words, Signs

It was a Monday evening in February 2009 and the end of what had been a long and unusually cold winter. Having just finished a two-hour Bible study on the coming of the Kingdom of God, the half a dozen elderly Brethren members who had attended the meeting closed their Bibles and began to share an informal time of Christian fellowship, chatting over tea and biscuits. As the evening came to an end, one of the leading men pulled on his reflective jacket, on the back of which he had written in modestly sized block capitals the phrase, 'JESUS SAVES.' Struck by the inscription and wanting to know more I said: 'I like your jacket, Gregor! Jesus Saves!' 'Oh,' he said, 'I just wrote that on the back so that someone might see it as I go about the village.' 'He's funny isn't he?,' his wife said to me beaming with admiration at her husband's quirky way of spreading 'the gospel.' Not wanting to betray the fact that I found Gregor's 'witness' a little strange, I said, 'It's good. I really like it!' 'It *is* good, isn't it?,' his wife replied, looking rather more serious. I nodded gravely and we left it at that, saying our goodbyes and heading for home.

We are in Gamrie, with Gregor, a retired fisherman in his early seventies who had worked his whole life at sea, becoming a successful skipper, and, by most people's standards, a wealthy man. But Gregor described himself not only as a fisherman, but also as a 'born-again' Christian. Raised in the Closed Brethren (CB), Gregor was 'converted through the preaching of the gospel' and later became a preacher himself. Over time, Gregor and his family distanced themselves from the CB movement, and, after two local splits, he helped reestablish the Braehead Hall as a small independent church. Despite his old age and ill health, Gregor continues to lead Braehead, preach the gospel, and 'witness' to all those around him about the saving power of the blood of Jesus. But why did Gregor spend two hours on a Monday night studying the Bible? And why was the topic that evening—the soon-to-occur apocalypse—of such immense importance locally? Why did he seek to 'testify' to the message that 'JESUS SAVES'? Why did he materialize such a message by inscribing it on his jacket? For whom were those words intended and how would they take effect?

This book attempts to understand what it is like to live and work as a 'sincere' and 'committed' Christian in Gardenstown—locally and hereafter referred to as Gamrie—a small fishing village of 700 people and six 'fundamentalist' Protestant churches, whose staunch religiosity is on the cusp of dramatic economic, social, and spiritual change. More than this, it is an attempt to show how the everyday religious experiences of Christians in Gamrie are animated by—but not reducible to—their social context by considering how local folk theologies relate to larger social processes occurring within Scotland and the north Atlantic. Arguing that religion is simultaneously ideational *and* material, my focus is upon the relationship between belief and experience—a relationship mediated, first and foremost, in and through the significance of 'The Word.' Where beliefs have objects and where objects 'have' *materiality*, beliefs are held to be essentially material. Equally, where material happenings are framed by theological (say, eschatological) *ideas*, objects and events are held to be unavoidably implicated in belief. Thus, this book presents an analytic of the relationship between local experiences of beliefs and objects, materiality, and language.

The Village

Gamrie is located on the coast of northeast Scotland, 45 miles north of Aberdeen and 15 miles west of the fishing port of Fraserburgh. The village itself clings to steep braes, creating a strange feeling that the dwellings could, at any moment, quietly slip down the cliffs and into the sea. During early pre-fieldwork visits to the area, I often felt (with some nervousness) that the village had a distinctly 'edge of the world' feel to it, this sense of isolation being reinforced by the fact that the village has almost no mobile phone signal, and by the curious glances visitors attract from inquisitive locals. The main approach road into the village winds its way past a number of huge 'fisher mansions,' moving down the brae and twisting off at bizarre angles toward the sea. The road branches at the foot of the cliff, with one track going left through the Seatown (figure 0.1) to a small, gray stone beach, and another going right, past dilapidated work sheds, to the tiny village

Figure 0.1   Gamrie's Seatown

harbor, home to the few remaining creel boats that come in and out with their modest daily catches of lobster and crab.

The older houses closest to the shore are arranged along narrow streets and feel like they are competing for what little space is available, like plants crowding each other as they grow toward the sunlight. As you wander up one street and down the next, first past the (now closed) post office, and then past the bakery-cum-general store, which sells sticky buns alongside Sellotape, the raucous sound of gulls serves as a constant reminder of the nearness of the sea. Not that such a reminder is ever necessary, with the air smelling of kelp (though not as strongly as it once used to), and strong winds bringing the salty taste of sea spray to the back of your throat. The rhythmic sound of waves breaking against the natural rock and harbor walls—which together close in upon the otherwise open mouth of the bay—give the village a sleepy feel in fair weather and a restless feel in bad. It is the sea and cliffs that define much of Gamrie, not only in terms of its striking scenery, but also in terms of its peculiar ambience and physical remoteness.

Despite the fact that Gamrie was set within a very rural region, with the newest houses at the top of the brae backing onto acres of farmland, Gamrics are quick to define themselves as a breed apart from their farming neighbors (cf. Cohen 1987: 108). Farmers were said to have an easy life compared to the working life of fishers—they did not work as long hours, always had the benefit of being near family and home comforts, and most importantly, never had to face the adversities of the sea. More than this, their moral character was said to be questionable; they drank heavily and used foul language and always worked on the 'Lord's Day'—'Sunday is just another day to them,' one informant told me with a real sense of scandal. Worse still, the churches that farmers went to (if they went at all) were thought to be hopelessly 'liberal'—'they're nae evangelical, church is a social club to them!' was a common comment used to write off farmers as apostate; 'their ministers are nae even saved; they dinna preach the Bible!'

Such rhetoric was said to be backed by historical precedent. When the ('liberal,' 'farmer') Gamrie Parish Church closed in 1992, the normal procedure would have been for the existing membership to simply transfer their 'lines' to the nearest Church of Scotland (CofS) congregation, in this case the ('evangelical,' 'fisher') Gamrie Kirk. But the elders at the Gamrie Kirk, convinced that many of those in membership at the Parish Church were 'unsaved,' asked them to join not by 'transfer' (a bureaucratic formality) but by profession of faith, that is, *as if new converts*, by going before the Kirk Session to 'testify' to how they had become 'born-again' believers. Perhaps unsurprisingly, everyone refused. Some now attend the (less strongly evangelical) Macduff Parish Church, while many simply stopped attending church altogether (this latter reaction further confirming to the Gamrie Kirk Elders that they were right to have been cautious). Such stories highlighted the 'deep spiritual divide' that was said to exist between the 'worldly' farmers and (in the words of one of my farming informants) their 'toffee-nosed, holier-than-thou' fisher counterparts.

This divide, although seldom articulated openly, ran deep, and was keenly felt by both sides, especially amongst children in the school playground and on the football pitch, where all socializing was conducted along occupational lines. There was almost no inter-marriage between the two communities as a result, with country folk said to find husbands and wives at Young Farmers' Clubs and fishers traditionally courting within the village's Kirks and meeting halls. Fishers and farmers also engaged in different leisure pursuits—farmers frequented pubs inland while Gamrie fishers generally avoided such places, spending what little time they had onshore at home with family. Fishers and farmers also had different shops. The Gamrie Spar ('Roy's Shoppie') was located in the village, sold no alcohol, and did not open on a Sunday. The Netherbrae Shop ('Cloudy's'), located a couple of miles out in the country, served the farming community, had a large stock of alcohol, and was always open on a Sunday.

The link between Gamrie's status as a fishing village (16 percent of Gamrie's workforce are currently employed in the fishing industry[1] compared with less than 4 percent in agriculture [SCROL 2001]) and the intensity of its religion will be an important theme throughout the book. Not only is the link strong historically—Brethrenism spread with the return of the herring fleet from England in the 1920s (Meek 1997)—but also in the present. 'Folk explanations' emphasized how going to sea meant risking your life on a daily basis; with men frequently injured or lost overboard, fishermen were said to be uniquely aware of their own mortality and thus their dependence upon God in times of peril. Where God was said to be 'protector,' he was also described to me by locals as 'provider.' Hunting invisible shoals of fish led men to rely on methods of filling their nets that sometimes fell outside the 'natural' limits of seabed mapping: 'When you're fishing, it's the Lord that puts the fish in...we haul [the nets] every two hours and we have to thank God for what we get, whether it's small or much,' one man explained. Such sentiments remained strong, especially where increasing competition for (and concentration of) quotas combined with the biting effects of a global recession—with fuel costs soaring and fish prices achieved at market failing to keep up.

Other local circumstances were important. Past experiences of serious poverty when fish stocks migrated away from British waters were said to have 'thrown people onto God's mercy.' I heard stories of 'godly old ladies receiving a word from God' to leave a pot of soup or a sack of potatoes outside so-and-so's backdoor only to hear how that particular household had been saved from hunger as a result. The precarious nature of making a living from the sea was said to foster not only a keen sense of God's leading and guiding,' but also created a close-knit community that was held together by shared worship as much as by shared hardship: '*Everyone* went to church in those days,' people would tell me. Less 'spiritual' explanations were also offered. Religious intensity owed much to a physical proximity attributed to Gamrie's history as a fishing village. The old fisher cottages, tightly packed among the cliffs backed onto one another; by looking out of your kitchen window you might easily look into someone else's bedroom. This gave rise to a strong sense of the community living in each other's pockets: 'In Gardenstown your neighbors are so close at hand that you hardly need to raise your voice' (Smith 1988: 204), commented one guidebook.

Such nearness was said to intensify an already strong 'small village mentality' by adding an additional layer of public moral surveillance. Certain places and spaces were monitored with particular closeness: Roy's Shoppie, the doctor's surgery, the harbor, the entrance to the hotel (and, by extension, the pub), and, of course, the Kirk and meeting halls. Local folk always knew where fellow Gamrics had (and had not) been and this was quickly extended to my own movements around the village. 'I didn't see you out at the Kirk on Sunday Joe—were you out somewhere else?' or 'How did you get on at the Watt's house—I saw you heading up their drive,' were typical lines of questioning. While nonattendance at church was particularly visible, as was frequenting the pub, Gamrics had a more general fascination with other people's business, to the point where many had binoculars resting on their window ledges, ostensibly for looking at boats in the bay, but which people also used (in my company) to see what others were up to further down the brae.

Anthropology, Religion, Christianity

The enterprise of theorizing 'religion'—a task that this book is also involved in—is not new, with many of the 'founding fathers' of sociology and anthropology giving much attention to observing, recording, classifying, and eventually defining the phenomenon we call 'religion.' The (perhaps immodest) quest of these men was to unearth the origins and latent functions of religion as a universal or natural human phenomenon: Marx (1977) told us that religion is alienating false consciousness; Tylor (2010) told us that religion is about belief in supernatural beings; Durkheim (2008) told us that religion is the worship of society by its members; Freud (2001) told us that religion is a kind of neurosis; Weber (1977) told us that religion is socially enacted values and ideals; and Geertz (1973), following Weber, told us that religion is a cultural system.

As will become clear, my primary theoretical sympathy lies with Max Weber and with the emphasis he places on the interrelationship between ideas and institutions, especially concerning economics and religion. I take my cue from Weber in other ways as well. In tracing the links between local experiences of life as a fisherman and life as a Christian, some of what I describe will echo Weber's (undoubtedly nebulous) thesis of 'elective affinity' (Weber 1968: 341). Drawn from the language of early nineteenth century chemistry and from

Goethe's novel *Elective Affinities* ([1807] 2008), this term—used by Weber to describe sociological association or attraction and thus a tendency to combine—is helpful in understanding the changing fortunes of Brethren fishing communities along the Aberdeenshire coast. Equally, in choosing 'enchantment' as a central trope with which to make sense of Gamrie ontology and cosmology, I again invoke Weber (1978c), this time with reference to his work on modern disenchantment. What I refer to by enchantment is a sense of life as animated—*made alive*—by constant intimate interaction with divine forces and cosmological purposes, that, try as one might, one cannot escape.

E. B. Tylor's definition of religion, now almost a 140 years old, also fits well with the ethnographic context of Gamrie, as well as my own understanding of what religion is. Asad (2003) and Ruel (2001) show how a *belief*-centric definition of religion is often a *Christian*-centric definition, and my sympathy toward Tylor is undoubtedly related to the fact that I am a Christian studying Christians. Christians, particularly (but by no means exclusively) evangelical Protestants, do indeed invest heavily in 'belief.' Yet, for many such Christians, religion is not 'belief in spiritual being*s*,' but belief in *a* spiritual being—God. Thus, although religion can be said to be 'belief in God,' for many evangelicals, belief may be defined more closely as 'faith,' and, more closely still, 'God' may well be spoken of as 'Jesus Christ.' This formulation—*'religion is faith in Jesus Christ'*—is clearly Christian-centric and thus runs the risk of seeming 'repugnant' (Harding 2000). Nevertheless, the resistance to a more general (comparative) category of 'religion' is not of my own making but taken from expressions of religiosity local to Gamrie. Consider the following extract from a Brethren sermon I heard preached by Sam:

> We're not really interested tonight in religion, because religion hasn't saved a soul—we're interested in *reality*! What would you offer God [on the Day of Judgment]? Your sincerity? It's not enough! It's only by *faith* that you are saved! Your religion? My friend, please don't do that—you still need to be saved...You need to be saved!

Where Sam makes a deliberate effort to subsume 'sincerity' and 'religion' into what are, for him at least, the much more potent rubrics of 'faith' and 'reality,' what is needed is a critical interrogation of this 'reality.' Where evangelicals speak broadly about 'faith,' anthropologists, perhaps even more broadly, still speak of 'belief.' Ruel's (2001) etymological history of the term is insightful. Where early (pre-Christian) usage of the term *pistis*[2] simply meant 'trust' or 'confidence,' the use of the word *pisteuo*[3] in the New Testament acquired a distinctly technical sense—'to believe' came to refer to an almost procedural notion of conversion. Crucially, such 'conversion' no longer simply referred to the personal trust of *pistis*, but also to trust in an event—that of the resurrection. Essentially:

BELIEF = PERSON + EVENT

Or rather:

BELIEF = JESUS + RESURRECTION

Later, the Early Church established a body of beliefs which, once codified by the Council of Nicaea, became orthodoxy, any deviation from which was heresy. The term continued to develop in the Reformation period through an emphasis on the interiority of personal faith. Thus 'belief' moved from trust in persons, to convictions about events, to corporately held orthodoxy, to the inward experience of faith (Ruel 2001: 101, 111). We can, therefore, rework Ruel's definition of belief as:

BELIEF = PERSON + EVENT + ORTHODOXY + INWARD EXPERIENCE

Or rather:

BELIEF = JESUS + RESURRECTION + CHURCH + FAITH

The core issue here is the way in which 'beliefs' find their mode of expression—that of utterly sincere and committed conviction. Žižek agrees, stating that ''fundamentalism' concerns neither belief as such nor its content; what distinguishes a 'fundamentalist' is *the way in which he relates to his beliefs*' (Žižek 2006: 385. Emphasis added). In essence:

> 'Fundamentalism' enacts a short-circuit between the Symbolic and the Real, that is, in it, some symbolic fragment (say, the sacred text, the Bible in the case of Christian fundamentalists) is *itself posited as real* (to be read 'literally,' not to be played with; in short, exempted from all dialectic of reading). (Žižek 2006: 386. Emphasis added)

Protestant Fundamentalism is *a religious anti-hermeneutic* (Marty and Appleby 1994), relating to its beliefs not as a 'symbolic fragment' but as a complete and perfect reality. 'We're interested in reality!,' the Brethren preacher shouted from the front of the hall. Thus we no longer have:

BELIEF = JESUS + RESURRECTION + CHURCH + FAITH
But rather:
REALITY = JESUS + RESURRECTION + CHURCH + FAITH

Where the previous five formulations seem to describe Ruel's (2001) understanding of the historical development of Christian theology in general, it is this sixth and final formulation that comes closest to describing the religion of Gamrie and thus the thematic content of this book. But how is this reality experienced by local Christians? And how might it be given an anthropological formulation? Some partial answers are sketched below as a way of opening the door to further discussion by covering the four overarching themes that run through the entire book, namely; words, immanence, imminence, and enchantment.

Words

How do words work and what are their effects? For the Christians of Gamrie, everyday religious life is experienced first and foremost through words and language. By 'words' I do not simply refer to the written 'Word' of scripture, nor to written words in general, but to all those words that are written and read, spoken and heard, subvocalized and thought, that together form language in general and religious language in particular. Where the ideational content of language within the Protestant context is well rehearsed (especially in terms of the theological content of 'belief'), what seems somehow less obvious is the material properties of words and language. I draw here upon the work of Coleman (2000, 2006, 2010) and Keane (2002, 2004, 2006) to show how words work insofar as they are not only unavoidably implicated in material *processes* but themselves have material *properties* and thus achieve real effects (cf. Austin 1962).

Immanence

How do spiritual realities come to be experienced as near and with what effects? Where Gamrie's Christians experience the world as controlled by God and the devil, my aim is not only to problematize the assumption that Christianity in general and Protestantism in particular is a religion of transcendence marked by a 'radical discontinuity' (Cannell 2006) between spirit and flesh, but to further suggest that immanence and transcendence co-constitute each other through the everyday interaction of words, bodies, and material objects. In speaking both of the 'immanence of transcendence' and the 'transcendence of immanence,' I deploy familiar Christian notions of the here and the hereafter but in the less familiar contexts of everyday objects (such as domestic appliances) and political eschatology (the European Union [EU], Israel). My aim here is unashamedly an anthropological cliché: to render the mundane things of the everyday as exotic (my washing machine is God's near presence) and the exotic things of the cosmos as mundane (the kingdom of satan is the Common Fisheries Policy).

Imminence

How are spiritual realities experienced as soon to occur and with what effects? Where the Christians of Gamrie divided over many theological and ecclesiastical issues, one thing that united all six places of worship was a deeply held attachment to the eschatological certainty that we were living in 'the last of the last days.' My aim here is to show how the present, when set against the distant (eternal) future, far from abolishing the near future (Guyer 2007), is actually reliant on this temporal middle ground as the very site where the eschaton is actively waited upon. In showing how the imminence of the eschaton shaped not only the search for 'signs of the times,' but also fed into intergenerational evangelism, the public preaching of the gospel, personal acts of 'witness,'[4] the frequency of demonic attack, and the success or failure of the Scottish fishing industry, this theme grapples with anthropological understandings of time, materiality, politics, and language.

Enchantment

How does the religion of Gamrie enchant the world and how does this enchantment relate to the disenchantment of Gamrie's non-Christian 'others'? Drawing on Weber's (1977, 1978a, 1978b, 1978c) notion of disenchantment as a 'loss of plasticity'—whereby one is robbed of the perception that life is cosmologically *rooted to* and *driven by* a unified sense of ultimate value—as well as Gell's (1992) work on magical efficacy, I suggest that the 'magic' of enchantment is seen in its conflation of sign and referent. Far from representing a basic philosophical error, such a conflation is, for my friends, simply a matter-of-fact recognition of a real state of affairs. I use the term 'enchantment,' then, to describe the process whereby the world is 'made alive with a kind of magic.'

This approach presents some important differences to Taylor's (2007) recent account of enchantment and disenchantment. Why was it 'virtually impossible' not to believe in God in 1500 when by 2000 such unbelief, for many, became 'inescapable' (Taylor 2007: 25)? Taylor answers by listing three hallmark assumptions of the 'premodern condition' now lost in our modern era: first, that the order of nature testified to God's 'purpose and action' in the world; second, that the order of society was conceivable only insofar as it was 'grounded in' God and His worship; and third, that 'people lived in an "enchanted" world of…spirits, demons, and moral forces' (Taylor 2007: 25–26). This movement from the premodern to the modern is, for Taylor, synonymous with the movement from enchantment to disenchantment, also indicating a profound reconfiguration in the ways we apprehend our own selfhood. Where our ancestors had 'porous' selves, vulnerable to meanings, forces, and objects outside the mind, we moderns now have 'buffered' selves, invulnerable to the spirits of old, being masters of our own internal meanings and ultimate purposes (Taylor 2007: 37–38).

I find this last idea, namely that enchantment produces a certain type of personhood, very stimulating, and will return to it in a later chapter. My contention here, however, is that Gamrie (and many other contemporary 'Western' societies), is both modern and enchanted. If 'pre-moderns' have no monopoly over enchantment, then it also seems plausible that they have no monopoly over porous selfhood; moderns too can be 'vulnerable to spirits, demons, [and] cosmic forces' (Taylor 2007: 38). This is because, finally, for religions defined by immanence and imminence, enchantment (unlike propositions about God's sovereignty over nature or society), exists not as a *feature of* belief but as the primary experiential *precondition for* belief. Thus, I argue that—in Gamrie today—preachers become the voice of God, the Bible is literally alive, and fishermen catch not only prawns but also the souls of men.

The role accorded here to materiality is central. The referent, that is, the 'Real' object, is accorded the kind of agency normally only attributed to human actors. While this is nothing new in the Christian tradition (aprons, holy water, and the incorruptible remains of the saints have been healing the faithful for centuries), I show the contemporary Protestant tradition as no less implicated in enchanted materiality than the Christian traditions of 'the premodern' era. Where the (Reformed) theological literature might cry 'idolatry' (Calvin 2007), the (modernist) sociological literature has tended to cry 'fetish' (Marx 1971). My own position seeks to avoid both of these judgments (as well as Taylor's 'pre-modern'/'modern' dichotomy) by examining how contemporary experiences of enchantment set up real relationships to the 'Real'—established in and through the deployment of words, bodies, and other objects.

Anthropology and Theology

Within the anthropology of religion, the absence of a strong and vibrant anthropology of Christianity has gone largely unnoticed until relatively recently. Apart from a few early exceptions, conventional anthropological wisdom had been to view Christianity as a religion that was both uninteresting and threatening. In terms of being uninteresting, Robbins (2003, 2006) and Cannell (2005, 2006) both suggest that anthropology decided some years ago that it knew what Christianity was about and needed to delve no deeper. Christianity was the Christianity of Weber's Calvinists—ascetic, dogmatic, individualistic, and driven by the interiority of cognitive belief and the exteriority of wealth accumulation. Christianity was as dull as Augustine was joyless (Sahlins 1996). If familiarity breeds contempt, the development of an anthropology of Christianity was always going to struggle, and just as much for cultural reasons as theoretical ones (Robbins 2003). Christianity, and particularly evangelical Protestantism, had been dubbed 'the repugnant cultural other' (Harding 1991). Thus, in terms of being threatening, Christianity was perceived to be deeply unsettling to the project of liberal secularism with which anthropology was often associated.

Further explanations for this hostility toward Christianity can be unearthed by looking at the history of anthropology. Anthropology was born, not only out of the 'monster' of political and economic imperialism (Asad 2003), but also out of its more spiritually minded sister institution, the Church, and her (sometimes no less 'monstrous') heralds, the missionaries. The desire to sever these colonial links was due not only to a political guilt complex, but also to the fact that anthropology desired to define itself as a 'science' that was utterly unlike the quintessentially metaphysical pursuits of theology. In this sense, anthropology ignored Christianity, in order to ignore theology, in order to ignore metaphysics, in order to define itself as a science. Because anthropology and theology were held to offer mutually exclusive accounts of humanity, anthropology distanced itself from Christianity because its theology existed, in Douglas's terms (1966), as an 'anomalous' and, therefore, 'dangerous' mix of familiarity and difference (Robbins 2003). To maintain this distance, anthropology sought to define Christianity as an 'impossible religion,' that is, as purely 'a religion of transcendence' (Cannell 2006: 43). Where anthropology tends to privilege the study of what people do rather than merely what they think about (Robbins 2006), and where Christians were seen as not really *doing* anything, Christianity was affirmed as a religion that was tediously consumed with belief and doctrine, and as lacking the excitement of the 'weird' and 'wonderful' rituals of the more 'primitive religions' so typified by Malinowski's 'savages' (1926, 1927). What is needed, it seems, is an enquiry into anthropology's own 'theological prehistory' (Robbins 2006), and a concerted effort to reevaluate the place of Christian theology within ethnographic accounts.

Thus, this book will examine the relationship between belief and experience. My concern is to describe and explain the folk theology of the Christians of Gamrie and in so doing, to analyze the relationship between the intellectual content of their religious beliefs (Keller 2004, 2007) and their experience of everyday religious life (cf. Jenkins 1999). By focusing upon enchantment—and by comparing and contrasting it to disenchantment—I take my cue from Weber insofar as I emphasize the central importance of ideas in shaping material experiences. Yet where Weber was concerned primarily with soteriology (and specifically with the Calvinist theology of salvation through predestination), my interest in the role of ideas is more general. In addition to examining different forms of soteriology, I also examine folk understandings of divine presence, demonology, eschatology, and local articulations of the doctrine of scripture throughout the book. Further, where Weber's intent was sociological, insofar as he sought to show how predestination had impacted upon the society and economy of much of Western Europe, my intent, being anthropological, takes a somewhat smaller scale. At times, then, I limit my scope to the local, to Gamrie, and its immediate coastal vicinity. At other times my focus is much broader, examining social and economic processes occurring nationally and globally.

A wider concern with the ways in which beliefs are created by the worlds in which they occur frequently draws my focus away from my (otherwise strong) commitment to analyzing the enchanting power of ideas and toward more materialist concerns. This too can be found in Weber, who, after all, was not just interested in the Protestant *ethic* but also in the development of *capitalism*. Here, the object under the anthropological lens is not theology but fishing. By looking at local experiences of the enchantment of labor—of trawling for prawns in the North Sea—I am, at the same time, looking again to the 'bigger picture,' that is, to issues of modernity and modern personhood. Attending to modernity, however, also requires that some attention be paid to what Weber frequently refers to as 'tradition' (Weber 1978d: 296). Does modernity—trawling for prawns on a truly industrial scale—bring 'detraditionalization' (Heelas, Lash, and Morris 1996) in the same way as rationalism is said to bring disenchantment? Might modernity herald 'the end of tradition' (Connell 1978)? Are the 'certainties' and 'securities' of 'communal' village life—'sustained by way of socialization within a closed environment' (Heelas, Lash, and Morris 1996: 4)—alive or dead? Are such 'traditional' forces immutable realities or delusional fictions?

In seeking to answer such questions by giving attention to the catching and sale of prawns, I show how the conceptual world of ideas (providence, testimony, and witness) is unavoidably implicated in the materiality of objects (boats, nets, diesel, and money). Yet, the role of materiality (and its relationship to theology) is not limited to fishing for prawns. Words too are regarded as enchanting objects not only through language, but also through the body. Words, and their relationship to language and the body, bridge my treatment of theology and fishing. This approach provides ethnographic and theoretical insights insofar as words and 'the Word' are of interest to both the anthropology of religion and the Christians of Gamrie. The subject (and object) of this analysis is language itself, that is, the shared concern for the importance of words, and, in the ethnographic context of northeast Scotland, their enchanting relationship to Protestants and prawns.

The Ethics of Methods and the Methods of Ethics

A number of years ago, during a discussion about religion in Scotland, a colleague said to me, 'Have you ever been to Gardenstown? You should go—there's an awful lot of religion going on in a very small place.' My interest piqued, I paid the village a visit when staying with family in the area. Having counted three churches in as many minutes as we drove to the bottom of the brae, I quickly decided that this would indeed be a good place to study conservative Protestantism in Scotland. Discovering another smaller church as we walked around the Seatown confirmed this, and I began to visit the village on weekends to attend Sunday services. The atmosphere of those early services made a strong impression on me. The slow doleful notes of the electric organ, the elderly ladies in their head coverings, the wall hangings declaring man's perilous spiritual condition outside of Christ, the long prayers, and the even longer sermons that communicated this same message of damnation and salvation with an emotional intensity, I had more readily attributed to American televangelists. It all seemed so foreign and exotic—and less than 30 miles from my own family home.

By my third or fourth visit to Gamrie I was clear in my mind that this was where I wanted to conduct an ethnography about Protestantism in Scotland, so I set about getting access the only way I knew how—by writing letters to the churches. To the Brethren, I wrote:

Dear Brothers,

I am...planning my fieldwork research into the Anthropology of Christianity in the northeast of Scotland...with a special focus on the various Christian communities of Gardenstown. By looking at the different churches in Gardenstown, I hope to gain some insights into how the daily life of the Christian is experienced in Scotland today.

I should also say that I am a committed Christian, having been blessed with Christian parents who brought me up to be a believer. I have for a number of years been a member of the Free Church of Scotland in Edinburgh. My choice of research into Christianity in Scotland comes out of something of a personal spiritual interest. Because the project will be an extended piece of work, I want to be able to reflect upon my own faith during the research process, rather than self consciously exclude it from my studies. I wish to show that the whole lived experience of the Christian is not a matter of arbitrary moralistic lifestyle choices but a matter of deliberate engagement with a personal faith in Jesus Christ; [...] the study would seek to listen rather than to assume, it would attempt to understand rather than to argue, it would seek to empathize rather than to judge.

If the study is to proceed, it requires the cooperation and good will of those whose lives I will seek to study. [...] Ideally I would hope to live in Gardenstown for an extended period of time (anything up to 18 months), and become over this period a part of the different Christian communities in the town. I would undertake to accomplish my work in a non-intrusive, respectful and confidential manner. [...] I hope...you and others at the Hall would be willing to participate. I am deeply aware that responding to my request will involve expenditure of time and effort on the part of those who participate.

Thank you for considering my request. I look forward to hearing from you.

Yours sincerely,
Joseph Webster

Having written to all six churches in the village, I quickly received positive responses from both the Gamrie Kirk and the Free Presbyterian Church of Ulster (FPCU). After a longer period of time I also heard back from one of the leaders at the Open Brethren (OB) who said he and others at the fellowship would be willing to participate. I never heard back from any of the three CB fellowships (Braehead, Seatown, and High Street) and assumed that establishing access to them would be very difficult. Despite this setback I proceeded to communicate with the Kirk, the FPCU, and the OB, requesting accommodation with a household within one of their congregations. I very quickly received an offer to lodge in a spare room of a local school teacher in the village—a divorced woman in her fifties who was a committed member of the local Kirk, but whose children and grandchildren did not live in the village. Once the details were arranged, there was nothing left to do but move into the village and begin the fieldwork proper, which I did on September 10, 2008.

Having moved into the village, I quickly fell into a routine based around the rhythm of writing, going for walks, and going to church. A typical day would start around 8 a.m. I would walk through the village to buy a morning paper and meet several others doing the same and pass the time of day chatting (in this way buying a paper could take anywhere between 15 minutes and an hour depending on who I met). I would come home and spend the remainder of the morning writing up notes from the previous evening's service and then take a walk down to the harbor where I would invariably meet some of the church elders who tended to take their walks together. In the afternoon I would visit elderly Christians in the village for a 'fly cup' where we would drink tea, talk about church events and current affairs, or sometimes read the Bible and pray. Evenings were the busiest and most structured part of any day where I would be out at a service or meeting almost every night. By week two of the fieldwork, I had established where each place of worship was and when all their various meetings were held. I actually drew up a rough timetable to make sure that I circulated around them fairly consistently so as not to favor one place and neglect others—something that became important as informants became more possessive of my time and attendance at *their* place of worship.

Unsurprisingly, much of my time was spent attending public worship and other church organized events. I would attend these meetings anywhere between seven and ten times a week, roughly four of which would be on a Sunday. As well as the main Sunday services (morning and evening) I would attend breaking of bread services, home Bible studies, church Bible studies, Bible readings, ministry meetings, prophecy meetings, Sunday and midweek prayer meetings, church rallies and conventions, missionary meetings, singing nights, gospel outreach meetings, and church socials as well as more informal men's breakfasts, coffee mornings, 'soup and sweet' fundraisers, church after-school clubs, church youth clubs for teenagers, and men's get-togethers for the retired.

As well as these explicitly 'church based' field sites I also worked across a range of other spaces. A month after arriving in Gamrie I attended a memorial service in Fraserburgh for several fishermen who had been lost during an onboard fire. The service was run by the Fishermen's Mission, and after asking around, it became clear that volunteering at 'the Mission' would be a good way to meet people, particularly since I was interested in the connections between Christianity and the fishing. Within a few weeks I had managed to set up a 'placement' at the Mission where I would shadow the 'Mission Man' and generally help out around the center. It was here that I met many folk with Gamrie connections who had left the village to find work. My work at the Mission turned out to be very fruitful, allowing me to collect many different people's 'born-again' 'testimonies.' I also volunteered at a drop-in centre for Filipino fishermen run by local Christian skippers. My time at the Mission also opened up two additional field sites—the fish market, and latterly, the boats themselves. On several occasions I went down to the early morning markets in Fraserburgh to chat to the fishermen, merchants, and auctioneers and photograph the various goings on, usually accompanied by Cameron, the 'Mission Mannie,' which made my presence easily explicable.

A few months before I left the village, for a week in September and a week in October 2009, I finally got the chance to work on the trawlers. Both skippers were Gamrie Christians (as were some of the crew) and both boats structured their entire working week around not going to sea on Sunday. These two separate week-long trips provided very rich and interesting data on many of the themes of the book, helped by the crew dynamic onboard, with discussions about binge drinking and sex, broken up with hymn singing, 'testimony,'[5] and debates about creationism and evolution.

Other field sites included the Gamrie harbor and summer café, Roy's Shoppie, Broden's Bakery, and various key informants houses. The Macduff harbor café also proved to be a good place to meet people, as did the Fraserburgh harbor. I could enter all of these places sure in the knowledge that sooner or later someone I knew would turn up for a chat. Much of my data was gained through these 'chance encounters' where people would stop to swap stories and 'muse awa.'

Within a relatively short space of time I had met and was on friendly terms with several of the leading men at the three CB fellowships and had started attending their services as well as those of the Kirk, FPCU, and OB. With access to all six churches established, I began to consolidate these relationships while also forming new ones with Christians from other nearby towns and villages, not only from Fraserburgh, but also in Macduff (a small fishing port, but with a large shipyard owned by a Gamrie Kirk elder) and Banff (home to one of the few successful charismatic churches in the area). I also had contacts in Sandend and Findochty to the west (where I knew some Brethren and Cooneyite Christians), and Peterhead and Boddam around the coast to the east (home to many independent evangelical churches).

The months seemed to pass slowly—I gradually filled a shoe box with little notebooks covered in worn brown parcel paper, each with the title 'Sermons' and then a number. I was on 'Sermons 39' with a week of fieldwork left. Each contained about ten thousand words of fieldnotes from church meetings and the 'daily round.' This routine of walking, chatting, drinking tea, and worshipping changed very little throughout the 15 months of fieldwork. Some of the more informal midweek meetings closed down over the summer as the evenings got longer and lighter and the men spent more time out in their creel boats fishing for lobsters. While this did give some sense of a seasonal round to the spiritual life of Gamrics, things continued, by and large, unchanged. At various points it became clear to me that my weekly routine had slipped rather seamlessly into that of a retired man. Getting the morning paper, going for walks round the harbor, collecting tiny sea shells along the tide line of the beach, popping into folk's houses for a fly cup, and going to the bakery at lunch time all became big events and rather second nature to me.

Intriguingly, despite the fact that I was about 50 years too young to be adopting such a lifestyle, nobody seemed to find it particularly odd, or if they did, they were too polite and shy to say. One of my few regrets was not having a dog to walk; it would have made being out and about in the village even easier—although not many of the older men kept dogs and did not seem to need one as an excuse to go for a wander. Perhaps the one thing that marked me out as a young person was my mode of transport—a jet black Vespa ET4 with full chrome tubing front, back and sides. Interestingly, this seemed to cause much more amusement than did spending most of my time with the elderly; a church goer riding a Vespa seemed to be more odd to my informants than a Vespa-riding Church goer, that is to say, it was the Vespa and not my 'old mannie' lifestyle that seemed to be the odd one out, especially given my own identity as a committed Christian. It is to this identity that I now want to turn.

One of the last pieces of advice I received before going into the field was 'Treat your fieldwork like a romance—you have to fall in love with them and you have to make them fall in love with you.' I left for the field knowing that the former was almost certainly going to be easier than the latter. In a sense I was already in love with the village with its little harbor and creel boats; the cliffs and seashore; the tiny Brethren Halls tucked away in amongst the old fishing cottages; the bakery that advertised Brooke Bond tea as if it were still 1950; the elderly men in twos and threes, walking bent over along the coastal path—it all seemed straightforwardly romantic. What I knew would be more challenging would be gaining the trust of Gamrie's Christians, who had a reputation for being shy and private people in the main, made more so by the religiously separatist strictures of much of their Brethren heritage. The solution, as far as I saw it, was two-fold: telling people I was a Christian and acting like other local Christians did.

First, then, I had to make it clear that I was a committed Christian by telling people so. 'So are you a Christian?' was the question that very often came when speaking to people in the village about my work (in a similar vein to the questioning of colleagues in anthropology who also generally require a personal biographical explanation for my choice of research topic). Having preempted the question, I attempted to spell out the answer in my earliest communication with Gamrie's key religious gatekeepers. This (written and spoken) claim to being a committed Christian, while clearly key to gaining access, was not straightforward or unambiguous, either to myself or my informants. Seemingly endless doctrinal and denominational divisions exist among conservative Protestants, producing just as many different shades of religious self-identity. Such variation inevitably caused (not uninteresting) confusion among my Christian informants, some of whom saw me as 'soundly saved' and 'a Brother in the Lord' and asked me to take full part in their religious lives. Some of them even asked me to preach to them (a request I carefully declined for fear of souring relations with other churches with whom they had bad relations). Others saw me as a Christian, but were unconvinced by my commitment. 'Are you *born-again*?'; '*When* was it exactly that you were saved?'; 'But do you really believe what *we* believe?'

My identity as a member of the Free Church of Scotland—a Presbyterian denomination in the Calvinist tradition—was both a help and a hindrance. With no Free Church near the village, local Christians did not find it odd that I was attending other churches. Yet attending six churches at once left me in an ecclesiastical no man's land—free to cross the boundaries (particularly of dress code and Bible version) that existed between them, but not fully involved in any one fellowship. Such vagaries occasionally caused conflict and embarrassment—experiences that were unpleasant in the moment but later turned out to be ethnographically insightful. For example, without realizing it at the time I created something of a stir in the local OB fellowship by attending Breaking of Bread meetings and actually receiving the bread and wine. One of the leading men supported my doing so, while another was strongly against it because I had not been baptized into their fellowship as an adult member. Others were unsure what to think. Things came to a head at the start of a Breaking of Bread service when one of the leading men asked me in private not to participate, saying that the sacrament was for baptized members only, further requesting that I did not tell anyone that he had made such a request. In the end, I did as he asked, neither partaking in the elements nor explaining my not doing so in relation to his request.

This and other encounters like it show that while I did speak about myself as a Christian, such words left some in the village unconvinced as to my salvation. What mattered more was conforming to a certain kind of Christian lifestyle by taking very specific steps to ensure my public conduct closely matched local expectations about what it meant to be a Christian. Most obviously, I was completely teetotal when in Gamrie. Despite living less than ten yards from the only pub in the village, I still, to this day, do not know what the inside of that building looks like—such was the strength of feeling against alcohol, and to drinking in public in particular. While this closed some doors (most notably the door to the pub and its ethnographic insights), it kept other doors open, namely the churches and the houses of those who attended them. Thus, just as someone conducting research within a women's refuge might find it difficult to maintain their access if they were to be regularly seen taking their leisure time in local strip clubs, I decided that frequenting Gamrie's pub would have required me to sacrifice a great deal of my access to Gamrie's Christians. More than this, it was also made clear to me that my 'Christian testimony' would be called into question ('*spoiled*' locally) if I was seen to associate too closely with certain people known to be alcoholics or drug users, as well as those involved in Gamrie's biker scene. Wherever possible, I did speak to these 'transgressive' groups, but always whilst bearing in mind the potential cost to other (more primary) research relationships.

In treating my fieldwork as a romance, then, I sought to 'court' the village—and especially its Christian residents—through a mixture of soft speaking and kind action. I always made sure to pay attention to the content of sermons, asking theological questions to communicate an interest in what was being said; I prayed aloud in prayer meetings (where permitted to do so according to denomination) to index the 'realness' of my own 'personal' faith; I volunteered at local youth clubs and gave my 'testimony' to the teenagers present when asked to do so by other leaders; I never drank or smoked or used foul language; and of course, I went to church more than anyone else in the village.

Over time, the results were striking, with local people (Christian and 'non') seeming to adopt me, almost universally, as 'an affa good lad.' Most of those I came into contact with in the village initially assumed I was living in Gamrie because I was training to be a Christian minister—and no matter how many times I assured people that this was not the case (explaining that I was a trainee anthropologist not a trainee minister), this locally intelligible identity simply stuck. For those in the village who knew me best and understood I was doing research at a 'secular' university, many continued to stubbornly assert that I would eventually quit anthropology and become a minister. One friend from Fraserburgh actually 'prophesied' over me, saying that the Holy Spirit had revealed to him that being a minister was my spiritual destiny.

Being the first person ever to have regularly worshipped at and befriended all the different Christian fellowships in Gamrie, several of my informants told me that they believed God had brought me to the village to unite the six churches as a precursor to revival. 'You are doing God's work,' I was told; 'you probably can't see it, but you *are*,' was their earnest assessment. When it finally came time to leave the village, the Kirk held a surprise goodbye party in my honor, inviting all the various denominations to attend. While it was said to be a remarkable ecumenical triumph that some members from one of Gamrie's (usually strictly separatist) CB fellowships attended, people also commented on some notably absent figures. Some of the key leading men stood to say a few words in my honor, again voicing the belief that I had done much to unite the Christians of the village. We sang a parting hymn and several of those present (myself included) began to tear up. And with the hugs, handshaking, and best wishes over, it was time to go home.

The assessment that I was 'doing God's work' was not just made with regard to the local village context but was also said to apply much more widely. My informants often sought to remind me that what I wrote in my book could, from their perspective, have a profound spiritual impact upon those who read it; it could cure their 'spiritual blindness' and 'bring them to saving faith.' People would pray in church meetings not only for me, but also for my book—that it would bring glory to God and expand His Kingdom. The longer I lived in the village and the closer I became to the Christians of Gamrie, the more extensively both my physical presence and academic work was appropriated back into the enchanted Christian cosmos of local believers. As far as my informants were concerned, God's bringing me to the village and His sending me out again was an act of 'providence' that united their local 'witness' and spread their global 'message.'

As I write this book, I am acutely aware that with such sincere friendship—backed by deeply felt religious emotion and expectation—comes with it a felt obligation to write a story that does not simply speak *about* the lived experience of the Christians of Gamrie, but *for* that experience. But it is commonly held within the social sciences that being an anthropologist and being an apologist are very different (even mutually exclusive) tasks. This is, by and large, a view that I share, and as a result, I do not see it as my job to 'preach the gospel' or 'teach the Bible,' regardless of my 'committed subject position' (Howell 2007) as a Christian anthropologist studying Christians. Nor, however, do I seek, as I described in my first letter to the churches in Gamrie, to 'self consciously exclude it from my studies.' My aim remains to 'show that the whole lived experience of the Christian is not a matter of arbitrary moralistic lifestyle choices but a matter of deliberate engagement with a personal faith in Jesus Christ.' Where I then spoke (in local terms) of examining 'personal faith in Jesus Christ,' I remain committed to the substance of this enquiry, but seek to undertake it through the sociological and anthropological lens of 'society,' that is, through the expressions of the community, in preaching, testifying, fishing, and watching for signs of providence, attack, and the end times.

As a result, some of what I will say in the chapters that follow may appear to some as 'too theological.' In treating the content of sermons or eschatological speculations as just as important as their cultural form, it may at times appear that I am more interested in the 'how' question than the 'why' question. In a seminar, when trying to explain *why* a woman named Elsa was weeping to the point of speechlessness in a public prayer meeting when praying for the salvation of the souls of her grandchildren, my answer was, and remains, because she sincerely believed that God would send her grandchildren to eternal punishment in hell unless they repented and became born-again Christians.

Whether we talk of 'folk theology' (Coleman 2000), 'ethno-theology' (Scott 2005), 'collective representations,' (Durkheim 2008) or 'belief' (Needham 1973) seems to matter little when attempting to grapple with the issue about how to deal with (that is, interpret) behaviors that we choose to define as religious. What matters more is providing an explanation that takes seriously the relationship between (a) indigenous cosmology (my grandchildren are going to hell unless they respond to the gospel) and (b) human action (public weeping). This is not to suggest in any simple way that (a) always provides a straightforward causal explanation for (b), just that the content of (a) needs to be considered alongside the content of (b) especially in a local Protestant context where theological 'truth' and Biblical literacy were held up to be of paramount importance, not only in the lives of individuals, but also in the lives of the village, the nation, and the world.

Yet much of what I say in the following chapters will almost certainly be deemed to have missed the point by my Christian informants, and although they would probably use the phrase 'man's fallen wisdom' rather than the phrase 'too anthropological,' the sense of indictment would be entirely the same. By suggesting that preaching is a kind of sacrificial eating of the totem, many of my informants will surely shake their heads at my abominable heresy and be left wondering if I listened to a word of what they had said to me during my 15 months in the village. And yet while this reaction might perhaps be expected (as may the reverse charge of being a 'theological apologist'), I want to suggest that both of these reactions may be helpfully brought into conversation with each other in an attempt to produce a new kind of ethnographic knowledge. What is needed is what Charles Taylor (1985) has called a language of perspicuous contrast. It is worth briefly lingering on this point in an attempt to see its import for bringing theology and anthropology (or indeed 'committed' Christians and 'secular' social scientists) into conversation with each other. In discussing the difficulty of cross-cultural understanding, Taylor has this to say:

> Although there is a strong temptation to by-pass agents' self-descriptions arising from the strong pull of the natural science model, any attempt to do so is stultifying, and leads to an account which cannot

be adequately validated. [...] The interpretive view, I want to argue, avoids the two equal and opposite mistakes: on one hand, of ignoring self-descriptions altogether, and...on the other hand, of taking these descriptions with ultimate seriousness, so that they become incorrigible. [...] But if not in their terms, how else can we understand them but in our own? Aren't we unavoidably committed to ethnocentricity? No, I want to argue, we are not. The error in this view is to hold that the language of cross-cultural theory has to be either theirs or ours. [...] But as a matter of fact, while challenging their language of self-understanding, we may also be challenging ours. [...] In fact, it will almost always be the case that the adequate language in which we can understand another society is not our language of understanding, or theirs, but rather what one could call *a language of perspicuous contrast. This would be a language in which we could formulate both their way of life and ours as alternative possibilities in relation to some human constants at work in both*. It would be a language in which the possible human variations would be so formulated that both our form of life and theirs could be perspicuously described as alternative such variations. (Taylor 1985: 123–125. Emphasis added)

Where Taylor envisaged his 'language of perspicuous contrast' being applied to the efforts of social scientists seeking after cross-cultural understanding, not only do I want to apply his model to this anthropologically conventional task, but I also want to take his idea a step further. My desire is to see not only the Christians of Gamrie brought into conversation with those who read this book, but, more than this, I seek to bring anthropology into a conversation with theology via the voices of those who inhabit its pages. I have sought to achieve such a dialogue by deploying a range of terms—some used by anthropologists, some by theologians, and some by both—to describe different ways of life 'as alternative possibilities in relation to some human constants at work in both' (Taylor 1985: 125). Many of these terms have already been discussed: 'words,' 'the Word,' 'testimony,' 'witness,' 'conversion,' 'sacrifice,' 'providence,' 'immanence,' 'imminence,' and 'enchantment'—these are the tools by which I hope to build up a picture of 'cross-cultural understanding' (Taylor 1985: 124) and cross-disciplinary dialogue.

Where Robbins and Engelke in their introduction to *Global Christianity, Global Critique* (2010) have suggested that putting 'Christian...categories back at the centre of debates about how to think about society and its potential transformation' has permitted 'critical thinkers not just to think *about* religion but also...*with* it' (Robbins and Engelke 2010: 625), it is my aim that by deploying a 'language of perspicuous contrast' throughout the chapters of this book, I might be able to bring something productive out of the two-fold charge that this book is 'too theological' and/or 'too anthropological.' The intention, of course, is that it be neither of these things, but instead would exist as an account of life, that, being constructed out of a language of anthro-theological 'give and take,' can make sense of what life is like as a Christian in a Scottish fishing village, not only by writing about religion, but also by writing with it.

Outline of the Book

Chapters 1 and 2 seek to situate Gamrie within its context. Chapter 1 addresses the historical and social context of the village by looking at different accounts of local history and at the recent sociological themes occurring within Christianity in Scotland. The churches as they exist today are described (theologically and in terms of church practice) as are the 'other Gamrics,' that is, those communities in the village who have little or nothing to do with the life and work of the churches. Chapter 2 considers how Gamrie is under three types of pressure—economic, demographic, and eschatological. In referring to this 'triple pinch,' I describe how Gamrie is facing economic uncertainty, demographic decline, and eschatological oblivion. I also pose a series of possible counter explanations for social change in Gamrie to show how the broader sociological picture, far from being one-dimensional, is actually made up of a complex constellation of social, economic, political, and religious currents.

Chapters 3, 4, and 5 examine the relationship between worship and 'The Word.' In the first part of Chapter 3, I examine two types of sermonizing—'preaching' and 'teaching'—and show how these map onto two different categories of persons—the unsaved and the saved. By asking the question 'why preach the need to be 'born again' to 'born-again' believers?,' I go on to show how, far from being a hermetically sealed event, sermonizing always requires the postulated existence of its opposite—'saved' persons at gospel preachings and 'unsaved' persons at Bible teachings. I end the chapter by suggesting how this requirement is eschatological in nature.

In the second part of Chapter 3, I shift my attention from speaking to listening and hearing. Where preaching was said to be an act of reverent worship, I argue that worship can be understood as a kind of sacrifice. Taking a new perspective on 'traditional' anthropological understandings of religious sacrifice as necessarily involving some form of eating (Robertson Smith 1972), I suggest that, in sermonizing, what is 'eaten' is not flesh but words. In this sense, hearing a sermon, while not construed as an entirely passive act, is also not experienced as an active negotiation between speaker and listener as equals. The aural relationship here is shown to be distinctly hierarchical, primarily concerning one's (personal) relationship with God, transforming preacher into prophet and congregant into a silent consumer of words.

Chapter 4 draws on fieldwork among Scottish fishermen and examines the performance of 'giving testimony' (the story of becoming 'born-again') as akin to Christian confession. Utilizing Susan Harding's evocative suggestion that conversion is not just conversion to a religion, but also to a language, I argue that it is by 'sincerely' testifying to a shared religious orthodoxy that the self is both known and made knowable. Key to communicating the sincerity of this performance is the public expression of gendered emotion as a 'folk' method for the unmaking and remaking of persons through embodied confession. Conversion narratives are not just directed toward the speaking self but are also explicitly concerned with the listening other. 'Giving testimony,' then, is also about 'bearing witness'; it is part of a larger programme of evangelism that seeks to challenge and thereby transform the identity of the hearing other.

Chapter 5, on the lived experience of trawling for prawns in the North Sea, is based on fieldwork conducted during two trips while working as a deckhand during my last winter in the field. In this chapter, I bring together my material on sermons and testimony to show how Gamrie's deep sea prawn trawlers can be 'read' as representing the village in miniature. Where both the 'saved' and the 'unsaved' were forced into physically close and relationally intense quarters, I show how the usually fixed religious and social boundaries of the village were constantly drawn, crossed and redrawn out at sea in a 'zero-sum game' of evangelism and counter-witness that magnified the daily politics of personhood while also bringing them into sharper relief.

Chapters 6 and 7 examine the relationship between religious immanence/imminence and enchantment, considering how encounters with God and the devil—in everyday life and in fulfillment of Biblical prophecy—constitute a challenge to the suggestion that modern life is experienced as disenchanted and secular. Chapter 6 examines local experiences of 'divine providence'[6] and 'demonic attack,'[7] showing how life resembles an enchanted struggle between God and the devil, with the Christian placed awkwardly in the middle.

In Chapter 7, I move from stories about the (enchanted) lives of individuals and their families to much larger concerns about the cosmic conflict between God and the devil being waged at the level of international politics. By making links between local fascination with and support for Israel over and against local fears concerning the EU, my aim is to show the multifarious nature of local eschatological anticipation, arguing that such a view of the future can only be understood when proper attention is given to how Gamrics experienced their present as 'the *last* of the *last* days.'

I conclude the book by discussing the relationship between words and objects and suggest that it is only by paying attention to the absolute and incommensurable (Lambek 2008) value of 'The Word' that an accurate picture of the enchanted religious experiences of the Christians of Gamrie is gained. Where it is the Bible that animates the enchantment of the logocentric cosmology of my Christian informants, it is this 'Word' that is shown to animate their religious lives. By arguing that the Christians of Gamrie inhabit an enchanted world within a disenchanted village, I suggest that it is this incommensurability that defines the lived religious experience of my informants. By framing my understanding of enchantment through the notion of consubstantiation—used in Eucharistic theology to explain how the body and blood are materially present *alongside* the bread and wine—I suggest that the cosmos of Gamrie's Christians is defined by the enchanted holism of the immanence and imminence of transcendence. Finally, it is the loss of this holism in the lives of Gamrie's non-Christian 'others' that defines the disenchantment of their own apparently 'secular' cosmos, while threatening to sound the death knell of the religion of Gamrie within the next generation.

Part I

Gamrie

Chapter 1

Situating Gamrie

Gamrie's history has been shaped by two dominant forces: religion and fishing. According to one of my informants, himself an amateur historian, the village of Powistown was renamed Gardenstown in 1721, founded by Peter Garden as a fishing village. While the village received its first mention in parish records in 1190 (the parish being called 'Gamrie'), the land was initially developed when a church dedicated to St. John was constructed to mark the place where, according to legend, the Scots defeated an invading Danish army in 1004. At this time (and for the next 350 years) Scotland was under the religious control of the Roman Catholic Church with Christianity having been first brought to Scotland by St. Columba in 563 during his efforts to convert the native Picts.

After the construction of St. John's churchyard, it was not until the mid-1500s that the official break with Rome was made during the Scottish Reformation. The religious and political upheaval of 1560 (which birthed the CofS in the same year) saw the rejection of the authority of the Pope, the outlawing of the celebration of the Mass, and the eventual instating of the (staunchly Calvinist) Westminster Confession of Faith. Yet, by 1582 the CofS was already experiencing its first internal fissure, with a section of the denomination leaving to set itself up as the Scottish Episcopal Church.

By the 1600s things began to change again (first in Europe, then nationally) with the development of Biblical Criticism. This form of thought was given its earliest voice in the *Theologico-Political Treatise* of 1670 in which Spinoza contended that the Bible was a natural text to be subjected to the rigors of intellectual reason and not interpreted through 'faith' via 'revelation.' Spinoza's approach gained credence with two key eighteenth century Enlightenment thinkers in Germany—Reimarus (1694–1768) and Griesbach (1745–1812)—who further developed the concept that the Biblical text was the product of a long history of human religious tradition and not of divine authorship (see Schweitzer 2009). Such ideas sent shockwaves through the strongly Reformed theology of the CofS, and, at the point where these new creeds converged with the arrival of the Scottish enlightenment by the mid-1700s, the liberalization of Scottish religious life seemed largely irreversible.

These pioneers of Biblical Criticism, as well as key figures in the Scottish Enlightenment such as David Hume—although not the subject of conversation among the Christians of Gamrie—were responsible for clearing an intellectual path that latterly opened up the way for a much more famous (and locally infamous) nineteenth century naturalist, Charles Darwin, to expound his views on the genesis of the human race. With his publication of *On the Origin of Species* in 1859 came the (essentially reactionary) formation of the Protestant 'fundamentalist' movement in America in the twentieth century, with opposition to the theory of evolution (described by some as 'the religion of the Antichrist') as one of its central tenets.

The 'Disruption' of 1843 (birthing the Free Church of Scotland from a major split within the CofS) set the tone for a period of 150 years of schism and popular revivalism across Scotland. With the Disruption came a significant weakening in the power and influence of the CofS, the national Kirk, which had been dominant in the northeast since the Scottish Reformation of 1560, subject only to limited regional competition from the (more moderate, Anglican) Scottish Episcopal Church, and, to a lesser extent, from Methodism. With many CofS Parishes in the west highlands experiencing secession, it became easier for Aberdeenshire fishing communities to openly express long-standing resentments toward their national Kirk. Ministers serving in the CofS were seen by many Gamrics as 'incomers,' who, having received an overly intellectual (and insufficiently 'spiritual') theological training at a secular university in one of Scotland's urban centers, came to their village with a misplaced sense of authority and superiority. Such men were resented for their educational background and scorned for being strangers to the physical labor of deep-sea fishing. The experience of being ruled over by a nonlocal Kirk minister was uncomfortable for many fishermen long accustomed to governing their own lives at sea. While the Scottish Episcopal Church retained supporters among the land owning gentry of inland Aberdeenshire, and the (staunchly Calvinist) Free Church grew rapidly among impoverished crofters in the highlands and islands, the fishermen of Scotland's northeast coast—lacking the cultural capital of Episcopalianism and resisting the theological autarchy of the 'Free Kirk'—was yet to find its own ecclesiastical 'glass slipper.'

Extrapolating from local origin myths, in the eighteenth and nineteenth centuries, something very close to a 'perfect fit' occurred between Gamrie's Christian fisherman and the (then new) Plymouth Brethren movement. Founded in Ireland in the late 1820s by John Nelson Darby (originally a curate in the Church of Ireland) and others, the group established their flagship church in Plymouth in 1831 (Coad 1968), arriving along the Aberdeenshire coast in the 1850s and 1860s (Dickson 1997). It took 70 years for this new millennialist sect—heavily influenced by Darby's dispensationalist eschatology—to gain any real foothold in Gamrie. A breakthrough occurred in 1921 when herring shoals migrated away from Scottish waters. A poor fishing season resulted, bringing serious economic hardship to the village, forcing Gamrie's fishermen to work English waters to fill their nets.

It was during what came to be called 'the 1921 Herring Revival' that Gamrics first came into contact with the 'open air' gospel preaching of the Brethren as they landed their catches in the harbors of Plymouth, Portsmouth, and Yarmouth. What they heard was a message of personal salvation and ecclesiastical separation, backed by an apocalyptic urgency that cast the present as 'the last of the last days.' Being Arminian, their salvationist message focused on the centrality of human volition—of *choosing* Christ'—thereby rejecting the Calvinistic predestinarian view of salvation by election proclaimed by their Presbyterian rivals, placing the onus instead onto each individual to respond to the 'preaching of the gospel' during these 'end times.'

This eschatology was (and continues to be) closely akin to the (strongly futurist) premillennial and pre-tribulationist dispensationalism Harding (1994, 2000) describes in her work with fundamentalist Baptists. Indeed, it was J. N. Darby who invented dispensationalism—the view that all human history can be divided into distinct 'dispensations,' determined by God's differential dealings with humankind on the basis of His establishment of different Biblical covenants. It is difficult to overestimate the importance of this theology locally; much of what makes life in Christian Gamrie 'enchanted' is the acute sense that not only is God immanent—spatially *close at hand*—but He is also imminent, that is, temporally *soon to arrive*. This combined assertion of the closeness and 'soon-ness' of divine (and demonic) forces made Brethrenism—and, over time, Gamrie—'alive with a kind of magic.'

Other elements of Brethren theology were important. A fully lay ministry was required—having professional clergy was a sin against the Holy Spirit insofar as it failed to recognize that God spoke through *all* saved men. In further contrast to Presbyterianism, communion ('Breaking Bread') was to be celebrated not once or twice a year, but *every* 'Lord's Day' morning, with anything less said to be willful disobedience to scripture. This 'act of remembrance' could be presided over by any 'soundly saved' Christian man; the elements being 'purely symbolic' required no liturgy, no consecration, and crucially, no minister. Yet, this symbolic view did not render materiality unimportant. The physical resurrection, for example, was stressed by all Brethren preachers, and cremation of the dead was condemned not only as a pagan practice, but also as a failure to properly anticipate the literal truth of 'the raising of the dead' on 'the last day.'

The 'doctrine of separation' was also a central feature of the Brethren message. All other Christian denominations were rejected as apostate by those early preachers who stood in the fish markets proclaiming escape from the coming judgment. Other aspects of social life were similarly treated—converts were generally discouraged from working with non-Brethren, for example, and marriage outside the group was prohibited. Politics was rejected as evil, with many Brethren to this day choosing not to vote as a matter of conscience. Latterly, newspapers, radio, and television were all shunned as 'worldly,' as were, in practice, much of the arts (most especially dance and instrumental music). This deliberately exclusionist platform left little room for ambivalence; those Gamrics who encountered Darby's followers were (rhetorically) presented with two choices—stay in the Kirk and burn or come out and be saved. It was after the 'Herring Revival,' during the 1930s, that many of Gamrie's fishermen made their choice. Conversions often occurred in blocs, first within individual boat crews, then spreading to immediate and extended kin (Meek 1997: 138). With large numbers leaving the Kirk to join the Brethren, the movement quickly established itself as a major player on the local religious scene.

Yet, despite what some of my more zealous Brethren informants wanted me to believe, this fundamentalist spirit cannot simply be attributed to the divine revelation given to J. N. Darby. Indeed, it seems that everything that had occurred up until that point—internationally, nationally, and locally—had been building to provide ideal historical conditions for the Brethren to flourish. The Reformation, breaking with Rome, began to assert the need for mass Biblical literacy over and against the public performance of religious ritual. This promoted the validity of individual interpretations of the Bible. The Enlightenment carried this process of personal discovery of (in this case Biblical) knowledge even further, and began the process of combining the search for material evidences of (literal and historical) Biblical inerrancy with the theology of dispensationalism and the eschatological search for 'signs of the end times.'

Nineteenth and twentieth century factors also played a part. The memory of the Ulster 1859 Revival ensured that spiritual awakenings were 'programmed into the mind-set of many east-coast fishermen' (Meek 1997: 138). It was through this same lens of religious fervency that the First World War—ending in the deaths of 15 million globally—was viewed as a sure sign of the coming apocalypse, sensitizing many to Darby's dispensational vision of the 'end times.' This was matched with a more general swing toward fundamentalism: the urgent need to have a personal 'born-again' conversion experience joined with the establishment of scientific six-day creationism as the theological response to the claims that evolutionism (ironically, like dispensationalism, itself a product of enlightenment thinking) had 'disproved' the Bible (cf. Harding 2000: 217).

Yet historical factors do not give a full explanation for why Brethrenism flourished. The sociology of 'elective affinity' provides another perspective, especially in making sense of the relationship between theological ideas and economic livelihoods. The material world of science and nature (omnipresent in the lives of men working at sea) were embraced as indexes of divine presence; individual conscience and the primacy of personal conviction became the highest court of appeal in all matters of religion; a patriarchal system of church governance was combined with a highly devolved system of leadership that placed all men in positions of equal authority over each other (and over female members)—permitting every man within this 'society of petty entrepreneurs' (Dickson 1997: 161) to aspire to be 'his own skipper' not only at sea, but also in church.

With each man in authority over everyone, no man, in effect, had the power to tell any other man what to do. Men who had taken orders from nobody during their working week at sea, only to come back to shore to sit under years of autocratic preaching by a lettered 'incomer' at the Kirk not only resented formal, educated, professional, top-down church leadership (cf. Just 1988), but were now being told that such ecclesial structures were blasphemy, and that it was their duty, as Christian *men*, to lead a newly revived 'body of believers' in whatever direction the 'Spirit of God' prompted. So powerful was the 'natural attraction' between the cosmologies of

Brethrenism and fishing, and so strong was their 'tendency to combine' (Howe 1978) that, between the 1860s and the 1940s, over 30 (Open and Closed) Brethren halls formed along the northeast coast alone (Dickson 1997: 164).

Religion in Scotland: Recent Social Themes

Over the last 50 years, churches in Scotland have moved from being one of the country's most influential institutions, to one squeezed by fierce competition. One explanation might be that Scottish churches have been increasingly affected by moral and cultural liberalization, while also becoming more in favor of (and dependent upon) ecumenicalism as a method of sustaining their lifespan. Yet the 'liberalization + ecumenicalism = secularism' paradigm actually seems to work in the opposite direction. Brown (1997), Bruce (2001, 2002), Hillis (2002), McCrone (1992), and Voas (2006) have all suggested that liberalization and ecumenicalism can be seen as largely a reaction to, not a cause of, the ways in which Scottish society has, since the 1960s, become ever more 'tolerant' and 'progressive' while growing less interested in the 'identity politics' that characterized much of the Scottish Presbyterianism of the past.

For Brown, the issue was one of changing trends in popular culture rather than any complex shifts in the modern Scot's cosmological outlook on life: 'it was lifestyle rather than ideology that seemed to instigate religious decline in Scotland' (Brown 1997: 3). For him, urbanization was the key social process that heralded the death of piety in Scotland, and, what better evidence of this than the unrivalled urbanity of Glasgow? 'By the time Glasgow was "European City of Culture" in 1990, and the pubs stayed open until three o'clock in the morning all year long, nobody doubted that religious Scotland was dead' (Brown 1997: 2). Further, urbanization brought with it 'a vast new range of occupations...leading to great variation in standard of living, popular culture and religion' (Brown 1997: 6). The argument is that 'the very instability of modern society seemed to threaten the tradition of communal worship and the tranquility of the agrarian life upon which piety and faith were founded' (Brown 1997: 8). Connell, commenting on rural life in interwar England, makes a similar point in his analysis of urban to rural migration in Surrey:

> The slower pace of life is the only index of change for most new residents; they cannot adopt a traditional country life style since even its semblance has long since gone.... Village life has become suburban life

and, for those who can afford the move, a pleasant rest from city life with just the merest hint of a lost country tradition [producing]...a new suburbia from which the simple life has gone. (Connell 1978: 214)

Brown and Connell's arguments seem clear: the nineteenth century process of urbanization, the twentieth century suburban development of 'new towns, and the liberalizing "modernity" that both of these processes brought with them' led to a more general 'undermining of the received role of religion' (Brown 1997: 166. cf. Connell 1978: 28–31). In the 1930s Scotland got the radio, in the 1950s it was television, and in the 1960s it was Bingo. It is not hard to see how this 'boom in...leisure' (Brown 1997: 166) began to erode some key aspects of Scottish religiosity, perhaps most obviously the Scots' willingness to adhere to the strictures of the Fourth Commandment.

Crucially, 'with religious decline came *ecumenicalism*' (Brown 1997: 7. emphasis added). The argument is again relatively straightforward—if your shack is falling over, you naturally begin to lean against the shack next door, and happily, no one has to sleep in the mud. Yet ecumenicalism had the effect of weakening religious identity in Scotland (Brown 1997: 7–8) by necessarily undermining denominational distinctiveness. Where church rhetoric tried hard to turn a necessity into a virtue, the shadow of decline was never far behind.

Further, liberalization in the wider culture did not go unnoticed by the churches. By the 1970s the Episcopal Church had stopped promoting the temperance movement, ceased its opposition to gambling, become more muted in its opposition to abortion, softened in its attitude toward homosexuality, and had become a leader in the antiwar movement. The Kirk followed and then overtook the Episcopal Church in its progressive politics, most notably in the decision in 1969 to ordain women, a policy that was not adopted by Episcopalians until 1992. The cumulative effect caused a 'moral metamorphosis' (Brown 1997: 169) in Scotland's churches:

> For those living through it, the impact of the cultural and then the lifestyle revolutions which started in the 1960s seem inescapably powerful for breaking *religious sensibility and the ecclesiastical grip on everyday life*. (Brown 1997: 174)

One way of understanding the radical transformation in the fortunes of Christianity in Scotland (and beyond) is to note the titles of some academic pieces written on the subject: 'Christianity in Britain, R. I. P' (Bruce 2001), 'God is Dead' (Bruce 2002), 'The Haemorrhage of Faith' (Brown 1997), 'Religious Decline in Scotland' (Voas 2006), and 'Bleeding to Death' (Brierley 2000).

The supporting evidence is strong. The 1851 census tells us that as many as 60 percent of the adult population attended church regularly at the time (Bruce 2001: 194). The figure, for England in 1998, had gone down to 7.5 percent (Bruce 2001: 195). Between 1900 and 2000 the number of clerics in Britain declined by 25 percent at a time when the population doubled (Bruce 2001: 199). In 1971, 60 percent of British marriages were conducted in churches; the figure in 2000 has almost halved (Bruce 2001: 199). The claim that decline in attendance at mainstream churches has been largely offset by growth in new religious movements (Davie 1994, Stark 1999) is difficult to sustain, accounting, as they do, for less than a sixth of the loss (Bruce 2001: 200). In the 1950s, 43 percent of the adult population believed in a 'personal creator God'—the figure in 2000 had declined to 26 percent. And unbelief in such a God had risen from 2 percent in the 1950s to 27 percent in the 1990s. If these current trends of decline continue, several mainline denominations (most notably the Methodists) will cease to exist in Britain by 2031 (Bruce 2001: 197).

But what of Scotland? 'It is evident that by *any measure* religious adherence in Scotland is lower now than in the past' (Voas 2006: 107). Religious mobility is flowing like one way traffic: 'The main movement [in Scotland] has been into no religion; whereas most people raised in no religion remain in that state, *many raised in a religion now have none*' (Voas 2006: 109). Protestantism has suffered most: 'for Protestants, it is clear that each generation has been less religious than the last' (Voas 2006: 111). With this change, we see a change 'from [Scottish popular culture] being more or less Christian to more or less not during the 1960s' (Voas 2006: 112).

And what of Aberdeen and the North East? The Aberdeen area now has the lowest church attendance in all of Scotland (Hillis 2002) despite a population explosion from roughly 73,000 in 1851 to 200,000 in 1991 (Hillis 2002: 709–710). In 1851 approximately 39 percent of Aberdeen's population went to Church. The figure was down to just 9 percent in 1994 (Hillis 2002: 711). Where the Aberdeen picture is bleaker for the churches than most, the Scotland-wide picture is far from rosy: 'One out of every two Scots sees themselves as neither a religious nor a spiritual person' (Glendinning 2006: 589). For Brown, the statistics suggest that we are likely to see a dramatic decline in its sociocultural significance of the Scottish churches. 'Very soon,' Brown argues, 'funerals will be the only occasion when the majority of Scots participate in a religious ceremony' (Brown 1997: 65). The result is that

> the stewardship of Scottish society is vested in generations which have become overwhelmingly "secular" in their culture and thinking. The churches may not disappear, but Scotland is sharing with the rest of Western Europe the rapid dissolution of Christian society. (Brown 1997: 174)

Is the God of the Scottish Reformation now only a God of funerals? What about Gamrie? With such a concentration of self-proclaimed Protestant fundamentalism, Gamrie is clearly not a very 'liberal' place. With six different churches, all of which have almost nothing to do with each other, Gamrie is clearly not a very ecumenical place. With Church attendance remaining at levels far closer to those reported in 1851 than to those of the 2000s, Gamrie does not appear to be a very secular place. Yet the religion of Gamrie is not what it used to be. Those in their teens, twenties, and thirties have largely abandoned the village Kirks and meeting halls, and while some have forged ties with Charismatic and Pentecostal churches in nearby towns, many of these young people do not now regularly attend any place of worship.

This demographic 'pinch' has brought other problems. With non-attendance of young workers comes a decline in what churches can expect to receive in weekly offerings, placing dwindling congregations under financial strain. With the failure of the young to 'convert to the faith,' come fears that Gamrie's religion is going extinct. Time, after all, is said to be critically short—Jesus is soon to come back, and then it will be too late. What was needed, my elderly Christian friends told me, was a vibrant 'witness' to God 'in this day and generation.' Yet, the grim reality, I was told, was one of demographic decline, economic recession, and eschatological crisis.

Much has been written about secularization in Northwestern Europe and North America, yet relatively little considers how 'macro' structural changes impact local landscapes of 'micro' religiosity in all their richness and particularity (cf. Cannell 2010). Bruce appears to hint at the need for this latter type of research in his recent book *Secularization* (2011), the opening comments of which open a space for religiosity *within* the secular. Bruce concedes that 'we should not foreclose on the possibility that religion may cease to be of any great social importance *while remaining a matter of some import for those who have some*' (Bruce 2011: 2. Emphasis added). Where the concluding 'some' in this sentence refers to 'religion as such' (Bruce 2011: 2), defined as: 'beliefs, actions and institutions based on the experience of supernatural entities...or impersonal forces...that set the conditions of, or intervene in, human affairs' (Bruce 2011: 1), Bruce's second concession, set in this context, is even more striking. He states: 'It is possible that a country that is formally and publicly secular may contain among its populace *a large number of people who are deeply religious*' (Bruce 2011: 2. Emphasis added).

How is it that 'religion may cease to be of any great social importance while remaining a matter of some import for...a large number of people who are deeply religious' (Bruce 2011: 2)? While such a statement is intelligible within certain sociological frameworks, to a social anthropological readership, this assertion is puzzling. The issue is one of scale. Bruce's suggestion that religion may be socially unimportant whist remaining important to large numbers of deeply religious people is sociologically plausible but anthropologically awkward because (and here I generalize), the former discipline has traditionally studied 'macro' social trends while the latter has more commonly addressed 'micro' social interaction. Indeed, as Weber was composing the original version of *The Protestant Ethic* in 1905, Radcliffe-Brown was preparing to embark on ethnographic fieldwork among the Andaman Islanders, a project which he commenced in 1906. Anthropology studied small villages within small archipelagos while sociology studied entire continents; in brute terms, then, the question becomes how we define 'of any great social importance.'

The significance of this question was again drawn to my attention in discussion with a sociologist of religion, who, in assessing the contribution anthropology had made to our understanding of religion, stated that while anthropology was good at telling *interesting* stories, it was not always very good at telling *important* stories. Whilst wanting to maintain some space for gentle academic facetiousness shared between colleagues from 'rival' disciplines, I still think this dichotomy between 'interesting' and 'important' is helpfully clarifying. Returning to Bruce's book *Secularization*, then, what makes religion 'important' is first and foremost a high degree of sustained institutional affiliation. While such institutional affiliation emerges *from* a shared culture that contains a shared belief system (Bruce 2011: 55), affiliation is also a measure *of* that culture (Bruce 2011: 99). Put simply, people go to church because they are part of a Christian culture, and yet their culture is Christian because they go to church. Crucially, the opposite trend is said to hold true:

> The secularization paradigm assumes that the decline of the Christian churches is evidence of more than just a loss of interest in attending

church. It is a sign that people have lost interest in the Christian faith, which, as Christianity has for centuries been the dominant form of religion in Europe, can be generalized as a loss of interest in religion. (Bruce 2011: 99)

For Bruce, religion is sociologically important exactly because it is socially unimportant, that is, religion is worthy of sociological investigation because its rapid decline into unimportance evidences an important social trend within modern industrial liberal democracies—secularization. Anthropology takes a different view, upholding that small (often peripheral) communities are important simply by virtue of their brute existence *as human communities*, showing limited concern for sample size, generalizability, or ability to highlight social trends. Equally, small communities are important not in spite of their peripheral location, but because of it. Such 'micro' communities, by inhabiting the periphery, tend to formulate modes of existence that differ from the more populous centers of human society where ('macro') social trends are generally imagined to take shape. Given these formulations, I want to suggest that Gamrie is 'important' for three different reasons.

First, Gamrie is *ethnographically* important simply by virtue of being the place where a number of people live out their lives. A study of Gamrie adds to an ethnographic record that currently knows surprisingly little about Scotland, its coastal communities, and the people who inhabit them. Furthermore, studying Gamrie not only informs us about a place—costal Scotland—but also adds to our knowledge of a religion—Christianity. While the anthropology of Christianity has been booming over the last decade, it still has no significant ethnographic record pertaining to Scotland, and none at all to the millennialist Scots-Presbyterianism and Brethrenism that this book examines.

Second, Gamrie is *anthropologically* important because, in adding to this ethnographic record, not only do we fill in discrete knowledge gaps, but we can then deploy this knowledge comparatively. Coming to terms with how Gamrie fishermen understand their 'calling' as prawn trawlermen illuminates the behavior of fishermen in other contexts—the Inupiat whalers of the Arctic Circle (Turner 1996), for example, have a very different ontology of sea hunting to Gamrics, a fact brought into sharp relief through comparison. Shift the scale, and understandings of salvation and their relation to religious language may be compared, this time with similarity coming to the fore. For example, performances of conversion narratives in urban California (Stromberg 1993) and Scotland appear closely akin. Drawing out the wider implications of these comparisons is another task with which this book is concerned.

Third, Gamrie is *sociologically* important because it speaks directly into the kind of 'bigger picture' sought by quantitative social scientists researching macro social trends. This is an argument I make below—taking up the entirety of chapter 2, but also present throughout the book—with reference to demographics, economics, politics, and millenarianism. The regional focus of this 'bigger picture' oscillates from Northeast Scotland, to Scotland as a whole, to Britain, to Europe, and the North Atlantic, and finally to more 'globalized' concerns (cf. Nadel-Klein 2003: 2). In widening this frame of reference as I do, the sociological is repeatedly folded back onto the ethnographic and anthropological, that is, the 'macro' is made to speak into the 'micro,' by considering, for example, how the EU threatens to destroy the Gamrie fishing fleet, and, in so doing, trigger the global—world ending—return of Christ. Gamrie is also of social importance, then, when its import is defined in terms of its capacity to inform key contemporary debates about religious radicalism, economic crisis, environmentalism, demographic change, and secularization—trends with which this book is also concerned.

Gamrie: Since the Revival

The radically individualist Protestantism that emerged in the nineteenth and twentieth centuries as a result of both the Reformation and the Enlightenment was highly schismatic, as the history of the churches in Gamrie shows (see figure 1.1). Many left the Kirk to worship with various Brethren sects, and of those who stayed, many appeared to have strong sympathies with Brethren theology. Since the 1850s, those in the Kirk have adopted Brethren eschatology largely in its entirety, are almost completely teetotal, and favor adult (believer's) baptism. Where Meek, discussing twentieth century religious revivalism in northeast Scotland, suggests that 'the fishing communities were tailor-made for the absorption and transmission of revival impulses' (1999: 138), the same can be said, it seems, for Brethrenism, which, after all, was built on revival.

The 'elective affinity' between Brethrenism and fishing goes beyond Brethren appropriations of the Biblical call to be 'fishers of men.' Ministers at the Gamrie Kirk and the Free Presbyterian Church of Ulster (FPCU) complained that their congregations, having been overly influenced by Brethrenism and a life at sea, were often defiant of their authority and disparaging of their profession. Gamrics, by and

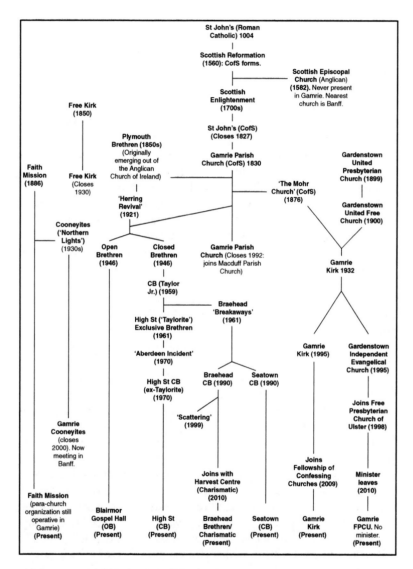

Figure 1.1 Diagram of church splits and mergers

large, agreed: ministers had '*nae idea*' how hard life at sea was, and, as a result, could never properly understand them as a people. Where being a Gamric meant being a fisherman, this entailed a sense of strong individual autonomy. 'I'm nae Free Presbyterian,' one man told me, explaining why he had left the denomination, 'I'm *free indeed!*'

In 1946, precisely because of this emphasis on the inalienability of personal religious freedom, the Brethren experienced their first major split caused by irreconcilable differences in theological opinion over adult (Open Brethren [OB]) versus infant (Closed Brethren [CB]) baptism. Having locally established the 'Open' and 'Closed' labels, baptism remains *the* distinguishing feature that separates the two groups. Another difference is the CB use of the Darby Translation of the Bible and the OB use of the King James Version. While not unimportant locally, this variance did not cause tension in the same way as views on Baptism did; both versions were held in high esteem by Gamrics for being 'very literal' (and therefore 'accurate') translations.

Since 1946, Gamrie's OB have not experienced further fission, largely because when theological or personality disagreements arise, an 'official' split is avoided by local dissenters simply leaving to worship at their next nearest OB hall. The CB, not permitting such internal disagreements to be dealt with by switching assembly but by excommunication or institutional division, have experienced more frequent schism, at points because of the influence of one man, Jim Taylor Jr., an early leader of the 'Exclusive Brethren' (EB), a sect considered to be fundamentalist even by the very conservative standards of the CB.

According to a number of my informants, Taylor Jr. pushed two particular Brethren teachings—on 'separation' from the world and on the liberty of Christians to consume alcohol—to their extreme, leading to the fragmentation of the CB and his own downfall. On 'separation,' Taylor Jr. introduced new rules that made even casual associations between EB and non-EB members almost impossible. Perhaps most controversially, an edict from Taylor Jr. that EBs could not eat with non-EBs led to situations where young children of those in the EB, who were not themselves 'in membership,' could not eat at the same table as their parents who *were* members. Crucially for Gamrie, those in the EB were not permitted to work with those outside the movement, meaning that many EB skippers who had non-EB crew were forced to sell their boats and give up fishing because of the impossibility of finding suitable EB replacements. It was this edict that caused the 1961 'breakaway'—made up of several high profile EB skippers local to Gamrie who refused to sell their boats and dissolve their business, instead reverting back to Closed Brethrenism as it existed before Taylor Jr.

The second split caused by Taylor Jr., the 1970 'Aberdeen Incident,' was as a result of personal scandal. Having promoted the use of alcohol among EB members as a key mark of 'Christian liberty,' many, having come from long lines of Presbyterian teetotalers, quickly fell into alcoholism. Taylor Jr. was also said to have developed the addiction with serious consequences to the credibility of his ministry. Things came to a head when Taylor Jr. was found, apparently drunk, naked, in bed with another man's wife. Days after the scandal hit the national tabloids, those in Gamrie who had remained loyal to Taylor Jr. post 1961 left the EB movement, reverting back to Closed Brethrenism, yet remaining as a separate assembly.

More splits followed, this time among the CB 'Breakaways' over a range of disagreements about how worship should be conducted— conflicts that were themselves exacerbated by personality clashes. Two families had personal connections to the Assemblies of God (AoG) and sought to bring this Pentecostal influence to Gamrie's Braehead Hall. A more explicitly evangelistic focus was sought by these 'modernizers,' as was the use of contemporary Christian music and instruments including guitars and a drum kit. Women were also given more opportunity to take part in the service and eventually a woman was asked to preach. Such changes caused two splits, the first in 1990, birthing today's Seatown CB Hall, and the second, in 1999 (known locally as 'the scattering'), which further fragmented the fellowship without leading to the creation of a new assembly. Since leaving the field in 2010, those dozen or so members who remained at the Braehead Hall have forged formal links with the 'Harvest Centre Riverside Christian Fellowship' in Banff, a charismatic church that is seeking to resuscitate Braehead by bussing in young Christians to hold contemporary 'worship celebration' services as an 'evangelistic outreach' for the 'spiritually lost' Gamrie youth.

Yet the Brethren have no monopoly on religious division in Gamrie. While the history of Presbyterianism in Gamrie during the late nineteenth and early twentieth century was a history of mergers (with the United Presbyterian Church merging with the United Free Church, which merged again with the CofS), the history of the last two decades has provided the opposite trend. In 1995 the Gamrie Kirk split over a decision handed down by the CofS General Assembly that 'homosexual inclinations' were not, in themselves, sufficient to bar a person from entering into training for the ministry as long as that person was not a 'practicing homosexual.' Some in the Gamrie Kirk, however, including Rev. Malcolm Davidson (the minister at the time), thought it was sufficient grounds for a bar and left the denomination in protest to set up the Gardenstown Independent Evangelical Church. Shortly after this departure, the new congregation made it clear to Rev. Davidson, that, despite having followed him out of the Kirk, they no longer wanted him as their minister. Davidson then left Gamrie, accepting a call to a church in America.

This marked a new chapter in the history of Presbyterianism in the village, with Gardenstown Independent Evangelical Church forming, as a result of personal connections, close (but informal) ties with the FPCU, the denomination founded by Rev. Ian Paisley in 1951. By 1998 an FPCU minister was sent to Gamrie for a summer to provide pulpit supply. When the congregation asked that he become their minister, he accepted their 'call' on the condition that the church give up its independent status and become Free Presbyterian. This was agreed and Rev. William Thompson became Gamrie's first FPCU minister. Over time the congregation's relationship with Rev. Thompson soured, some say as a result of his unwavering faithfulness to the theological principles of the FPCU, and others as a result of personality clashes. The situation hit a low during the 15 months of my fieldwork, and, just weeks after I left, Thompson accepted a call to a FPCU congregation in Northern Ireland, leaving the very much diminished Gamrie FPCU to consider its options. The congregation remains without a minister.

During this time, the Gamrie Kirk underwent a crisis of its own as a result of the appointment of an openly gay minister to Aberdeen's Queen's Cross Church, who planned to move, with his partner, into the manse. The Gamrie Kirk, having remained relatively united during the decision making process by joining the evangelical pressure group 'The Fellowship of Confessing Churches,' may well split from the CofS in view of the fact that Aberdeen Presbytery formally appointed a gay minister to one of its churches as a result of a General Assembly ruling in May 2011. No formal action will be taken by the Gamrie Kirk, however, until the publication of a report by a 'Theological Commission' on human sexuality in May 2013 clarifies the denomination's official stance on the ordination of gay clergy.

There are also two other groups who appear 'orphaned,' without any connection to other local churches. They are the 'Free Kirk' and the 'Cooneyites,' (known locally as the 'Northern Lights'). The 'Free Kirk' (about a mile outside the village, in the countryside) was the one church about which I could glean almost no information. Local people were not sure if this was originally a Free Church of Scotland, a United Presbyterian Church of Scotland, or a United Free Church of Scotland. All I could establish with any degree of consensus was that it opened in 1850, only to close again in 1930, for what reasons I am unsure. The church—now used to house old farming machinery—elicited about as much local interest as my questions did useful information.

Finally, beyond the fact that they are a breakaway from the Faith Mission, I also know little about the Cooneyites (locally, the 'Northern

Lights'), having only attended their meetings half a dozen times with a friend in Gamrie who, up to 2000, hosted a small fellowship of 'Northern Lights' in the village. The tiny Restorationist sect, founded by William Irvine (in Scotland) and Edward Cooney (in Ireland) in the early 1900s, refuses to take any official name for itself and rejects all other churches as apostate. Similar to the Brethren, they also reject the idea that the ministry should be a paid profession, but unlike the Brethren, they further reject the use of permanent church buildings, choosing to meet in rented village halls and the homes of followers. Unusually, the group permits women to preach—the majority of their itinerant evangelists (who practice 'homeless ministry') are women. Perhaps most controversially, Cooneyites claim that salvation can only be gained by listening to their own preachers, leading many Gamrics to view this group not as a sect, but a cult. The group folded in Gamrie in 2000 due to lack of members and now meets in a home in Banff.

Gamrie's Churches Today

Whilst all Gamrie's churches have slight differences in doctrine and worship, what they hold in common is a strong attachment to 'the need to be saved' (a personal and deeply transformative rupture of the old sinful self from the new 'born-again' self, defined by a life of ongoing repentance), 'believing the Bible' (literal interpretation and personal application), and 'spreading the gospel' (where all of daily life is redefined evangelistically).

To outsiders, all six churches have a distinctly 'fundamentalist' feel to them. Sermons, sometimes lasting over an hour, are the focal point of most services (figure 1.2) and are centrally concerned with human sinfulness and the need to be 'washed in the blood' of Jesus. The buildings are remarkably bare, with almost no adornment save banners and posters displaying various Biblical texts (see figure 1.3). Old-fashioned revivalist hymns are sung either without music or, where instrumentation is permitted, with an electric organ. While quiet chatting is permitted before the service at some churches, others expect silence to be kept at the outset. Almost all of those in attendance (including children) bring their own Bible to church, many of which, despite being leather bound, are well worn, tatty looking, and often heavily annotated (cf. Bielo 2009). For many in Gamrie, then, the Bible one carried acted as a key index of salvation.

The religion of Gamrie, while not misogynistic, was unapologetically patriarchal. In most of Gamrie's places of worship, women were required to wear long skirts and head coverings, and in some

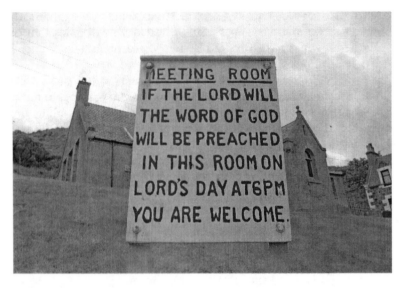

Figure 1.2 High Street (CB) Hall

Figure 1.3 Gamrie Gospel Hall (OB), showing baptismal tank open

churches were not permitted to speak during worship. Gamrie's Christian women, as with their men, felt strongly that the Bible clearly defined the different roles men and women were to fulfill in church life. I often heard local women from the Brethren and FPCU criticizing 'liberal' churches for allowing 'wifey preachers'—'it's nae Biblical,' came the simple but stinging indictment. Opinions in the Gamrie Kirk were softer, but not by much. Women were allowed to offer public prayers and readings of scripture, but could not be elders, and were never allowed to preach.

The Braehead Hall seems to be the exception to this rule, as was often the case more generally due to their being influenced by Pentecostal and charismatic Christianity. In the other five churches, men dominated all aspects of formal and informal church life, maintaining this position on the basis that such a model was (according to the vast majority of my male and female informants) the only truly Biblical one. This is even the case in the Gamrie Kirk despite the fact that the CofS as a national denomination has ordained women ministers since 1969 and strongly expects all churches to have both male and female elders. Clothing was also strongly gendered: many wore (as a matter of conscience) plain, muted clothes; men wore suits and women wore (generally unadorned) blouses, skirts, and hats. Where clothing was most strongly gendered among the Brethren (women were not permitted to wear trousers, were discouraged from wearing jewelry and makeup, and were required to have their hair long and covered), this was not as strictly enforced in the Kirk, where women wore trousers and makeup and many choose not to wear hats.

Outwith the formal setting of public worship, gender roles were less strictly policed. While women *were* expected to manage the domestic sphere—raising children, keeping the home comfortable and clean, and being in a constant state of readiness to provide 'Christian hospitality'—they were also sometimes managers in a different sense. As 'fisher wives,' these women, owing to the fact that their husbands were constantly away at sea, became, in many respects, de facto heads of household. Not only did this involve the disciplining of children (a task normatively understood as falling to fathers) but also, in some cases, family finances—the mortgage, utility bills, and taxes. In more than one case, where female informants were married to local skippers, boat repayments, and crew wages were also administered not by these men but by their wives. One friend told me (I think only half jokingly), that he and many other skippers did not have the slightest notion of the state of their family or business finances—'I just catch the fish and the wifey does the rest!' Yet, the other men in the village

Local Name	Denom.	Size	Dominant Age	Gender Roles	Bible Version	Music Style	Dress Code	Communion Practice	Baptism Practice	Views on Alcohol
Kirk	CofS	80+	Some young children and middle aged. Mostly 60+ Relatively large Sunday school (n = 30)	M only leadership (informally and contra to national CofS policy) F can pray aloud and do readings	Mainly NIV with others	Organ and hymns Some modern choruses	Various. Older dress more formally	Open to all professing Christians. Six times a year?	Officially infant baptism yet no babies baptized in living memory. Adult ('believers') baptism strongly favored	No official line. Many teetotal. Drinking in moderation expected but not backed by formal church discipline
Gospel Hall	Open Brethren	40	60+ Very small Sunday school (n = 4)	M completely dominant F silent apart from hymn singing.	KJV in general	No instruments Mostly 19th and early 20thC revivalist hymns	M dark suits. F head coverings and long skirts	Closed table. Open Brethren membership or letter of introduction generally required. Weekly.	Adult ('believers') baptism only	Strictly teetotal. Condition of membership
Irish Church	FPCU	30	Some in late middle age. Most 60+ Very small Sunday School (n = 6)	M leadership and dominant F can pray aloud	Strictly KJV only Trinitari-an Bible Society member	Organ. Mostly 19th and early 20thC revivalist hymns	M dark suits. F head coverings and long skirts	Open to all professing Christians. F generally required to wear head covering. Monthly?	No official position. Left to the conscience of individual ministers.	Strictly teetotal. Condition of membership

		No.	Age/composition	Gender roles	Theology	Music	Dress	Communion	Baptism	Alcohol
Seatown Hall	Closed Brethren	20	Some children and middle aged. Mostly 60+ No Sunday school	M completely dominant F silent apart from hymn singing.	Darby	No instruments Own ('Little Flock') hymn book	M dark suits. F head coverings and long skirts	Strictly closed table. Closed Brethren membership and letter of introduction always required. Weekly.	'Household' (infant) baptism of the children of members	Alcohol permitted and used relatively widely. Moderation expected
Braehead Hall	Brethren/charismatic	12	60+ (some teens- 30s bussed in). Youth service (developed post-fieldwork).	M dominant in the past, now much more equal F can lead, preach, pray etc.	Wide range	Piano and other instruments Various hymns and choruses	Generally informal. Older dress more formally	Open to all professing Christians. Weekly.	Adult ('believers') baptism only	No official line. Many teetotal
High Street Hall	Closed Brethren	6–8	All 70s–80s. No Sunday school	M completely dominant (only two M in attendance) F silent apart from hymn singing.	Darby	No instruments Own ('Little Flock') hymn book	M dark suits. F head coverings and long skirts	Strictly closed table. Closed Brethren membership and letter of introduction always required. Weekly.	'Household' (infant) baptism of the children of members	Alcohol permitted and used relatively widely. Moderation expected

Figure 1.4 Summary of various aspects of church life and practice broken down by denomination

had the last laugh, telling me how my friend could not control his wife, who was unusually domineering. When the church he attended with his family divided, his wife refused to attend the newly created meeting that resulted from the schism. For a long time the family did not attend any church as a result. Eventually, his wife got her own way and they began to attend a different denomination entirely. 'Why?' I asked. 'Because his wife wouldn't submit,' came the gravely disapproving reply.

Looking beyond gender, the similarities that exist between the different churches and halls are more numerous than the differences (figure 1.4). While some used an organ and others did not, many of the hymns sung in the Kirk were also sung among the different Brethren groups, with the same slow pace and somber tone. The lyrics often focused on human sinfulness, the crucifixion, and the Second Coming. While each church had its favored hymnal, each had similar topical indexes—'worship,' 'the Godhead,' 'the Holy Scriptures,' 'the Gospel,' 'consecration and holiness,' and 'the Lord's coming.' Attitudes toward alcohol were also a common denominator, often becoming a local litmus test for the health and orthodoxy of anyone—and any church—claiming to be Christian. While the CB did permit moderate consumption of alcohol, all the other fellowships were, officially or unofficially, teetotal. Public consumption of alcohol was strictly taboo and bars and pubs were abhorred as 'the devils lair.'

Yet it would be wrong to assume that these local similarities in ecclesiastical form emerged from a fixed parochial mind-set that resisted, on principle, all influences from outside the village. Not only did each place of worship support overseas mission work—in, for example, Argentina, Kenya, Spain, and Papua New Guinea—but missionaries came to Gamrie to preach and update congregants on the progress of their work. Beyond this global network of missions, Gamrie's Christians often left the village to travel with work or on holiday, seeking out suitable places of worship wherever they went. Informants of mine had connections to halls or churches in the Faroe Islands, in Tenerife, in Romania, and elsewhere. Most especially, local Christians' eschatological interest in, and political support for, Israel opened up several avenues for forging global Christian connections. The Gamrie Kirk ran pilgrimages to the 'Holy Land,' while several of those in the Brethren toured Israel independently. Christian Zionism extended beyond villagers' trips to the Middle East, to consumption of (and financial giving to) global Christian broadcasting stations such as God TV. Many of my informants were avid consumers of

Christian television, regularly watching American preachers such as John Hagee and Joel Osteen deliver sermons on topics of contemporary interest.

Religion, in short, was everywhere—not only in churches and meeting halls, but at home, in the streets, on the boats, in what people spoke about, how they dressed, what they read, where they went on holiday, who they gave their money to, and what they watched on television. Combine all this with a general atmosphere of seriousness and reverence and it becomes easy to understand how Gamrie has a local reputation for stark religious intensity. Looking beyond the immediate bounds of the village, the 65 mile stretch of coast running from Boddam in the southeast to Findochty in the west contains dozens of churches and meeting halls, the majority of which are Brethren, Pentecostal, or independent evangelical; it is within this coastal Protestant fishing region that Gamrie is geographically and 'spiritually' situated.

Other Gamrics: The Village of the Damned

Yet the village is not entirely elderly nor exclusively staunchly religious; it is a diverse place, home to an assortment of different communities making up a collection of socially very different Gamries. Take the local teenage boys, for example, who, being too young to drive or without cars of their own, spend their summer evenings playing football at the park and their winter evenings hanging around the bus shelters, chatting and joking, and smoking cigarettes. Or the older lads who spend the early evening cruising up and down the braes in their modified cars and then park at the harbor late at night to play music from their stereos. Most of these 'loons,' in their teens and early twenties have not only their youth and boredom in common, but also their work—going to sea, making money, and spending it as they please. These young boys and men are conspicuously absent from the churches, are vocal about having no interest in Christian things, and are happy to flout the taboos their parents and grandparents observed, particularly regarding alcohol. Today, when a 'blackening' occurs[1] it is now accompanied by heavy public drinking, much to the chagrin of the older generations.

Another noticeable subgroup within the village is the art community. These well educated, middle class, generally English retirees buy houses in the Seatown and travel to Gamrie to spend their summers painting, bird watching, and drinking wine on the seafront. Artists have attracted other artists, and there are now several small 'galleries' where these seasonal residents occasionally show and sell their work to each other and to day-trippers. This community is largely isolated from Gamrie's religious life—'we don't bother them and they don't bother us,' commented one painter when I asked what contact she had with the Christians whose CB hall was just yards from her studio. Such is the established nature of this group, that one couple have actually set up the 'Creative Retreat,' a business where they teach, hold exhibitions, and host professional artists by offering a 'winter residency' scheme.

Holiday makers come to the village, some for months, others for a week or less. Many are walkers and keen photographers. These transient guests have no real sense of the religion in the village and do not, as a result, follow informal expectations with regard to Sunday observance. The same is also so with local day-trippers, some of whom are said to come to the village to launch kayaks from the harbor during the Sunday services because they know none of the trustees (all retired Christian fishermen) will be present to collect the relevant fee. Other 'incomers,' with boats berthed in Gamrie harbor, choose to distance themselves from local religiosity in more enduring ways, with one man naming his vessel *Evolution.*

With a relatively numerous supply of council houses in the village, and (at one time) fairly cheap private properties for sale— several young families from England have moved to the area in search of the 'good life.' These families, with no religious affiliation, found it almost impossible to integrate into school and community life, especially given the level of anti-English sentiment said to be particularly strong among young local families. Finally, some 'incomers' without children moved to the village not in search of the 'good life' *per se,* but due to environmentalist convictions. The Cetacean Research and Rescue Unit, is a Scottish charity based in the village that conducts research into the dolphin and whale populations who inhabit the surrounding coastal waters. As with the artists, these environmentalists had little contact with Gamrie's Christians, using their site in the Seatown as a base of operations rather than a place of permanent residence.

Perhaps the most controversial 'sub-culture' within Gamrie was the bikers. These (generally middle aged) 'rockers,' both Scottish and English, were—by virtue of being highly visible—an often talked about minority. Leather jackets, tattoos, piercings, shaved heads, thick heeled and metal rimmed boots, flashing chrome, and roaring exhausts all combined to make this group the seeming antithesis of the quiet but staunchly religious elderly Christians of Gamrie.

I remember attending a 'breaking of bread' service one Sunday morning at the OB when a dozen motorbikes flashed past the pitted glass windows of the hall with a deafening thunder of engines. An elderly woman turned to me, presumably noting my surprise, and mouthed the word 'bikers!' nodding with a frown only to turn again to the front platform. The local reputation of these individuals was not good. Many were accused of being 'druggies,' and with locally high incidences of heroin addiction in Gamrie and the surrounding towns, some were also suspected of being drug dealers. I became friends with one of the bikers during my fieldwork, largely on account of my own method of transport. The fact that I rode a scooter did not seem to bother him—'two wheels is two wheels,' he used to tell me.

What joined all of these 'others' of Gamrie—the boys at the bus shelters, the young men in their modified cars, the artists, the 'English incomer' families, the holiday makers, the kayakers, the environmentalists, and the bikers—was, as far as my main group of Christian informants were concerned, the fact that they were all 'unsaved.' These groups were, in this sense, united insofar as they constituted the village of the damned. This was the case because the 'gospel message' was starkly described in terms of being either 'for' or 'against' Jesus; 'heaven bound' or 'hell bound'; 'born-again' or 'dead in sin.' What mattered, for my Christian informants, was that these neighbors of theirs were heading for a 'lost eternity.' Thus, while on one level there were many Gamries typified by many different subcommunities, on another level, there were really only two kinds of people in Gamrie; the saved and the damned. It is this tension between social heterogeneity and religious duality that animates much of the context of this book. Having looked at how the present is experienced as a product of the past, let us now consider how the future is imagined as a product of the present.

Chapter 2

The Triple Pinch

In terms of religion, Fraserburgh[1] and Peterhead[2] feel like large versions of Gamrie. Both towns have several conservative Protestant churches, many emerging from a history of schism. Fraserburgh alone has 18 churches, including the Assemblies of God, Baptist, Elim (Pentecostal), Immanuel (charismatic), United Reformed, Open Brethren, Closed Brethren, Salvation Army, two independent evangelical churches, four CofS churches, a Jehovah's Witness Kingdom Hall, and a Roman Catholic Church. Historically, as with Gamrie, the Brethren were very influential, with Peterhead being home to the only Exclusive Brethren hall remaining in Scotland's northeast today.

The role of the fishing industry is also prominent, with Fraserburgh Harbor remaining the largest shellfish port in the United Kingdom and Peterhead its largest white fish port (FIS 2009). In 2001, 5 percent of Fraserburgh's workforce and 4 percent of Peterhead's workforce were employed in the fishing industry (national average 0.3 percent) (SCROL 2001) and in 2008, Peterhead landed 113,000 tons of fish (at a total value of £100 million) and Fraserburgh 28,000 tons (total value £52 million). Such facts are particularly striking for Fraserburgh, given that between 1996 and 2008 the port suffered a 28 percent loss in its total fish landings (FIS 2009). This is in part explained by the fact that shellfish values in the northeast have increased by over 94 percent since 1996 (FIS 2009).

Because of the continued presence of the fishing industry in the northeast, Fraserburgh and Peterhead each have a 'Fishermen's Mission'—a Christian charity that provides chaplaincy services to the industry—despite the fact that many other Mission centers across the United Kingdom have closed in recent years. Both centers have an evangelical (and largely male) leadership, with both, at various times, also functioning as churches in their own right. But while fishing—and the religion of fishermen—is a significant element of the contextual picture of northeast Scotland, it is not the only element.

The Christians of Gamrie, while clearly not the only social subgroup in the village, were unique in so far as they found themselves teetering on the edge of a three-way precipice, looking down into economic, demographic, and spiritual oblivion. My friends were acutely aware of the situation they faced: intense economic insecurity, a demographic time bomb, and the imminent apocalypse. These forces were hemming them in, producing a powerful sense of foreboding about the future. In presenting the 'bigger picture' of Christian Gamrie in terms of a 'triple pinch,' there is a danger of giving a contextually overdetermined view of its religious life, too flat and tidy to properly encapsulate the confusion—the sense of being spiritually and socially 'out of place' in one's own village—that was so often described to me by my elderly Christian informants. To recapture this sense that the village was 'like a foreign land these days,' I want also to consider some alternative explanations in order to highlight both complication and contradiction.

Pinch One: Economy

Of Gamrie's 733 residents, 302 are in some kind of employment, over a third of whom are employed within the 'skilled trades' occupations. Only 38 percent are classed as 'employees' (national average 51 percent) whereas 20 percent are 'self employed' (national average 7 percent). Of those aged between 16 and 74, 40 percent have no educational qualifications (national average 33 percent) and only 16 percent have a degree or other professional qualification (national average 19 percent). Further, the average working week for men in Gardenstown is 55 hours—significantly higher than the national average of 43 hours. The picture is different for women (working 28 hours a week compared to a national average of 32), many of whom are left to run the household while their husbands are away at sea. Despite some shrinking in the fishing industry across the northeast, fishing still directly accounts for 16 percent of the local workforce (national average 0.3 percent). The village is also increasingly dependent on tourism: Gamrie has six self-catering cottages, a bed and breakfast, and a hotel. The local economy appears strong by many of these indicators; with no one in the village of working age having 'never worked' (national average 9 percent) and less than 2 percent classed as 'currently unemployed' (national average 4 percent) (SCROL 2001).[3]

There are clear advantages in providing a materialist reading of Gamrie's 'religion of fishing,' showing, as it does the importance of local money. Key here is the strong presence of 'nonconformist' Protestantism characterized not only by freedom from state interference (the charge often leveled against the 'established' religions of Episcopalianism and the CofS), but also as free from the control of ordained ministers. Brethrenism was said to be *'free indeed!'* because it was governed by as wide a body of local men as was possible. These men were not required to have any formal theological (or any other kind of) education and undertook no training before entering into public leadership. Far from being a weakness, this was held up as a strength—the laity were said to be reliant 'neither on books nor on Man's wisdom' but 'upon the Holy Spirit alone.'

Where this emphasis on the centrality of the Holy Spirit emerged, in the case of the Friday Masowe (Engelke 2007), because of a rejection of material objects (including the Bible) as mediators of divine presence, Brethren emphasis on the Holy Spirit emerges from a rather different rejection of supra-individual ecclesiastical authority. While many Brethren halls did have *de facto* leaders, such figures were frequently challenged by other men in the assembly. Where internal conflict was irresolvable, splits occurred. Some in Gamrie were unconvinced by this radically devolved model of church leadership: 'They're their own bosses at sea and their own bosses in their [religious] meeting[s]; every man is his own skipper and he can go *wherever* he likes,' said one Presbyterian leader with pointed criticism.

What this mutual critique (of fishermen by clergy and vice versa) agrees on is the existence of a strong degree of 'affinity' between life at sea and life in the Brethren. In this context, freedom of movement and freedom of conscience amount to much the same thing: an unwillingness to be governed by the will of another. Men did frequently tell other men (and, of course, women) what to do—the point is that submission to such instruction was voluntary. The same applied, in my experience, on board Gamrie's trawlers. Skippers gave orders, and crew, by and large, followed. Yet crew followed not because the authority of their skipper was sacrosanct, but because the content of an order was deemed sensible. Orders deemed (economically) disadvantageous were argued against, with a debate—not unlike a discussion of doctrine at a Brethren Bible reading—allowing a range of opinions to be stated, most especially among older, more experienced, crew. Where compromise was unachievable, undesirable, or both, skippers—and often 'leading men' in the Brethren—had the final word. Crucially, however, freedom of movement/conscience remained unviolated: congregants or crew feeling regularly or seriously aggrieved protected the moral supremacy of their individual autonomy by leaving a hall or boat that caused offence. On land and at sea, fellowship and friendship, while valued strongly, played second fiddle to self-determination.

Where fierce adherence to the 'singular truth of the Bible' collided with multiple interpretations of both Word and Sacrament, conflict arose and splits occurred, birthing various new Pentecostal, charismatic, and independent evangelical churches. These then proceeded to split and split again, giving rise to the dozens of Protestant groupings scattered across the northeast coast of Scotland today. With this highly 'Free' form of Protestantism (unable to draw support from a wider national denomination) came a heavy dependence upon those who made up the local congregation. Such dependence was not only about committing one's time, but also one's money. Whilst ministers' wages were not required, meeting halls needed to be rented and heated, preachers had their travel expenses paid, and missionaries abroad and full time evangelists at home needed support, none of which came cheap. Local religion, being locally funded, was (and is) dependent on the health of the local economy in order to 'stay in business.' Were the economic foundations of fishing to go into decline, the impact on Gamrie's religion would be marked—foreign missions would cease, gospel campaigns would dry up, and halls would close and fall into disrepair.

For now at least, the economic foundation appears relatively stable. This may explain (within the confines of the Scottish context) some of Gamrie's continued religiosity in contrast to the 'heathenism' of other parts of the east coast further north. Wick, where the fishing industry has all but died, appears to have very little religion in general and independent Protestantism in particular; with no Brethren halls, the Kirk maintains a dominant role. Moving west to Ullapool, Gairloch, Skye, or Lewis, the ecclesiastical (and industrial) picture is different again. The fishing industry, while not having reached Wick's irretrievable low, is struggling in these places nonetheless. Yet the religion remains very much alive, dominated, as it is, by the centrally funded Free Church of Scotland. While Gamrie, Fraserburgh, and Peterhead's fisheries seem to be standing firm, the slow creep of industrial change cannot be denied. Three forces of change are being exerted upon the fishing industry of northeast Scotland: regulation, competition, and concentration.

First, the (hotly contested and highly politicized) issue of decline in fish stocks has led the EU to regulate fishing methods and introduce quotas. This has squeezed many skippers economically as the cost of buying quotas increases and species that are caught without a license must, by law, be dumped. During my time working on the trawlers, dozens of tons of (drowned) fresh fish were thrown back to sea because either the boat's quota had already been caught or the boat did not have a license for a particular species. Such centralized bureaucratic control contravened local Christian sentiments about the moral importance of personal autonomy. This problem of 'throwbacks' was 'read' as a sign of the end times, based on a belief that the EU was the Antichrist (and that the devil was using the quota system as a way of gaining control over food production in order to enslave the human race via a future imposition of worldwide famine). Whether or not the EU had ulterior spiritual motives is irrelevant to our discussion here. What matters is that EU regulation of Scotland's fishing industry was hurting skippers and their crews economically and causing them to worry about the long-term viability of the industry.

Second, increased competition from foreign fisherman (particularly from Norway and the Faroe Isles) and the Scottish and international oil industry was putting the fishing industry in financial difficulty. Fish prices were being pushed down, as, for example, herring caught in Norwegian waters was being sold in Peterhead. Equally, as boys in their mid teens prepared to leave school to enter the labor market, increasing numbers were 'going into the oil' as opposed to fishing. The same was true of some veteran fishermen who made the sideways move from the trawlers to the rigs and supply boats, attracted by higher, more secure wages, and better working conditions.

Third, the end result was that fishing in northeast Scotland was becoming increasingly concentrated in the hands of fewer skippers. Those who managed to stay in the industry built bigger, more efficient vessels that required greater start-up capital and cost more to run. As boats grew in size the real commercial fishing was done from Fraserburgh and Peterhead—the tiny Gamrie harbor could still support small inshore creel boats (mainly the preserve of retired, 'hobby' fisherman) but certainly not the trawlers that for many years had dominated the industry. The demographic implications were obvious: young (economically productive) Gamrics tended to move to where the work was, drawing the few church going families with young children away from the kirks and halls, toward the more lively charismatic and Pentecostal churches, such as the Assemblies of God (AoG) in Fraserburgh, which to this day has a large, young, and very wealthy congregation. To the extent that the regulation, competition, and concentration of the fishing industry in the northeast of Scotland exert their own pressures, the suggestion that Gamrie might be facing 'the last of the last days' industrially seems not so much doomsday pessimism as economic realism.

One possible contradiction rests in the simple fact that Gamrie, as a fishing village, has experienced considerable economic prosperity ever since the boom in the industry in the 1960s and 1970s. With this first wave of money came widespread car ownership and geographical mobility that in turn brought about the early stages of social transformation. This highly religious, relatively close-knit (and closed) community became more open to the influences of migration, tourism, and secularism. Television in particular was said to increasingly take precedence over attendance at Sunday worship in this new modern era, especially in households with children and teenagers. Churches previously filled to bursting with people eager to hear 'an old fashioned [fire and brimstone] gospel message' seemed increasingly out of touch with these newer forms of consumerism.

Many people (fishermen and others) told me—some with pride, some with horror—that Gamrie had, as a result of this past boom, more millionaires per head of population than anywhere else in Scotland. 'Fisher mansions' at the top of the brae were custom built, commissioned by very wealthy skippers, seemingly with the aim of affording maximum comfort when onshore for short spells before going back to sea. Luxury furnishings inside and powerful cars outside, as well as regular foreign holidays (summer and winter) signaled to others that these households were doing well for themselves despite the squeeze on the northeast fisheries. These bigger properties, built on more spacious plots of land, seemed to mirror some of the morally dubious socio-spatial characteristics that my fisher informants attributed to their (now not so distant) farming neighbors. Perhaps then, we are not seeing the last days of the fishing, but the last of the 'old days' of fishing so synonymous with poverty, close-knit community, and 'tradition'?

Where young children with smartphones and designer clothes, and teenagers with brand new cars well before they passed their tests were not uncommon, it is important to note that some skippers had huge debts, tied not only to the mortgages on their boats, but also to their modern lifestyles of conspicuous consumption. Yet there were others, who, working on enormous pelagic boats capable of catching £1 million of herring per trawl, were paid astronomically high wages. Deck hands no more than 18 years old were rumored to be earning upward of £80,000 for working six to eight weeks a year. With few if any family commitments and a taboo on working a second job for the other ten months of the year,[4] some of these wealthy

young men turned to fast cars or drugs—and sometimes both—
in an attempt to spend their wages. Stories circulated through the
channels of gossip and local newspapers of the disastrous (social
and spiritual) consequences of the reckless actions of these imma-
ture youths unable to handle their wealth. Old people shook their
heads at seeing the kinds of things they imagined only happened in
big cities (drug dealing, joy riding) occurring in their 'own village'
among their 'own folk.'

Such prosperity was only possible because of the concentration of
the fishing into the hands of an ever-shrinking list of skippers, many
of whom were from Gamrie. While some crews went out of business,
those resilient (or 'lucky,' or 'blessed') enough to remain in the industry did very well for themselves. So why were Gamrie's Kirks and halls
struggling to keep their doors open if many Gamrie fishermen continued to prosper? The answer is straightforward—those currently
making big money in the fishing were either unconnected to any
fellowship ('too busy,' I was told by their critics, 'to have any time
for God') or were attending only on a nominal basis but not 'tithing'
their earnings. 'Money is their God,' my elderly friends would say,
giving a stern warning to those, such as myself, who appeared willing
to listen. The *existence* of prosperity among Gamrie's skippers was
certainly not being debated, but rather the *effects* of this new found
(and uniquely modern) wealth. Gamrie's ageing Christians were in
agreement: 'Prosperity has been the death of religion in this village;
the young folk have so much money that they've lost sight of their
need of God.'

The 'elective affinity' between nonconformist Protestantism and
deep-sea fishing appeared—at least in part—to be breaking down.
Trawling for prawns had become much safer; with the advent of
steel hulls came more sheltered 'closed deck' vessels, and later, ships
equipped with collision avoidance computer systems. Equally, sonar
technology made hunting for previously invisible shoals of fish more a
subject of science than it did a matter of religion and superstition. The
logic held by many of my older informants was that with closed decks
and full wallets, the God of protection and provision was no longer
the priority He once was.

Where the economic rewards of trawling rose, so too did the over-
heads. By the 1980s, with considerable rises in the cost of steel and
diesel, the size of mortgages fishermen had to secure to start or expand
a business grew exponentially. Today, an average sized trawler costs
around £2 million, with much larger pelagic boats costing around
£25 million. Such massive financial outlays meant that the traditional

six-day week at sea—crucially leaving Sunday ('the Lord's Day') free for worship—was largely abandoned in favor of much more fuel efficient trips that lasted anywhere from two to eight weeks. With more time at sea (and less time in church) profits from catches continued to overtake expenditure and the lifestyles of fisherman rose accordingly, causing the 'natural attraction' (Howe 1978) between subsistence fishing and a certain kind of austere Protestantism to grow ever colder.

Prosperity not only brought the development of more efficient trawling technologies, but it also brought radio and television, tagged, as an informant of mine reminisced, with the advertising slogan 'bringing the world into your home.' It was the arrival of modern 'worldliness' (with all its associated ungodliness) that my elderly Christian friends mourned bitterly. Not only was the world brought to Gamrics, but through, among other things, widespread car ownership, Gamrics were brought into the world.

In the 1990s, a property boom corresponded with the boom in the fishing industry causing small traditional 'fisher cottages' in Gamrie's Seatown to be sold (at enormous profit) to wealthy English urbanites who sought rural summer retreats (cf. Connell 1978: 208). With the Seatown desolate for ten months of the year, newly prosperous skippers built ever bigger 'fisher mansions' at the top of the brae, consolidating the demographic change that had already occurred at the bottom of the brae with the arrival of 'English incomers' (who now make up 11 percent of the resident population) (SCROL 2001). These new 'white settlers' (Jedrej and Nuttal 1995)—who inhabited the 'village of the damned'—brought with them new modern, secular ideals and ways of life. Sunday work, nonchurch attendance, and public consumption of alcohol became increasingly the norm, with 'traditional values' becoming little more than a distant memory within two generations.

With the local fishing industry seemingly an industry of extremes, offering either bankruptcy or enormous wealth and very little in-between, the future economic possibilities do not bode well for the religion of Gamrie. As Nadel-Klein points out, the local, national, and global narratives that surround the fishing industry tend to paint a picture of 'perpetual crisis' (2003: 133. cf. Cohen 1987: 152). For Gamrie, where 'the love of money' is no longer assumed to be 'the root of all evil,' a Goldilocks-type resolution—with neither too much money to turn people off their 'need of God,' nor too little, choking the supply of funds needed to remain solvent—seems unlikely. Such was the pinch of economy.

Pinch Two: Demography

The village's first census in 1841 recorded 90 dwellings and a population of 420, which had grown to 170 dwellings and 1200 people by 1901 (GENUKI 2011). The resident population of Gamrie, according to the 2001 Scottish Census (SCROL 2001), is 733 (comprising 304 households), ethnically white, and aging. Of those aged 16 and over, 55 percent are married (national average 44 percent), 5 percent are divorced (national average 7 percent), only 22 percent have never been married (national average 31 percent) and just 3 percent cohabit (national average 7 percent) (SCROL 2001).

Yet local demographics, as with the economy, are changing. Many people in their twenties are migrating to Aberdeen or elsewhere in search of work, and, as already described, more boys in their teens are choosing to work in the oil industry rather than the fishing. Another strong indicator of out-migration is the falling roll at Bracoden Primary School, which serves Gamrie and the surrounding countryside. There are currently only 56 pupils enrolled and 3 teachers (including the head teacher) on staff. While part of this decline is to be explained by a lower birth rate, my landlady (herself a teacher at Bracoden during my fieldwork) explained the shrinking roll in terms of families moving away from the village to the bigger centers of Banff and Aberdeen.

This situation is complicated by the relatively new trend of in-migration. With 11 percent of the population being 'English incomers' who either come to buy retirement homes or arrive with young families in search of a better quality of life, older Gamrics complained to me how the close community of days gone by had given way to a sense of social estrangement and decline. Such trends were said to have corresponded with a growth in economic inequality, a rise in petty crime and vandalism, and the spread of drink and drug abuse. Discussing 'how times have changed' was not the preserve of the elderly—those in their thirties and forties also spoke to me of dramatic shifts in the 'spiritual,' social, and industrial configuration of the area.

Yet, the Christians of Gamrie were growing old and they knew it. Many of my informants were elderly people who had long since retired. It was these older folk who made up the majority of the congregations I spent so much time with during fieldwork. The sons and daughters of these older people, themselves in their thirties and forties, were noticeably absent from church. This meant (assuming religious 'revival' did not break out among the young) that several of the fellowships in the village were on the brink of extinction, a fact of which my friends were very much aware.

The Braehead Hall was a classic example of this, with a congregation of about 12, the youngest of whom was in her mid sixties, the majority being in their seventies and eighties. I remember one particular meeting when the agedness of those gathered was on display for all to see. There were only seven of us at the Bible study that evening; several of the others were not well enough to come out on a cold October night such as it was. Mitchell (a man in his seventies), slowly pulled a chair round to face where he sat, placed a cushion on the seat, and lifted his right leg up to ease the chronic aching that plagued him. Keith (who looked to be in his late sixties), sat beside me, wheezing—'I'm affa breathless tonight Joe,' he told me with a pained expression, holding a hand to his mouth. Rhoda told us all that she had been struggling this week with headaches and dizziness. Gregor—the *de facto* leader of the fellowship—sat stiffly in his chair not mentioning the fact that he had a serious heart condition that meant he was regularly in and out of hospital with severe chest pains. Harry was the last to join the circle that night, but within minutes his entire body was shaking with a horrendous wracking cough and was eventually taken home. The meeting was abandoned after only a few prayers because of the lack of able bodied people needed to sustain the study. 'You have to laugh!' Carol chuckled, commenting on our disastrous attempt at holding a meeting that night. 'That's right,' Rhoda said with a more somber tone 'otherwise you'd cry.'

The pinch of demography did not just concern the presence of old age within the churches, but also the absence of youth. All of Gamrie's churches were mostly made up of grandparents. The middle aged, by and large, did maintain some limited church connection by attending special 'one-off' meetings but were generally much less committed to public worship than their parents. As mentioned above, the pressures of modern fishing was an often given explanation (or 'excuse' depending on who was talking); bigger boats meant bigger mortgages that meant longer trips to sea to meet repayments, and this meant more time away from the village. Weekends at home were precious and skippers often chose family over church commitments. This was said to have a profound impact upon their own children; where fathers did not go to church, mothers would often stay home as well, leaving teenagers with little reason or encouragement to go to church or Bible class. Boys in their mid to late teens were often out on the boats with their fathers in any case, and girls frequently chose to stay at home with their mothers.

In this sense, nonattendance did not seem to emerge from any atheistic conviction (it was not uncommon for parents who did not themselves attend church to send their young children to Sunday school simply as a form of free childcare) but rather out of pragmatism and lack of interest. The onus, as a result, was firmly placed back on the grandparents to do the real work of 'household evangelism.' The recipients of these spiritual efforts were not their own (now grown up) children, but their grandchildren. Heartbroken women who prayed for their families through tears prayed mainly for their grandchildren who were pitied for having no strong example of Christian leadership in the home. The demographics of this evangelism were not incidental. Elderly parents who were themselves committed Christians had all but given up on their children 'converting'; those in their middle age were seen as having made their decision to 'reject Christ' despite having been 'raised under the influence of the gospel.' The efforts of my elderly Christian informants had shifted focus onto their grandchildren who were, after all, 'the future of the church.' Yet, as we shall see with the pinch of eschatology, the pinch of demography made it abundantly clear that time was running out.

Gregor and Carol, Mitchell and Rhoda—these older Christians could not expect to be on this earth for much longer; they were growing old and were 'heaven bound.' The time they had left was all the time that there was to secure the continued future of the church; if their grandchildren did not convert, the local religion would die. Parents—too busy with making money at sea or running the household—could not be relied upon to 'send forth the Gospel call' to the next generation, so it fell to the grandparents, through the sacrifice of their preaching, of their prayers, and of their 'daily life of witness,' to make the most of this last chance. As their bodies aged and failed, so too did their hopes of living to see the spiritual revival they so anxiously desired to be 'poured out upon the land.' If nothing changed soon, the only foreseeable path was numerical decline followed by extinction; 'There's only old ones left now Joe. Soon we'll have to close the door for good,' one man said as he locked up the hall after a prayer meeting. Such was the pinch of demography.

Out-migration, as discussed already, is something of a problem for the churches of Gamrie. Some young families have left the village to live in the larger towns of Banff and Fraserburgh. Others, while not moving residence, have chosen to worship there rather than attending any of the churches or halls in the village. Banff has a large charismatic church able to attract young families with a contemporary 'worship band,' and an emphasis on youth and children's work. Likewise, Fraserburgh is home to several lively Pentecostal churches that are personnel and cash rich. These churches seem to be bucking the wider regional and national trend toward decline in church attendance, a feature that is in some measure explained by the fact that these congregations are growing (in part) due to their ability to attract members away from other struggling churches, such as those in Gamrie.

Other complications regarding in-migration arise. While many of the 'incomers' to the village have no church connection at all, others do. In general, those not born and brought up in the village, if they were to go to any place of worship in Gamrie, would choose to go to the Kirk, it being the largest and most 'mainline' fellowship. Several of my Christian informants fell into this category and some had become highly involved in the life and work of the church. The Kirk Sunday school and (interdenominational) 'Crusaders' after school club also attracted several children from incomer families, even where their parents were not themselves attending any place of worship.

The FPCU offered a slightly different slant on the process of in-migration. Several of their key members were Northern Irish farmers who had sold their land in Ulster and bought much larger farms in Aberdeenshire where land was cheaper. These families represented the 'gathered' section of this congregation—far from being local, some undertook a 60 mile round trip to attend what Gamrics said felt like a church run by and for Northern Irish expats. Others, such as members of various Brethren groupings whose own halls had been forced to close because of numerical decline, came from neighboring towns and villages into Gamrie each Sunday for worship. Others still came to Gamrie not because their own Brethren meeting had closed, but because they had fallen out with those who ran the hall nearest their home.

Patterns of church attendance were neither bounded nor stable. While some left Gamrie every Sunday to worship outside the village, others came in, and still others did both, attending one church for a period of months (or even years), then moving elsewhere in search of a warmer welcome, a freer (or more conservative) doctrinal outlook, a different style of worship, or simply a change of scene. When it came to the churches of Gamrie and the surrounding region, the reasons for coming—as well as the reasons for going—were just as various as the people who held them.

Pinch Three: Eschatology

In the year 1145, Halley's Comet passed over Belgrade, with its gaseous tail burning bright in the night sky. Its cosmic light was so alarming, that, according to the Italian Renaissance historian Bartolomeo Platina, Pope Calixtus III ordered that special prayers be said for the city to avert the 'grievous pestilence' that would surely follow this onslaught of 'the wrath of God' (Emerson 1960). Calixtus's decree had its intended effect and Belgrade stood firm. About 200 years later, however, God's anger was rekindled against Europe, again in the form of Halley's comet. Yet on this occasion the prayers of the faithful did not meet with mercy but with an eruption of vengeful sickness so fierce that it struck down a third of the continent by 1350, as many as one hundred million souls. This bubonic plague—this blackest of deaths—was seen by many as The Almighty enacting judgment upon the whole earth in a way that could only but remind these Medieval Christians of the fate of Old Testament Egypt at the hands of Moses. By 1910, over half a millennium later, with the reappearance of the comet over Europe, the French astronomer Camille Flammarion predicted (albeit with 'scientific' intent) that Halley would finally bring about *la fin du monde* as a result of a highly poisonous gas that was said to be emanating from this increasingly infamous astral body. His prophecy—with hindsight, a little hasty—led to the panic buying of gas masks and 'anti-comet umbrellas' (Etter and Schnelder 1985) as fear took hold and people waited for either deliverance or death. Neither, in the end, arrived.

Many of my informants constantly sought to remind me that we were all living in 'the *last* of the *last* days' by which they meant that Christ would return (literally) 'any day now' to judge the world with fire from heaven. But what do the Christians of Gamrie have in common with Pope Calixtus III, the Black Death, and anti-comet umbrellas? They share, it seems, a concern with 'signs of the end times.' The Bible was the first place my informants looked to find these precursory warnings, and it was to the 'prophetic scriptures' of the Books of Daniel and Revelation that they normally turned. Yet—to borrow a phrase from Geertz (2000: 168)—if these texts were the menu, what my friends really wanted was a meal. To satisfy this hunger, the 'secular' world of Scotland compelled Gamrics to look not to astronomy but to modernity for evidence of the nearness of the 'last days'; it was politics, as opposed to comets and plagues, that provided the best proverbial meat of the imminent apocalypse.

It is this belief—that humanity is on the cusp of Armageddon—that forms the core of the final 'pinch,' and asks the question, how is everyday life to be lived in the present when any (and all) sense of the near future (see Guyer 2007) is either abandoned or endlessly qualified with the phrase 'assuming Jesus hasn't come back'? How does this unceasing anticipation of deliverance from imminent annihilation frame the way in which wider social, demographic, and population changes are viewed? Clearly, these eschatological beliefs promote enormously urgent and hugely pressurized efforts of evangelism: because time is said to be so critically short ('we are,' I was reminded time and again, 'living in the *last* of the *last* days'), the salvific stakes could not be higher.

The pressure my Christian friends felt to 'witness' to 'the need to be born-again' was enormous; the 'day of grace' (the time that remains *before* Christ's return in judgment, up to which salvation can still be received) was running perilously short and could be cut off in an instant, leaving, so I was told, millions if not billions of souls to (eternally) die in their sins. These were not the souls of some imagined and far off 'heathen,' but the painfully close and personally precious souls of 'unconverted loved ones'; husbands and wives who 'had not yet made a decision for Christ'; sons and daughters, now in their middle age, who 'showed no interest in the gospel'; and grandchildren, who 'were far, far away from the Kingdom.' From the perspective of the Christians of Gamrie, although they yearned for the return of the Christ who would usher them into heaven, this return was double-edged insofar as it also marked the beginning of an eternal separation from unsaved family members.

It was not just the shortness of time that made the stakes high; the 'pinch' of eschatology was also sharply felt because of the consequences of the decision that had to be made. Casually neglecting to respond to 'the call to be saved' amounted to the same thing as outright rejection—'a lost eternity in hell.' 'There is no sitting on the fence!' was the message I heard from dozens of gospel preachings in all six churches; 'You either accept Christ as your Savior or you reject Him!' Acceptance meant that those issuing 'the call to be saved' could be assured of 'enjoying an eternity of fellowship' with those who had responded positively in this way. Rejection meant eternal material separation from husbands and daughters and grandchildren who had 'been born-again.' Salvation and damnation, far from being predestined, were the products of human volition; personal events decided upon by the hearts of morally autonomous individuals, known to others (and thus indexed as 'real') either through 'giving testimony' or by 'living a life of sin.'

The weight of sorrow that this lived experience put on elderly Christians whose families were not 'saved' was heartbreaking to witness. I can remember attending a weekly prayer meeting at one particular church that was, like all the other meetings, mainly made up of folk in their sixties, seventies, and eighties. One woman, whenever the time came for open congregational prayer, would plead with God

to save her grandchildren. Her words expressed a deep sense of help-lessness; she had shared the gospel to no avail; their hearts were 'stub-born and hard'; they had, up to now, 'rejected Christ.' Her prayers were, almost without fail, cut short when stifled tears gave way to speechless weeping, leaving other congregants to step in and take up the same theme on behalf of their own 'unsaved' love ones. These were tears borne out of the tension between the instantaneous and the unending; between making a decision that took immediate effect and one that would also have permanent consequences; 'Time is run-ning out! Accept Christ as your Savior *tonight* and spend eternity with Him in heaven *tomorrow!*,' was the refrain of many a preacher. Such was the pinch of eschatology.

Practically (and prophetically) speaking, it has been 'the last of the last days' in Gamrie for decades. The Second Coming of Christ has been 'utterly imminent' since the Brethren arrived in the village in the 1850s, spreading their millennial vision through street preaching and home Bible study. Yet even a moderate amount of historicism allows one to see that the application of 'end times' Biblical prophecy to con-crete happenings 'in the world' is rather fickle. The title 'Antichrist' is an informative example: for a great number of years after the Scottish Reformation of 1560, many of those who broke with Rome espoused that the Roman Catholic Church in general, and the Pope in particu-lar, was the Antichrist. That is to say the Papacy was held to be the pro-phetic fulfillment of 'The Beast' spoken of in the Book of Revelation; a puppet of the devil designed to lead people into blasphemous wor-ship directed toward a demonic and counterfeit savior.

There was, for some time, broad consensus among the generations of followers of Luther, Calvin, and Knox in this regard, with the Papacy enjoying a spell of about four hundred years in the Protestant eschatological limelight—with some in Gamrie still subscribing to this view today. The next major figure to take the name 'Antichrist,' Charles Darwin, did so out of an intellectual creativity first made possible as a result of the Enlightenment, causing his theory of evolu-tion to be dubbed 'the religion of the Antichrist.' With the national and political upheavals of the twentieth century and the arrival of modernity, Darwin's unholy honor was lost during the war years to Nazism, which, because of its determined efforts to destroy the Jewish peoples of the world, was seen by many Christian Zionists (and not a few other Protestants) as the Antichrist. After the Second World War and the rise of the USSR, because of its ideological zeal and unfavor-able treatment of Christianity, communism replaced Nazism as the new and certain face of the Antichrist. The EU (then the Common

Market) was next to take the stand as the latest uncontested Antichrist with its unification of economic markets and a legal and bureaucratic structure centralized in Brussels. And then September 11 rocked the global political order, placing Islam, in the minds of many 'funda-mentalist' (and some evangelical) Protestants, as the clear and present manifestation of the Antichrist.

With the arrival of each new 'evil empire,' the old assertions that such and such was, without doubt, *the* Antichrist were forgotten, pav-ing the way for the demonization of a new institution or previously ignored religion or individual as the devil incarnate. The interpreta-tion of Biblical prophecy was (and is) sufficiently vague to allow for a highly malleable 'real world' application (cf. Thompson 2005: 29). In discussing 'the last of the last days,' no date or time is given and no specific disprovable threshold is offered; my informants told me that we were simply living through the 'end times.' 'Do you think we are living in the last days?,' I would ask my Christian friends. 'Of course we are!' came one particularly insightful response 'but the question is: are we living through the *last* of the last days? I think we most definitely are. *Most definitely.*'

But what happens when prophecy fails, to borrow from Festinger's (1956) famous study of an end of the world UFO cult? The obvious answer is that, in the context of Gamrie, it simply never does. The indefinite is always offered in place of the definite and, as a result, the general theme of future predictions—that we are living through the end times—triumphs over the specific details of how the Papacy or the EU or Islam fits into the picture (cf. Tumminia 2005). It is not the eschatological answer that matters but the act of reasserting the need to ask the question: Are we living through the last days? In the religious context of Gamrie, such a question can only ever be answered, *'Of course we are!'*

As the Christians of Gamrie looked into the future, all they could see was eschatological deliverance or economic and social destruc-tion. The likelihood of 'going out with a bang' seemed slim; these 'last of the last days.' being so small, promised only a whimper, that is, 'assuming'—as the endlessly sincere qualification to all future predic-tions went—'that Jesus didn't come back.' 'It's in the Lord's hands,' one man told me; 'God is still on the throne—we just have to wait on Him.' It is to the nature of this 'waiting time'—defined locally not by passive inaction but by the urgent activity of preaching, 'giv-ing testimony,' and evangelism—that we turn to in the second part of this book.

Part II

Words

Chapter 3

Preaching

*Then he said to me, "Son of man, eat this scroll I am giving you and fill your
stomach with it." So I ate it, and it tasted as sweet as honey in my mouth.*
(Ezekiel 3:3)

Gamrie's Christians often described Christianity as a life of worship and a life of sacrifice. But what does a life of sacrifice look like
and how is it related to worship? My friends explained how *'unsaved'*
persons were entirely guided by the sinful 'lusts' of the flesh, whereas
Christians (the *'saved'*), although still in possession of this 'fallen
nature,' sought instead to be guided by the righteous yearnings of
the 'spirit.' The activity of sermonizing reflected this divide. Sermons
that catered to the saved were referred to as 'Bible *teaching*' whereas
sermons directed toward the unsaved were referred to as 'gospel
preaching.' This differentiation between preaching to the unsaved
and teaching the saved was made sense of with reference to the consumption of different foods. Drawing on Pauline thought, preaching was likened to 'milk'—the food of unweaned babies—since the
simplicity of this gospel message of 'born-again salvation' was held to
be the only suitable sustenance for such spiritual infants. The saved,
being more mature, while also partaking of this milk, 'hungered
for' the 'meat' of Bible teaching—the deeper truths of the Bible—
which, when 'feasted upon,' would, like protein, help them grow and
develop. These four pairs of concepts—'unsaved' and 'saved'; 'flesh'
and 'spirit'; 'preaching' and 'teaching', 'meat' and 'milk'—help us to
see how sermonizing can be understood as a type of sacrifice.

Preaching as Sacrifice

*Sacrifice is a religious act which, through the consecration of a victim,
modifies the condition of the moral person who accomplishes it, or that of
certain objects with which he is concerned.*
(Hubert and Mauss 1968: 13)

So say Hubert and Mauss. But note how Gamrie's Christians—for whom the prototypical sacrifice of the crucifixion was *self*-sacrifice— seem to be folding each level of their famous typology back onto the Protestant individual. In their life of worship, the sacrificial '*victim*' is the flesh of the Christian. The ritual specialist (the '*sacrificer*') is not only the preacher, but also the ordinary listening congregant. The '*object*' of sacrifice is Christian personhood, and the beneficiary (the '*sacrifier*') is the one to whom that (now born-again) personhood is ascribed.

Sacrificing the 'sinful lusts of the flesh' was said by local Christians to involve the 'starving' of bodily desire and the 'feeding' of the life of the spirit. The flesh referred locally to various 'natural' (and thus 'fallen') corporeal 'lusts' for food (especially meat, seen as stimulating libido), dancing, sex, alcohol, tobacco, and violence, as well as various other forms of bodily stimulation and gratification. Amy showed me her mother's 'Pledge Certificate' that solemnized her vow never to drink alcohol, a vow that Amy herself had taken. William spoke to me of his strict disapproval of dancing, even at weddings. Gavin spoke of his ongoing struggle against smoking, something that he saw as a God-dishonoring bodily addiction that he needed to conquer 'in the power of Jesus' Name.'

The spirit, rather than naturally desiring the things of the body, supernaturally desired the things of God—typified locally as prayer, hymn singing, Christian fellowship, and of course, the reading and exposition of 'The Word.' Gavin's struggle with nicotine was a battle he could always hope to win, no matter how many setbacks he experienced, because, unlike his non-Christian friends, his 'flesh' (and its desires) was slowly being transformed as he prayed, read the Bible, and heard 'The Word' preached. It was through the speaking and hearing of sermons, then, understood as acts of sacrificial worship, which granted my informants a mediating category with which the 'spirit' and 'flesh' could be traversed. But what was being sacrificed? And how? And with what outcomes?

First, *what* was being sacrificed? The local answer was the 'lusts of the flesh.' Corporeal pleasures were condemned from Gamrie's pulpits and prayer halls for their demanding immediate and repeated physical gratification regardless of the impact upon the credibility of one's 'testimony.' It was the 'free and easy' 'indulgence' of bodily desire— the 'sins of the flesh' as my informants frequently called them—that were to be sacrificed. These were the 'sinful lusts' that so many of my older Christian informants imagined would eventually cast their grandchildren into hell. Such was the necessity of the sacrifice.

Second, *how* was it being sacrificed? Sacrificing the flesh was said by local Christians to involve the 'starving' of the sinful desires of the body and the 'feeding' of the life of the spirit. The sacrificial life of Christian worship, then, like all 'traditional' forms of sacrifice, involved a kind of killing—the killing of the flesh. This is evidenced by the fact that my closest informants who spoke to me about personal struggles in their 'walk of faith' portrayed their 'life of worship' as an 'ongoing battle with the flesh,' seen in Gavin's fight against smoking or in Amy's vowing to never drink. The needful task of the Christian was described to me by these friends as explicitly involving a 'putting to death' of the flesh: 'Be busy killing *sin* or sin will be busy killing *you*!'

I want here to draw some parallels between Gamrie's folk-theological model of self-sacrifice-as-mortification-and-feasting and the model described by Robertson Smith (1972: 252, 255) and elaborated by Durkheim (2008: 251) that states that sacrifice necessitates, in some form or another, the eating of the sacred being. Thus, where Robertson Smith states that

> everywhere we find that sacrifice ordinarily involves a feast, and that a feast cannot be provided without a sacrifice [...] when men meet their god they feast and are glad together. (Robertson Smith 1972: 255)

I suggest a similar process of ingestion is at work within the sacrificial worship of Gamrie's Christians. Where the work of (totemic) sacrifice seeks to forge 'fictive kinship' (Carsten 1997) bonds between the worshipper and the divine through the sharing of food, for Gamrie's Christians, the sacrificial 'killing' of the flesh is in large part achieved through a (very Protestant) take on Robertson Smith's ancient Semitic sacrificial feast. Where my informants constantly pressed upon me the necessity of 'feasting upon the Word of God,' and where preaching, praying, and reading the Bible were all seen as central aspects of 'feeding' the new spiritual life of any Christian in Gamrie, like so many methods of sacrifice, the sacrifice of the flesh requires a kind of eating. But—and this is where I significantly diverge from both Robertson Smith and Durkheim—it is not an eating that necessarily involves the literal imbibing of food through the mouth, but rather involves the figurative imbibing of words through the ear. The 'flesh' that Gavin, Amy, and William sacrificed through a life of reverence was *transformed* into words and then *re-embodied* ('feasted upon') through the key religious ritual of sermonizing. It is this re-embodiment—this eating of words through the ear—that constituted, for my friends, the sacrificial meal of the speaking and hearing of sermons.

Third, what was the *outcome* of such a sacrifice? The answer again lies with the duality of Christian personhood locally conceived. The first outcome was a 'putting to death' of the flesh—experienced through my informants' (figuratively) violent destruction of the physical compulsion to gratify the desires of their bodies, seen in their (literal, material) abstention from those forms of life already mentioned above. The second outcome, connected to the first, was my informants strengthening of their life in the 'spirit' through the 'feeding' of spiritual desires to pray, sing hymns, share Christian fellowship, witness to the unsaved, read 'The Word,' and hear it preached. Mortification of the body followed by sanctification of the self followed by mortification of the body . . . a sacrificial process that was imagined to occur and reoccur until the commencement of 'the hereafter.'

This sacrificial 'killing' of the flesh and its sinful desires was undertaken by a kind of figurative 'starving' and 'feeding.' The flesh (the '*victim*' in Hubert and Mauss's terms) was 'put to death' through the strict denial of corporal desire through the normative expectation of teetotalism, celibacy outside marriage and prohibitions on smoking, foul language, violent behavior, and so on. In this sense, sacrificing the flesh by starving it of corporeal appetites is closely akin to the related phenomenon of mortification. Indeed, my informants seemed to conflate sacrifice and mortification through their reading of scripture, most especially Paul's epistle to the Romans in which first-century Christians are entreated to *'present your bodies as a living sacrifice, holy and acceptable to God, which is your spiritual worship.'* Among Gamrie's twenty-first-century Christians, this 'presentation' of the body is double-edged; as with 'born-again' conversion, it requires that a death (to 'self,' 'sin,' and 'flesh') takes place before new life can occur. In local folk-theological terms, abstaining from sensual gratification was both mortification and sacrifice because it 'crucified' the flesh and, in so doing, presented the body to God as a sacrificial offering of self-renunciation.

The Christians of Gamrie are not alone in pursuing this model of mortification-as-sacrifice. William Christian (1972), in his analysis of *promesa* ('promise' or 'pledge') prayers among Catholic peasant farmers in northern Spain describes a similar process of self-renunciation as sacrificial penance. 'The sacrifice of pride,' for example, occurs through mimicry of monasticism by shaving the head and donning a 'sacrificial habit.' Other examples include sacrificing resources of time and money in prayer and alms giving, as well as sacrificing bodily comfort and pleasure by undertaking pilgrimage barefoot (Christian 1972: 119–120). So too among Catholic peasant farmers in Portugal, where:

> A concern for satisfaction of bodily desires alone would give rise to *vicios* [evil]...These have to be tempered by restraint and order, by sacraments, the household, social norms....Peasant society is not merely concerned with the procurement of a bountiful life, but rather with a bountiful *and* orderly 'social' life. (Pina-Cabral 1986: 124)

In Protestant Gamrie, as in Catholic Spain and Portugal, these abstentions were only part of the picture; there was also a more constructive method for encouraging 'restraint' and creating 'order' beyond a 'killing' of the flesh, namely 'feeding' the 'life of the spirit.' Being a *'living* sacrifice,' my friends would tell me, meant living a life of reverent worship characterized by a pursuit of the spirit that was received into their renewed bodies by feasting upon the words of scripture. Eschatologically, what my friends sought was a joining of their human bodies and selves with the very body and self of Christ, who, at the point of His soon arrival at 'the end of days,' would rapture them—bodily—into the heavens.

Where preparation for this 'Rapture' often centered on the stomach—on the 'eating' and 'digesting' of scripture—it should be borne in mind that such lofty gastronomic goals are far from new, existing, as Caroline Walker Bynum (1987) vividly describes, as a central aspect of medieval religious symbolism. By virtue of being the primary preparers (as opposed to consumers) of food, medieval women were able to develop—in its very refusal—both a culturally acceptable form of asceticism and a highly effective form of manipulation (Bynum 1987: 191–192). Crucially, this manipulation was not just exerted over their own bodies, but over the entire cosmos:

> Fasting...was part of suffering...which redeemed both individual and cosmos. Women's inedia...can be understood only if we understand the late medieval notion of *imitatio Christi* as fusion with the suffering physicality of Christ, and late medieval notions of the female as flesh....[To these female pietists] the point was pain because the pain was Christ's. (Bynum 1987: 207, 212)

Moreover:

> Food was a multifaceted symbol in medieval spirituality...[F]ood basically meant flesh; flesh meant suffering (sometimes ecstatic, delicious

suffering); and suffering meant redemption. Fasting, feeding and feasting were thus not so much opposites as synonyms. Fasting was not flight
from but *into* physicality. Communion was consuming i.e., becoming,
a God who saves through physical, human agony.... [Medieval women]
frequently called this journey "eating" or "hungering", because to eat
is to join with food—and God is food, which is flesh, which is suffering, which is salvation.... To eat was to consume, to take in, to become
God. And to eat was also to rend and tear God. Eating was a horribly
audacious act. Yet it was only by bleeding, by being torn and rent, by
dying, that God's body redeemed humanity. To become that body by
eating was therefore to bleed and to save—to lift one's own physicality
into suffering and into glory. (Bynum 1987: 250–251)

The parallels between the religious devotions of these medieval
women and the Christians of Gamrie are striking: both take food—
starving, eating, and feasting—as key religious symbols. Both cause
'the flesh' to suffer in order to achieve communion with the divine.
Both, ultimately, seek a salvation that is rooted in the here (in 'physicality' and materiality) and the hereafter (in cosmological redemption
and in heavenly 'glory'). Yet there are also important differences. In
Gamrie, God is *food* only in the sense that He is *Word*—the quint-
essential 'spiritual nourishment' that is 'hungered for' by all 'true
Christians.' And for Gamrics, God is certainly *not* flesh—for this
means fallen corporeality. Indeed, although Christ became flesh, His
flesh was special; it was made of words; He became the *Logos*, the
Incarnate Word.

In Gamrie theology, not only did Christ's flesh become 'Word,'
it also became a book, in the 'living,' 'breathing' pages of the Bible.
Humans, tragically, were the ones made of fallen flesh; God, on the
other hand, was *text*. Where Bynum suggest that, for medieval female
ascetics, 'the point was pain because the pain was Christ's' (1987:
212), in Gamrie, *the point was Word because the Word was Christ's.*
Or perhaps 'The Word *was Christ*,' suggesting not just ownership
but existential union. Indeed, on one occasion, I met a man who,
seeking to bring about my conversion, leveled his gaze at me and
said: 'If you want to know Jesus, *here He is*,' as he placed his Bible in
my hands. To the extent that he meant for me to take what he said as
literally true (and I think he did), it seems that my informants' imitation of Christ, rather than fixing upon the redemptive nature of pain,
focused instead on the differently stimulating processes of words and
language. It was words (preached, prayed, read, sung, and witnessed
to), that granted oral and aural routes to self-sacrifice, mortification,
salvation, and glorification.

What of communion—of 'breaking bread' at the 'Lord's table'?
And what of that quintessentially Protestant get-together, the after-
church 'bring-and-share' meal?[1] Over the duration of my fieldwork,
I noticed with interest how the ritual of communion seemed to be
an almost entirely representational event, whereas church suppers and
times of fellowship and hospitality in the homes of Gamrie's Christians
were very material celebrations of food. One of the first explanations
I heard for the Brethren 'breaking of bread' service, offered by Lachlan
during an OB 'Bible reading' only weeks after I arrived in Gamrie is an
insightful local account of the meaning of communion:

> [We read here in Mark 14 of] the institution of this very precious feast:
> the breaking of bread and drinking of the cup. I've never ever got over
> the simplicity of remembering the Lord Jesus. Simply bread and wine;
> and it's a wonderful thing that His people down through the ages have
> done this. *We must stress that this is only emblems....* The additions of
> man spoils everything.... It's [only supposed to be] a loaf of bread and
> a cup of wine, and men have spoiled it. *It's nae a re-enactment, it's a
> remembrance....* There is a day coming that's going to be very joyful:
> when we see Him [face to face, at the point of the Second Coming] *we
> will na need bread or a cup.*

As a restatement of the communion-as-purely-symbolic 'Memorialism'
commonly associated with the early Swiss Reformer Huldrych
Zwingli, Lachlan's description of the Eucharist as, variously, 'only
emblems,' 'a loaf of bread and a cup of wine,' and 'a remembrance'
that will not be needed after the Second Coming, seems to leave
little room for the celebration of actual (nonsymbolic) practices of
eating and drinking as a real gastronomic event, either in religious
ritual or the everyday. Nor is Lachlan alone in his estimation; all
the churches in Gamrie broadly shared this view of communion as
an act of remembrance that used bread and wine to symbolically
memorialize the death (and soon return) of Christ. The wider context here—historically and in present imaginings—is a critique of
Roman Catholicism and its supposed 'reenactment' of the crucifixion through an assertion of the nonsymbolic 'real presence' of
the body and blood of Christ via the doctrine of transubstantiation.
These 'additions of man' were held by the Christians of Gamrie to be
unscriptural and therefore corrupting innovations. 'The simplicity of
remembering' had been 'spoiled,' and it was their task, as '*true* Bible
believers' to faithfully (and accurately) observe 'this very precious
feast' until the coming 'joyful day' when neither loaf nor cup would
be required to remember.

But until then, what else were the Christians of Gamrie putting in their stomachs apart from huge quantities of words and tiny amounts of bread and wine? Occasions for congregational feasting were plentiful. Sunday services would almost always end in (or be transitioned by) cups of tea and trays of biscuits; one church went as far as to have a communal meal at the end of every Sunday evening service. After-church fellowships—commonly marking the arrival or departure of special guests—would always center on the sharing of food, with vast spreads of savory and sweet dishes provided (usually by female congregants) in grand displays of culinary skill. 'Soup and sweet' church fundraisers were equally popular; hearty soups and dozens of deserts would be topped off with piles of home-bakes and washed down with endless cups of milky tea. Meals in the home also featured prominently in the Christian lives of my friends. Sunday lunches and teas were major gastronomic events and occasions for competitive hospitality, with women attempting to outdo one another in what sometimes felt like an arms race of home economics.

The Christians of Gamrie were not straightforwardly ascetic—not when it came to food at any rate. My friends nourished their bodies with a varied (and sometimes rich) diet of meats, vegetables, sweet puddings, and, of course, the best quality fish and shellfish. This culture of plenty worried some; 'the kingdom of heaven is nae meat and drink!' one man said to me in scornful criticism of another hall's emphasis on hosting communal meals. Others were concerned that jovial conversation over food after church allowed the devil to snatch away the words of the sermon before they could be 'digested.' Similar anxieties surrounded bountiful harvests of prawns at sea; although this food was mainly shipped off to the Continent, profits from catches—and thus the embodiment of 'worldly' standards of, for example, dress—had increased. Other forms of bodily consumption remained taboo for local Christians; alcohol, tobacco, and tattoos, despite their cultural prominence among fishermen, were shunned. Heroin addiction, widely visible within the bigger fishing towns of the northeast (and said to be rife among younger generations of Scots fishermen), was also universally condemned—often as a 'demonic craving,' that, like alcoholism, was said to emerge from the sin of gluttony.

As these storms of worldliness and sin raged around them, the Christians of Gamrie continued to meet around the 'Lord's Table' to break bread, to remember, and to wait. The elements themselves were not particularly consequential. Some churches used wine, others grape juice, still others port. The Brethren favored round uncut loaves of bread, the Presbyterians cut squares of bread from presliced loaves. Leftovers were thrown away without ceremony—one man I knew actually took the scraps of bread home in a little bag to feed the birds, rather than waste good food. Where the symbolic resonance between the Lord's Table and the dinner table is especially strong among Highland Presbyterians (seating reserved for communicant members is traditionally marked out by draping white fabric—strongly reminiscent of table cloths—over pews, an act known as 'setting the table'), this was not an emphasis within the churches of Gamrie.

Yet, far from indicating a disenchanted view of communion and of food, the 'Memorialism' my friends avowed was of such importance that ritual participation fully demarcated the boundaries of the Christian community. I was not allowed to break bread in three of Gamrie's four Brethren halls; being non-Brethren and a newcomer left them unconvinced that my life and faith befitted my claim to being a Christian. The other three congregations, conversely, signaled their acceptance of my claim to faith by allowing me to partake of the elements. In Gamrie, as across Christendom, food—and the ritual sharing of food—was emblematic of salvation. Indeed

> meals...symbolise proper behavior among social groups in relation to one another and in relation to God....In establishing precisely who eats what with whom, commensality is one of the most powerful ways of defining and differentiating social groups. (Feeley-Harnik 1994: 2, 11)

Which is why the EB 'separate tables' edict (debarring members from sharing *any* food or drink with nonmembers, including children within the immediate family) was so controversial and led many to leave. Here, food sought not only to demarcate the limits of Christian community, but sought to do so through 'the destruction of kinship' (Feeley-Harnik 1994: 141). But why take food—bread, wine, the dinner table—as the key establishing symbol? Feeley-Harnik's work on early Judaism and Christianity is helpful:

> Food was the embodiment of God's word, his wisdom, for a people who would have no graven images. The food God provided was his word....God's word, as represented in scripture, was not a dead formula. The word was realised in creative, life-giving, death-dealing speech, which transformed wisdom into practice, as food is transformed into flesh. (Feeley-Harnik 1994: 107)

Indeed, 'food was the word and food law was the law' (Feeley-Harnik 1994: 107). But if food is a type of word, can the opposite really be true? Can words be food; can words be eaten? Feely-Harnik says not, arguing that during the intertestamental period gastronomy had the advantage over language: 'food, as opposed to…scripture…could be eaten' (1994: 167). Being unable to comment on ancient Palestine, I want to limit myself to Gamrie and to the present by returning to my suggestion that it was words that my Christian friends came together to eat as they sat in the pews listening to scripture being preached. Communion, being '*only emblems,*' was a symbolic affair. Preaching, on the other hand, existed as a very real kind of eating, and scripture as a very real kind of food. Not only was Christ—the God-man— both human and divine, he was also the Incarnate Word; a 'living page'; a book 'still warm with the breath of God.' The Eucharistic call to eat His flesh and drink His blood, then, was not primarily fulfilled by eating bread and wine, for there was memory there, but no real power—and certainly no 'Real Presence.' Communing with (and consuming) God—achieving commensality with Him—was, for my friends, a state best realized by feasting upon the 'milk' and 'meat' of the Bible, through the 'preaching' and 'teaching' of 'The Word' made text.

This textual incarnation—this word-made-flesh-made-text—gave birth to a new kind of Eucharistic consubstantiation, for it was here, in the pages of scripture, that my friends encountered both the 'Real Presence' of the divine *and* the material presence of the everyday. The immanence of its bound pages and leather cover made the Bible a human object; the transcendence of its textually incarnated divinity made it an object of God. As was said to be true of Christ's body, both sets of presences occurred simultaneously; scripture was both a book, and, in an extreme formulation I heard on more than one occasion, a part of the Trinity—'Father, Son and Holy *Bible.*'

As a result of the enchantment of conversion, moreover, Christians themselves could expect to undergo their very own textual incarnation. Being 'born-again' meant becoming what one informant described to me as a 'living epistle.' His logic was in clear agreement with other Christians in the village: 'People will na read the Bible, but they will read your life!'; 'We may be the only Bible they read!'; 'We pray that our very lives might be as The Word!' Being a 'living epistle,' then, meant becoming a kind of book—an epistle incarnate—that could be read *by* the 'unsaved' through observation of Christian conduct and read *to* the unsaved though the giving of Christian 'testimony.' Thus, one difference between the 'saved' and the 'unsaved' was that the saved person, by being 'born-again,' had begun to develop a different kind of body that contained a different kind of substance—'The

Word.' Salvation came to be experienced (created *and* maintained) as bifurcation; 'The Word' entered the newly 'born-again' body, but the 'flesh' remained. The result was a copresence, which, like Gamrie's folk theology of the Bible-as-textual-incarnation, mirrored the Eucharistic doctrine of consubstantiation by positing immanence (bodies, bread, books) and transcendence (spirit, salvation, scripture) as concurrent and interchangeable.

In positing the existence of a transformed body made not of flesh but of words, I do not want to suggest that this body is essentially 'metaphorical' and thus 'really' yet another example of the supposed 'pure transcendence' of Christianity. In the very different context of the Catholic Philippines descried by Cannell (1999), devotions offered to *Ama* (a life-sized wooden carving of the 'dead Christ') allows 'a process...of becoming like Christ...and so transforming oneself' through an 'identificatory logic' where 'one's identity is actively merged with that of the holy figures' (182). For Gamrics, the process of transformation-by-identification is similar, but involves words as opposed to wood, producing a new kind of logocentric immanence that no longer dichotomizes flesh and spirit, but actually conflates them. The sacrificial outcome is both the immanence of transcendence and the transcendence of immanence.

Preaching in Context

> God [is] sanctifying his people in every age through the preaching and the teaching of the Bible....Take seriously the preaching of the Word of God Sunday after Sunday in this place! Take it seriously because you are being prepared for heaven...through the teaching of the Word of God....This is a preparation for eternity....As you come to sit under the ministry of God's Word, don't reject that ministry. Take it on board and say "Lord, it's not the minister who's speaking to me here; it's *you* who is speaking to me through your Word..." Act upon what is taught in the Word of God....Whatever God says to you in the preaching and teaching of the scriptures *do it* and be obedient to what God tells you!

It was the second week of May, a Sunday, and I was sitting in the Gamrie Kirk. It was my fourth church meeting of the day and the eighth of that week. The preacher spoke with a high pitched urgency as he pleaded with us to submit ourselves to the truth of God as it emanated from the pulpit—itself an impressive structure that towered a full 12 feet over the congregation. But what does it mean to 'take seriously the preaching of the Word of God'? Why is listening to a sermon 'preparation for eternity'? And how is the experience of listening to what is said from the pulpit transformed by the view that it is not the minister who speaks but God?

Having 'sat under' roughly four hundred sermons during my time in the field, I left the village with a strong sense of their importance within Gamrie religiosity. Crucially, there existed different types of sermons according to the perceived spiritual condition of the (often imagined) target audience. Morning services catered for the 'saved.' At the churches (Kirk and FPCU) the sermon was designed to teach and encourage believers. At the halls (OB, CB) there was a 'Breaking of Bread' service for those who were 'in the meeting' (born-again *members*) that would often have a 'wee wordie' (short sermon) aimed at explaining afresh some aspect of the act of breaking bread.

In the afternoon in the halls there would be either a 'Bible reading' (where certain leading men would discuss a portion of scripture while the majority of men and all of the women would sit in silence and listen), or there would be a 'ministry meeting'—a sermon similar in function to the morning services at the churches. At the end of the day (generally 6 p.m.) gospel preachings (called the 'glad tidings'[2] by the CB) would occur at every place of worship in the village. These were aimed at the 'lost' and were the best attended because many 'unsaved' would maintain a church connection by going. I also heard sermons preached at informal 'prayer meetings' in folk's houses, on streets and in town squares, at youth clubs, during men's get-togethers, at old folks coffee mornings and played on CDs in living rooms; I even heard a sermon preached in a local fish market to celebrate the launching of a new boat. With such variety comes the need for a definition.

Tomlinson—who defines sermonizing as 'a genre of ritual speech performance in which explicating Biblical texts is a central goal' (2006: 129)—provides a helpful starting point. Sermonizing *is* a 'ritual speech performance' insofar as it is a kind of 'religious formalism' spoken in front of an audience (Durkheim 2008: 35). But, like many conservative Protestants, my informants would strongly object to the suggestion that their preaching was 'ritual,' for fear of being associated with Roman Catholic forms of worship. Explicating via exegesis was central; 'I'm not reading *into* the Bible, I'm here to read *out of it*!' was a common way of rhetorically framing this aspect of sermonizing. While formal public delivery of Biblical exegesis was deemed to be essential, preaching was what it was because there was also an audience—a congregation of listeners. Sermonizing was not only a 'ritual *speech* performance' (Tomlinson 2006: 129), but also closely bound up with the practice of *listening*; it was the ear, just as much as the tongue, that was involved in the preaching of the scriptures.

Despite the plethora of different 'worship services' listed above, I want to consider the sermons that I 'sat under' during my fieldwork not as an endlessly diverse system of species and subspecies, but rather as reflecting a dual typology—that of (i) 'preaching' and (ii) 'teaching'. These are two distinct practices that need to be explicated as such. While I am aware that this dualism is in danger of underemphasizing both sameness (the sense that preaching really is something of a coherent whole) and difference (insofar as there are more than two 'types' of sermon), its retention is justified insofar as the dual categories of 'preaching' and 'teaching' did exist 'on the ground' in order to cater for (and create) two distinct audiences—and types of person—the 'saved' and the 'unsaved.'

Preaching the Gospel

Attending a Gospel service at one of Gamrie's CB Halls for the first time left quite an impression on me. Proceedings began when a man called Martin slowly rose to his feet, walked to the front of the hall, and stood behind the lectern. He gave out a hymn number, and, after the singing, three readings, and a short prayer, he began to preach:

> God in his glad tidings tonight is the way of peace! It is a way unknown to Man naturally! Man cannot walk in it...because Man walks by sight and knows nothing about the path of life!...Man is lost! Guilty! Born in sin! All have sinned!...We [the saved] have been redeemed by precious blood!...Dear friends, does everyone in this room believe that God raised Jesus from the dead? Oh the ransom price!...Have you ever stopped to contemplate the glories of the Lord Jesus? If you do not know him this is your opportunity to find him tonight! Has everyone here bowed the knee to Jesus?...We are living on the threshold of great events.... *Now* is the accepted time [to be saved]: tomorrow might be too late! This world is ripe for judgment! And how soon will it be? We do not know, but He could come tonight and it will be too late!...May we know what it means to have Him as our personal savior! May you accept Him tonight, for His namesake.

The 'fundamental' message of Christianity I heard over dozens of gospel preachings was this: human beings are born as enemies of God, are under the curse of Adam's sin, are naturally ignorant of 'the things of God,' and, because they cannot help but delight in evil, are bound for everlasting punishment in hell. But, roughly two thousand years

ago, the Son of God came to earth, lived a perfect life, and then sacrificed himself on the cross to 'pay the price' for the sins of humanity. As a result, anyone who has 'come under the shelter of the blood'
by being 'born-again' through 'personal faith' in Jesus has had their
rightful punishment transferred onto Him and will escape the wrath of
God that is soon to be poured out upon the world when Jesus returns
in judgment. These 'born-again' believers would either go to heaven
when they die, or, if they live to see the unfolding of 'end times prophecy' (as was assumed to be the case locally), they would vanish from the
face of the earth having been 'raptured' (bodily) into heaven. Those
who 'refuse to recognize their need of a savior' would either 'die in
their sins' and enter a 'lost eternity' or, if alive at the point of the rapture, would suffer seven years of 'tribulation' on earth and then be cast
eternally into hell. Such was the 'seriousness' of the gospel message.

My liberal use of exclamation marks in the transcription is not an
exaggeration of his oratorical style, but is meant to accurately con-
vey the level of intensity with which Martin preached—and he was
no exception. All of the men I heard preach the gospel did so with
extreme verbal (and bodily) intensity. Such delivery ran against normal conventions of speech—these elderly fishermen were not bold
and brash by habit, but shy and reserved in general conversation. Yet
their sermons were marked with a sense of power, feeling, and considerable volume. '*Thump it oot!!*' would be the (only half joking)
advice given to preachers on the evening they were due to 'take the
gospel.' Men's faces often went puce as they shouted from their platform about the immediate imperative of being 'born-again.' 'Man is
lost! Guilty! Born in sin!' Martin roared at us from the front of the
hall with the occasional fleck of spittle shooting out of his mouth and
catching the light as it descended on those sitting in the front row.
A preacher would take his Bible in his hand, waving it in the air to
emphasize a point with particular authority, and, on occasion, might
actually thump the cover with his fist as he 'sent forth The Word'
with almost hysterical zeal.

Sermons were not monologues but interactive in the sense that
preachers also often fired (albeit rhetorical) questions at the congregation as a way of drawing them in: 'Dear friends, does everyone in this
room believe that God raised Jesus from the dead? ... Have you ever
stopped to contemplate the glories of the Lord Jesus?' Such questions
were also linked to an appeal: 'May *we* know what it means to have
Him as our personal savior! May *you* accept Him tonight' By starting with the first person plural and ending with the second person
singular, a preacher would seek to evoke both shared responsibility

and direct confrontation. '*There's a heaven to be gained and a hell to be avoided!*' Add to this the fact that time was deemed to be incredibly short—'We are living on the threshold of great events....He could come tonight and it will be too late!'—and we begin to see why the message that Martin delivered was designed to sound like an utter emergency. But why did Christians like Martin preach the gospel in the first place?

The reason for preaching the gospel was because there existed a category of persons called 'the unsaved' who urgently needed, before the end of the 'day of grace' to be 'born-again' and thereby join the ranks of the 'saved.' This is why Elsa, weeping to the point of speechlessness when attempting to pray for the conversion of her grandchildren, was not praying for their salvation in the abstract, but was rather praying specifically for the preaching of the gospel. Praying for their salvation meant praying for the preaching; that 'the gospel would be proclaimed with convicting and converting power'—a phrase that Elsa and others used frequently. The gospel existed 'to do a saving work,' and it was for the efficacy of this work that she 'prayed over' with tears of anguished sincerity. Without this category of 'unsaved' persons, the preaching of the gospel would be superfluous.

Friends who shared with me their 'testimony' very often referred to their 'moment of conversion' as coming during a sermon. Doug described to me how he was restored to 'saving faith' after hearing the text 'Seek ye first the Kingdom of God' preached about on three occasions in as many days. Luke, a friend who struggled with learning difficulties, spoke of how he was saved from abandoning his faith when he eventually learnt how to read when in his thirties. Reading the Bible for himself for the first time meant he could finally understand the preaching. His 'hunger' for 'The Word' grew and he sought to be spiritually 'fed.' Stewart, another friend, used to attend worship services with me at a local nursing home for patients with severe dementia, and always left feeling dejected. 'It's just so *depressing*!' he said '*none* of it's going in—they don't understand a *word* the preacher is saying!' Stewart later explained that if they were not saved before they had 'lost their minds' then 'there was no hope for them now—how could there be? They canna understand and respond to the gospel.' These dementia sufferers could not be saved, then, because they could not 'hear' the gospel.

Doug, Luke, and Stewart help us to see that listening is just as important as speaking. In order for preaching to foster the kind of salvific 'hope' that Stewart spoke about, the right kind of words and feelings were required to allow one's ears to be 'opened' and one's heart to 'respond.' But what importance was accorded to the *eyes*? What kind of *sight* did preaching grant the sinner? Doug, Luke, and many others described how hearing the gospel granted them sight of their sin, that is, it brought a sincere conviction to their 'heart' that they were 'in need of a savior.' Preaching brought sight that brought conviction that brought conversion. The gospel was preached because there existed this category of 'the unsaved' who were 'blind' and needed to receive 'spiritual sight' so that they would 'be given conviction of sin' and experience salvation via conversion. Without the category of 'sinner' everything else collapses in on itself.

Does the preaching of the gospel lose its urgency (and perhaps even its intelligibility) when all those listening are 'saved'? When attending High Street CB gospel preachings, the 'glad tidings' would be 'sent forth' despite the fact that there were only six or seven people present, all of whom were publicly recognized (through their participation in the breaking of bread) as fully committed Christians. Despite the spiritual security of the tiny congregation, the same intensely urgent message would be 'sent forth.' The burning imperative of becoming a 'born-again' Christian would be stated and restated for the entire duration of the sermon. Even assuming that this particular CB group was, at times, less than fully convinced that I myself was a 'true believer,' these gospel preachings had been happening faithfully (in my absence) every Sunday night for years to these same six Christians. So why preach the need to be 'born again' to 'born-again believers'?

The highly standardized style and totally inflexible format of these sermons is insightful. 'We just have to keep preaching the glad tidings,' the preacher would say to me as we filed out the hall. A woman, apparently embarrassed by the tiny size of their meeting said to me on my arrival: 'Well Joseph, there aren't many of us, but we just go on—we have to be faithful,' explaining that because the sign outside their hall stated that The Word of God would be preached every Lord's Day at 6 p.m., it was their spiritual duty to do so regardless of who attended. 'We are always hopeful of visitors,' another woman commented, despite the fact that I never saw a single visitor apart from myself during my 15 month association with their hall. The shift in thinking is profound. The imagined (potential) audience, that is, the conceptually present but physically absent category of the 'unsaved' was, for my friends, more real ('real' in the sense that it directed action in the world) than the audience sitting facing the preacher. It wasn't the 'soul state' of the congregation that mattered, but the brute existence—'out there' in the world—of the category of the 'unsaved' that determined what and how and why men preached. The method of delivery (preaching) and the subject matter (the gospel), were, in a sense, the same thing. Preaching was, by definition, preaching the gospel.

Yet for those 'saved souls' who sat silently in the pews, listening to the gospel was an act of worship. 'You never get too old for the gospel!' was a stock phrase often voiced at the end of a sermon by ordinary congregants; 'it's always the same but you can never hear it enough!' This was the case, my friends would tell me, because the gospel represented 'the basic diet' of any 'true believer'—like the drinking of milk, it was held to be both a necessity and a joy for all. 'You never grow out of it!' was the summary of another ordinary congregant. Such was the enchanted experience of listening to preaching as an act of worship that it was characterized by both the immanence of personal 'fellowship with Christ' and the transcendence of being 'transported to the Pearly Gates.'

But '*teaching* the Bible' was held to be a fundamentally different kind of activity (which provided a different kind of sustenance—not milk but meat) because it was itself defined by a different category of person—the 'saved.'

Teaching the Bible

There is only one piece of furniture in the most holy place. It's important....This is divine revelation. There is the ark and the mercy seat. The mercy seat was made of pure gold....The Ark speaks primarily of the Lord Jesus Christ....He's the God of heaven and He must have the pre-eminence....The Tabernacle was a place where God might dwell, so it was fundamental to the worship of the Israelite...and Christ is fundamental to our worship. The shittim wood speaks about His humanity: it was imperishable, it was incorruptible, it didn't rot, and that speaks about His sinless nature. And [the wood] was clothed with gold: [which speaks of] humanity clothed with deity. But with Christ it was the other way around; deity clothed with humanity....The manna speaks of spiritual food: it is white [which speaks of] His purity....And Aaron's rod spoke of resurrection. And we have that [assurance of resurrection] in our hearts today, that we are going to see our loved ones again [in heaven]....[And] we are going to see Him [Jesus]. We are going to see Him! Why am I so sure? Because it was his prayer!

* * *

The great thing in our Christian life is not heaven, but to *see* our Savior first of all! There's no retirement in this business, no retirement in the Christian life! [We are] never satisfied with the spiritual [condition of the present; we are] always seeking more ground to be possessed. We're all getting older, but the Lord is the same, he never changes....Encourage the saints! To encourage them is to give them heart!...It's a good thing to be able to put the saints at peace....What am I trying to do here in Gardenstown today? I'm trying to put *heart* into you! What is ours by promise we should make ours by possession!...It's good! What is Hebron? Fellowship!...Fellows-rowing-in-a-ship! That's what it means! All rowing the same way! We're going home!

Above are two sections of transcript taken from two different 'ministry meetings' I heard at the OB. Both preachers, like most of the men at the hall, were retired fisherman. The first sermon explained the symbolism of the Ark of the Covenant as described in the Book of Exodus. The second was a call for the congregation to 'follow the Lord with a whole heart.' Where preaching the gospel involved an (often imagined) dual process of 'conviction' and then 'conversion,' teaching the Bible was also, by and large, said to have two distinct processes at its core—that of the 'equipping' and 'encouraging' of believers.

Where *preaching* existed because of the (logically prior) existence of 'sinners' who needed 'saving,' *teaching* existed because of the (no less logically prior) existence of Christians who needed 'feeding.' But how might a sermon about the symbolism of the Ark of the Covenant 'equip' believers? And what might it equip them for? The answer was described to me in terms of 'spiritual warfare'; Christians needed to be 'well fed' with Bible teaching so that they would be 'ready to do battle with the world and the devil.' For the Christians of Gamrie, learning about the material properties of the exact type of wood used in the construction of the Ark was not an object of curious trivia, but rather an act of divine communion and self-renunciation. The purpose of such a sermon was that the act of hearing—of listening to and studying the Bible—equipped believers to be 'living sacrifices,' that is, it gave them what they needed, or, perhaps more accurately, it gave them the *words* they needed, to live for God and fight the devil.

Such teaching, far from being subject to the kind of critique that derives from the fallibility of 'ordinary' words was accorded a special place within the speech community. Thus the Christians of Gamrie, as with Coleman's charismatic Faith adherents

do not regard themselves as *interpreting* the Bible or inspired sermons, but *receiving* them, thus gaining determinate understandings that can be shared by all who apply so-called spiritual ears and eyes to sacred words. (Coleman 2000: 127)

Where Coleman views sermonizing as 'internalisation' and 'exter-nalisation' (Coleman 2000: 127, 131), I propose that the preaching of the Word is an act of worship that transforms both the ('internal') self and the ('external') world through the dual notion of teaching and preaching. This worship was enchanted because it had real trans-formative effects—it 'saved souls' and 'fed' and 'built up' the believer. Where preaching as worship was said to be sacrificial (my informants stressed the need to 'submit to the Word') receiving teaching from the Bible became an act of renunciation and edification, with the self both stripped away and built up at the same time. Indeed

> deploying language becomes, according to this logic, *both a loss of self and a gaining of access to a language from God* that, in its bodily (and other material) effects, transcends the need for interpretation. (Coleman 2000: 133. Emphasis added)

The category of the 'saved' remains central, insofar as it was only 'born-again believers' who would ever be able to 'really worship' at ministry meetings. Bible *teaching* was for the saved because it equipped them to live lives of sacrifice and reverent worship, things that the 'unsaved' could never do. As already described above, mature believers were said to be 'fed' from the 'meat' of Bible *teaching* and unbelievers from the 'milk' of gospel *preaching*. Importantly however, 'mature' Christians did not only eat 'meat' from the Word—they too needed the 'milk' of the Bible, but in a different form from unbeliev-ers. They needed the milk of encouragement.

In speaking of the 'milk of encouragement,' I refer to the type of Bible teaching that had as its aim the 'building up' and edification of believers. Encouragement was spoken of as a specific 'spiritual gift' said to be the mark of a good preacher. The value of such a gift was linked to the general perception that Christians in Scotland were living through hard times; society was said to be 'against the things of God' and was growing increasingly intolerant of a 'Biblical Christianity'; 'This warld is nae wir hame, we're jist passin through till we get to the other side,' friends would say with real yearning. Teaching from the Bible did not only mean imbibing 'The Word' as an act of increasing one's knowledge of scripture—sometimes referred to disparagingly as 'head knowledge'—'feeding on the Word of God' was an activity that was also directed toward the heart:

> And Aaron's rod spoke of resurrection. And we have that [assurance of resurrection] in our hearts today, that we are going to see our loved

ones again [in heaven]....[And] we are going to see him [Jesus]. We are going to see him! Why am I so sure? Because it was his prayer!

It was sermons such as these that elicited the strongest feelings of enthusiasm and support from regular congregants. Some of the women at Gamrie's OB Hall spoke to me about their joyous anticipation of heaven as we filed out of the building after sermons such as these. They told me with unusually unrestrained smiles how old age would no longer hold them back—they would have new and perfected ('sinless') resurrection bodies, experiencing a closeness of worship unlike anything on earth. Not only would they be reunited with loved ones who had 'gone home,' but they would also be 'in the physical presence of the Lord forever.'

While they remained on earth, being in the hall and hearing 'The Word' taught took them as close to Jesus as they could hope to be 'this side of eternity.' Other friends spoke of being 'transported into the very throne room of heaven' when listening to the Bible being taught. Still others described listening to such teaching as 'a real feast,' sometimes turning to me at the end of a sermon and remarking with a smile 'now that was a good meal wasn't it Joe?' It was listening to 'The Word' being taught that gave these ordinary church members the greatest reassurance of their salvation ('we're going home!') and the strongest reason to 'persevere in the faith.' After all, as my friends often sought to remind me, the weekly 'meals' we enjoyed at the hall as the Bible was taught would one day be replaced by the eagerly anticipated 'perpetual feast' to be eternally consumed in the presence of the 'Incarnate Word' in heaven.

All of this reinforces our earlier suggestion of the centrality of two types of person—the saved and the unsaved—for 'going home' means going to heaven, and the men who stood and preached that message of encouragement and hope did so with only one audience in mind—the 'saved.' It was only with 'fellow believers' that this heavenly 'home' and 'feast' would be shared. There was no 'equipping' to be offered to the 'unbeliever' through Bible teaching and certainly no encouragement to be offered to them unless they responded to the 'glad tidings.' They were already fully prepared for their lost eternity and could only be rescued from their fate through the preaching of the gospel, which was their equipping, their encouragement, their mode of conviction, and their means of conversion all in one.

Yet there is a danger of my suggesting a picture that is altogether too monolithic by giving insufficient attention to disordered performances and the messy reality that follows. What happens if a gospel sermon is lackluster or a ministry meeting is discouraging? Might it be possible for a gospel sermon to entirely miss the point by neglecting to mention the need to be saved? Sermons are a kind of performance, and as such, are liable to failure (Tomlinson 2006, 2009). Yet in Gamrie, sermons were generally failures not because they were heretical but because they were simply the wrong kind of performance. For example, I once heard a man called Amery Moran—from Ireland, but living and working in a nearby town—preach a sermon entitled 'running to win,' which, despite its encouraging title, was all about 'the solemn reality of Christ's final judgment'. What followed was an intense 40-minute tirade against those who called themselves Christians but were 'not true believers':

> You are either a card-carrying Christian or a cross-carrying Christian, and if you are only a card-carrying Christian, you are in trouble! There are going to be those who stand before Christ [on the Day of Judgment] and they are going to be in a heap of ashes! There is one thing that God detests more than anything else, lukewarmness! If you feel this word [sermon] is for you, then go on your knees and pray!

The congregation, it being a morning service at the Kirk, was predominantly 'born-again' members, and as such, came to church hoping to learn something new about the Bible and have their souls encouraged. But they received neither, leaving with a sense that they had been wrung out by a visiting preacher who suspected them all of being lukewarm fakers. The cool reception Amery received as everyone filed past him at the door was palpable. The message 'wasn't a helpful challenge' a man said to me a few days later, but simply felt 'judgmental.' 'How did they ever expect to have any young folk in the church with sermons like *that*?' he asked me, shaking his head.

'Rituals that focus on the articulation of achievement of meaning can also suggest meaning's boundaries and, perhaps, violate those boundaries' (Tomlinson 2006: 140). Yet Amery's sermon seemed to be a direct violation, not of meaning—the congregation seemed to know all too well what he *meant*—but rather of the appropriate content for the occasion of worship. Amery wasn't the only one who fell into such a trap. One man in the village was frequently criticized for his preaching—he spoke for too long; his sermons were boring and 'too heavy'; they felt like 'lectures' that 'lacked heart' and 'went over everyone's heads.' He was also accused of no longer giving 'an old fashioned gospel' but instead preached sermons that were discouraging and devoid of love. 'You canna fault his Bible knowledge,' people would say to me, 'he kens it *all*. But that's the problem, ken, it's all head knowledge, there's nae love in it ataw you ken.' As with Amery, this preacher was disliked for both his content and style. Their failure seemed to be a failure of 'emotional enskilment,' that is, a failure to produce the right emotional reaction within the right context. Teaching the Bible to Christians through a sermon that contained 'no love' and 'no heart' was an error that proved fatal—it was said that Amery would probably not be invited back to preach, while the other preacher eventually left Gamrie to minister elsewhere.

But sermons were also deemed to be failures because they were off point. On one occasion at a gospel meeting at the OB, a native Argentinean missionary preached about Jesus' last days in Jerusalem by using a 3D wooden map that he had erected at the front of the hall. He then proceeded to reenact (in differently sounding hushed voices) the conversation between Jesus and the disciples at the last supper. It was not until right at the end of the sermon that the preacher mentioned the gospel message—after a long description of how antivenom is extracted from snakes to cure those who have been bitten, the preacher suddenly leveled his gaze at the congregation and simply said 'the blood of Jesus Christ is the only antidote to the poison of sin...so you, this evening, can accept Him before it is too late and you end up in the lake of fire!' And that was it. The sermon was over and there was a prayer and a hymn and the service ended. 'Well that was different!,' a man wearing hearing aids said to me, I think rather more loudly than he realized. But it was his embarrassed grin that said more than his actual comment, and judging by the conversations I had with folk over a cup of tea after the meeting, everyone in the hall agreed—a 'full gospel' had simply not been preached.

Sermons can and do fail. They can fail by being discouraging or at odds with the imagined spiritual condition of the audience. Performative success was in large part determined by a preacher's ability to maintain a clear distinction between the need to *preach* and the need to *teach*. Yet 'preaching to the converted' was a common occurrence, and not one that was deemed a performative failure on that basis. This is because listening to the gospel was an (enchanted) act of worship insofar as it was described by ordinary churchgoers as a foundational part of their Christian 'diet,' which, because it 'always gave an impression of Christ' that took them 'into His near presence,' was an act of hearing that one 'never grew out of.' Such worship, then, was characterized by the transformative effects of both immanence and transcendence.

Where preaching the 'glad tidings' was described as 'coming under the sound of the gospel' and where teaching the Bible was explained as 'coming under the sound of The Word'—with both being described as (albeit different kinds of) 'meals'—the link between words and hearing and eating was undeniable. Friends often spoke of the unsaved as 'hungry souls' and the saved as 'hungering after the Word.' I remember on one occasion, how, during a gospel preaching, the sermon reached its climax when the minister proclaimed: 'It is an ambition of mine to see this church *filled* with people *hungry* to do business with God!' What are we to make of this language of hunger and eating? Coleman (2000), writing on the 'internalisation' of the Biblical text among charismatic Protestants in the Word of Life church in Sweden, makes the following observation:

> 'Internalisation' refers to the process of *incorporating* language within the self in a way that is…embodied. It is a form of self-inscription (as opposed to description) that leads believers to understand themselves as 'words made flesh.' (Coleman 2000: 118)

Internalisation is a kind of embodiment. Words are incorporated within the self to the point that they actually begin to constitute the flesh of the believer who undergoes their very own textual incarnation. Not only does Coleman describe the embodiment of the Word, but also its being eaten:

> Perhaps the most striking example of how the Word is invested with physical qualities is evident in the way many faith adherents *describe the process of reading the Bible as a form of ingestion akin to eating*. One can hunger for or 'get filled' with the Word…In this view, the text is embodied in the person, who becomes a walking, talking representation of its power. Eating is an especially powerful image because it points to a notion of internalising truth directly, bypassing the distorting effects of both social context and intellect.…*Internalisation therefore refers to an incarnational practice* [whereby] people came to regard themselves as physically assimilating and thereby actually being taken over by scripturally derived…words. (Coleman 2000: 127–129. Emphasis added)

It was not until one Sunday in September, having been in the field for almost a year, that I found myself wrestling with the relationship between 'hearing' and 'eating' as locally salient tropes of worship. And then I 'sat under' two separate sermons on the topic of hearing in the space of a few hours and then a further two over the fortnight that followed. The first sermon I heard that day was at the FPCU. The minister preached on the Queen of Sheba's visit to Solomon's temple and gave the following words of introduction:

> Our purpose on going up to God's house should be to hear what God has to say to us.... Prepare your heart to hear from Him.... *The act of worship is the act of hearing!* Listening to God, listening to what God says to us. God speaks from His Word!... *It is an act of worship to hear....* Worship is listening! Worship is hearing! Listening to what God will say.... As we come to the House of the Lord we should pray "Lord, speak to me, open my ears, open my heart.... Lord, speak to me!"

Having left this service to attend a CB 'Bible reading,' I was taken aback when, at the end of the meeting, the main speaker summarized the discussion of the preceding hour by stating: So the secret really is in that verse 18: *'take heed therefore how ye hear.'*[3] [It] depends what kynd[4] we hear.

The third occasion occurred when attending a funeral service in the village. The preacher was describing the conversion of Lydia in the Book of Acts: 'she had to have *this* open first,' he said emphatically, giving his ear a dramatic series of downward tugs; 'She opened her *ear* to God's messenger.'

Hearing 'properly' was made possible through the medium of emotion. In this sense, there is no real difference between hearing and listening—hearing 'properly' means 'really' listening, namely, listening with one's heart and whole body. If one is not listening, then one is not 'really' hearing. During 'good' sermons, emotions ran high, with some congregants often providing their own barely audible commentary—'yes Lord'; 'thank you Jesus'; 'yes, amen'— over what was being said. Others stared intently at their feet, nodding their heads; others closed their eyes, apparently in prayer; still others sat forward in their seats, gripping their Bibles tightly as if their excitement required them to hold onto something to keep their balance. The obvious comparison here with Hirschkind's (2001) brilliant analysis of cassette-sermon audition in Cairo is interesting, extending not just to embodiment, but also to ethics and specifically to the hope of moral transformation, both of the self and the other.

What, then, of the deaf? Can they be 'saved'? The answer, given the power accorded to reading, is yes. My friends described how God spoke to them through 'The Word'; a voice that was internally audible to Christians during private silent scripture reading. The blind too were said to have access to this same kind of hearing-by-reading.

A story circulated during my fieldwork of a Christian man who suffered terribly as a result of an accident that left him burned, blind, and deaf. Eventually, his only way of 'hearing The Word' was by reading a Braille Bible with the tip of his tongue. The story, echoing our epigraph from Ezekiel, often ended with the teller commenting upon how 'sweet' those words of scripture 'tasted' to the man.

It might be objected, that, in my analysis of the practice of listening, much of my ethnographic evidence emerges not from those who hear, but those who speak, that is, from preachers and not from 'ordinary' congregants. In Gamrie, however, there was no strict division between speaking preachers and listening congregants, for, although only men preached, it was also the case that all male members were actively engaged in both preaching and teaching. Thus, men who preached also constantly sought to remind their listeners that they were also preaching to themselves, for they too needed to hear the message that God would have them proclaim. Preaching and teaching, then, were forms of listening and hearing. Consider, finally, a fourth preacher:

> The Bible says that *faith cometh by hearing and hearing by the Word of God*.... Faith is to trust in what you have *heard* and not what you have seen. What you've heard us pray about! What you've heard us testify about! What you've heard us speak about!... God has communicated to us and what we have is the book the Bible.... It liveth and abideth forever and ever! All I'm doing...is communicating to you what is in this book.... Base your decision on this book! *Faith cometh by hearing and hearing by the Word of God!*

Hearing 'the Word' was a mode of sacrifice; a life built upon the dual process of 'starving' the flesh and 'feeding' the spirit. 'The Word,' as the 'sacrificial meal' (Robertson Smith 1972) was to be 'feasted upon' like any other, but with the difference that the 'eating' was done not through the mouth but through the ear, by hearing and listening. The flesh was 'killed,' transformed into words, and then re-embodied by being eaten through the ear in sermonizing, giving my Christian friends a new body and a new self. This seems less surprising the more we realize that not only is the sacrifice of Christian worship *living*, but so also, to many evangelicals, is the Bible. Inasmuch as Jesus was locally understood as word-made-flesh-made-text via the consubstantiation of the Bible (sheets of paper *and* the 'Real Presence' of God), Christians too experience this enchanted doubling by becoming 'living epistles'—bodies filled with words that could be read *by* and read *to* the 'unsaved.'

Four main conclusions emerge. First, 'faith,' which, for my informants, was synonymous with being a Christian, 'is to trust what you have heard and not what you have seen.' Second, it is not 'the eye of faith' but the ear that is most active in this process; 'she had to open *this* first...she opened her *ear*,' the preacher insisted to a congregation of mourners. Third, this is why it is of the utmost importance to 'take heed therefore how ye hear'; the Christian is defined by their faith that is itself defined by hearing. One can only listen if one's ears are open, and further, if one is listening in the right way; 'it depends what kynd we hear,' that is, it depends on the nature (or disposition) of our hearing. If it is not only hearing that matters, but also the way in which a believer hears; 'taking heed' is nonnegotiable. Fourth, this is all the more the case when we realize that 'the act of worship is the act of hearing,' which, I have argued, was also held to be an act of sacrifice.

To this end, the intended purpose of the last preacher I quoted was clear—he was calling himself and those who listened to him (as, indeed, they were 'calling' themselves just as he was 'hearing' himself) to sacrifice their 'flesh' to 'The Book'; to forsake all others in a self-renouncing and worshipful commitment to the incarnate Word-made-flesh-made-text. In hearing these words preached, my informants were enacting a life of self-sacrifice: 'putting to death' the flesh by starving their bodies of its sinful desires. And insofar as the act of worship was said to be an act of hearing, this sacrifice was undertaken by 'feasting upon' the *preaching* of the gospel and the *teaching* of the Bible, by eating words through the ear.

Chapter 4

Testimony

*I couldnae come out my bedroom this morning without speaking to my
Lord. If I didnae have Jesus with me just now I couldnae speak to you.
But I know that's he's.... [starts to weep]. Its emotional, you ken, with
me, I mean, I'm a strong man, dinna get me wrong, I'm a powerful
man ... but when I'm speaking about my Lord, I cry.*

(Alasdair, retired fisherman, northeast Scotland)

Alasdair is 65, a 'born-again' Christian and former fisherman who
lives to 'speak to as much people as I can ... [about] the Lord.' But
what does it mean when committed Christians like Alasdair describe
themselves as 'born-again'? And why would Alasdair make it his mission in life to speak about 'the Lord'?

Among Gamrie's fishermen, 'giving testimony' (the story of how
one became 'born-again') redefines the self not only in terms of
'born-again masculinity,' but does so through emotional acts of self-
revelation to then mobilize that self to convert others to the faith.
By displaying gendered conversion narratives through a highly con-
ventionalized (Crapanzano 2000) and emotional (Luhrmann 2004,
2010) performance, the 'born-again' Christian makes sense of daily
life, not by creating a uniquely emergent story of personal religious
identity, but rather by publicly identifying with a shared religious
orthodoxy. Equally, 'giving testimony' needs to be understood
within its local context as forming part of a wider project of modernity (Keane 2007), and as such, as an idiom for the struggle to make
sense of rapid social, economic, demographic, technological, and religious change occurring in Scotland.

In entering the debate about conversion as continuity or
change, I echo Robbins (2003) and Engelke (2004) by suggesting
that the 'born-again' Christian does indeed experience religious

transformation as real discontinuous change. Within the context of Scottish Protestantism, this transformation was said to be so total that local people insisted on speaking of their 'born-again' experience as a literal 'conversion,' not from one *religion* to another (it was said to be much 'deeper' than that) but rather from one *kingdom* to another—from 'satan's kingdom of darkness to God's glorious kingdom of light' as my friends would tell me (cf. Bielo 2011, Bialecki 2009). Such transformation, experienced as ontological, suggests that within the Scottish context of 'born-again' Protestantism, the radically discontinuous nature of some forms of religious conversion might still be eluding anthropology today.

By considering the relationship between embodiment and linguistic practice through the recounting of 'born-again' conversion narratives, I follow Luhrmann (2004, 2010) in emphasizing the central importance of bodily emotion. Contra to Luhrmann, however, I cannot maintain that such 'metakinetic' practices 'imply quite different learning processes than those entailed by linguistic and cognitive knowledge,' nor do I agree that they represent 'different kinds of learning' that are 'psychologically distinct' (2004: 519) from each other. The deployment of words and emotions, language, and the body are to be understood not in terms of psychological distinctiveness, but rather in relation to their sociological inseparability. I want to show this by viewing the practice of 'giving testimony' as analogous to a certain type of Christian confession—one that is dependent upon a dramatic conflation of word and body through the deployment of gendered emotions.

I also question a trend within the anthropological literature on conversion narratives to focus empirical analysis upon the speaking ('testifying') self to the neglect of the listening other. In viewing conversion as 'always a process of becoming' (Engelke 2004: 104), the perpetual state of transformation experienced by the 'born-again' Christian, is not, contrary to Stromberg's (1993) seminal work *Language and Self-Transformation*, wholly (or even principally) focused upon transforming the *self* (Stromberg 1993: 3–4, 29–31, 124–129). In the Scottish context at least, 'giving testimony' is also, *by definition*, an act of 'witness.' In the Christian's recounting of their 'born-again' conversion narrative, language and the body are always engaged in an explicitly evangelistic exercise that seeks to transform not just the self-identity of the speaker, but also the identity of the hearing other.

In this chapter, I present data from just one interview. Although I interviewed dozens of Christian fishermen, Alasdair's story seems typical of many of the highly emotional conversion narratives I collected while in the field. In choosing to focus upon Alasdair, I aim to encap-sulate something of the stories of people like Grant, a man who was converted at sea when his boat ran aground and his father and three of the crew were lost, or the stories of Toby and Fraser, two best friends who had owned and skippered a boat together, and who were con-verted within a short time of each other as young fishermen. I deploy Alasdair's (auto)biography not as a 're-presentation [of] epistemology' but rather in a way 'which places the emphasis on indigenous ontology' (Tsintjilonis 2007: 173). Not only do I treat Alasdair's words as capable of speaking to the wider themes of Scottish Protestantism found in the testimonies of other northeastern fishermen, but do so in a way that focuses not upon (theological) theories of knowledge, but upon local affective experiences of 'conversion-as-being-in-the-world.'

'I Got Saved at the Sea'

JW: Maybe you could tell me something about how you became a Christian?

Alasdair: Well, I was born in [northeast Scotland]…and I went to church with my granny and granda and to Sunday school. All my pals were away on a Sunday afternoon playing football and I used to rebel to my mother [saying]: "Look, I need to be with my friends"…so when I was 14 I stopped going to the church completely. At 15 I went away to sea…and I just went with my pals…drinking and all the stuff young fellas do. Then when I was 21 I [married] my wife and…I come home this day and said to my wife I says, "I'm finished with this drink—this is nae a life—I need to be with my family"…I [also] used to swear, but my fam-ily didnae, and I says, "well Alasdair, you've stopped drinking and you dinna miss it, [so] you could stop swearing" and I did [**voice breaking: looks away**] and a couple of years after that I got saved. I got saved at the sea. I came to the Lord at the sea and I gave my heart to the Lord at that time.

Living in Gamrie allowed me to hear many different people 'give their testimony' in formal church meetings as well as to each other in casual conversation. These performances of testifying relied on the reproduction of predictable forms of narrative. Every testimony, almost without fail, began with the words 'I was born.' They con-tinued by describing early spiritual experiences and later times of rebellion and would culminate with a statement about the moment of conversion, such as: 'I got saved at the sea.' I started collecting these narratives a few months after arriving in the field when a local friend of mine suggested that I should hear so-and-so's *testimony*—this person, he said, had had a dramatic conversion experience and would be happy to share it with me. The interview went well, and, noting my enthusiasm, my friend quickly gave me a long list of other people who would be willing to 'share their testimony.' All I had to do was busy myself with asking the question 'could you tell me something about how you became a Christian?,' which, without fail, produced conversion narratives where I would sit and listen for anything from 20 minutes to several hours.

For Stromberg, the reason for this 'remarkably high level of co-operation' is clear: the reiterative speech act is itself 'a central element of the conversion' (1993: 3). To recount their conversion story

> was, for these believers, not a chore but rather a central ritual of their faith. The conversion narrative offered an opportunity to celebrate and reaffirm the dual effect of the conversion, *the strengthening of their faith and the transformation of their lives.*' (Stromberg 1993: 3. Emphasis added)

While I agree that this dual self-directed motive was present, I also think a third process—central to a properly relational understanding of conversion—was occurring, namely that the sharing of such narratives was not just about transforming the speaking self but also the listening other.

The Spurious Quest for the Uniquely Emergent

An obvious objection arises here: if I was so quickly given a list of people who would be willing to tell me how they were 'born-again,' does that not indicate that the data to which I was given access— the retelling of the rehearsed testimony—was in some sense nothing more than a shallow 'official line' that simply parroted the 'canonical language' (Stromberg 1993: 124) of conversion so heavily invested in by the religious groups I was researching? As Crapanzano (2000) has observed, commenting on the context of Christian fundamentalism in America, the 'once I was lost, now I am found' narrative is hardly in short supply when examining what he calls '*prêt-à-porter* testimonies [which]...are, for the most part, conventional [yet]...concealed by their intensely personal quality' (Crapanzano 2000: 31–32). Was it not my job to avoid having the verbal wool pulled over my eyes (or perhaps ears) by, as a colleague suggested, seeking out something more 'uniquely emergent'?

I actually think not. This is because in looking for the uniquely emergent, what is sought is a narrative unrestricted by form and unencumbered by past retelling, that is, something without convention and without history—a narrative free from structure. Looking for such a narrative is misplaced because no such narrative exists. Harding's classic work *The Book of Jerry Falwell* (2000), which examines religious and political rhetoric among Christian fundamentalists in America, gives some instructive context on this point. By describing conversion 'as a process of acquiring a specific religious language or dialect' (2000: 34), Harding shows us how 'giving testimony' necessarily draws upon a preexisting structure, and in so doing, becomes not an epiphenomenon of some other (hidden) cultural phenomenon, but rather exists as a distinct linguistic practice. If conversion is conversion to a language and not just to a religious orthodoxy, then the search for the uniquely emergent is indeed the search for that which does not exist.

This critique of the intellectual quest for the 'really real' (or uniquely emergent) narrative—free from the trappings of form and rehearsal—also echoes Keane's (2002) analysis of the Christian's quest for transcendence, that is, a 'truer' emergent meaning that lies just below the 'surface' waiting to be discovered; a narrative free from structure, meaning free from an intended audience, and agency free from rehearsal (Keane 2006). The Protestant quest for transcendence and the intellectual quest for the uniquely emergent amount to much the same thing—a search for 'sincerity.' The (in Keane's terms [1997a], very Protestant) suspicion of the 'surface narrative' is articulated thus: in listening to those 'giving testimony,' anthropologists are liable to miss the point because those who recount them might be being *insincere* by parroting a 'readymade' surface narrative in order to hide the 'really real' story of their (so called) 'conversion.' The quest for sincerity and the quest for the uniquely emergent share the same anxiety about the way in which the surface can mask that which is underneath. This matters, according to both of these quests, because that which is underneath (the inner *self*) is that which '*really* matters.'

These dualisms privilege a certain Western ontological view of 'authenticity…in both commonsense and anthropological ideas about culture' (Handler 1986: 2). The 'shallow' is shunned in favor of the 'deep.' The 'true' is prized over the 'false.' 'Mere appearances' are derided in favor of 'real substance.' What is 'really below the surface' is sought over and against that which is 'just on the surface level.' The 'rehearsed' performance and the 'structured' narrative are seen as suspect where the 'uniquely emergent' may be accepted with implicit trust.

Yet, if 'giving testimony' is not properly understood by searching for some uniquely emergent narrative but is to be analyzed in terms of an inherited and thus preexistent linguistic structure, and if conversion is about conversion to a specific religious language (Harding 2000: 34), how does this fit with Robbins' (2004) theory of Christian conversion as cultural discontinuity? 'Giving testimony' is not just about registering a standardized statement of conversion within the confines of a specific local linguistic structure (in this sense conversion is not just about the way in which change is subsumed within fixed cultural particularity) but is also about 'real' (discontinuous) change. If we are to take seriously my informants' deliberate conflation of the 'born-again' Christian experience with that of 'conversion,' it seems that within the context of Scottish Protestantism, what is going on is more radical than the pouring of new wine into old wineskins (Engelke 2004).

Despite the fact that conversion is narrated through convention and thus retains a social history (being embedded in a preexisting linguistic performance that is locally intelligible exactly because it is not uniquely emergent), the language and experience of being 'born-again' also necessarily claims an absolute break with the past. As the preachers in the previous chapter made abundantly clear, one is born *in sin* and then dies *to sin* by being 'born-again' *in Christ*. This process was explicitly held by local Christians to be fully synonymous with the process of conversion. The question 'when were you *converted*?'—asked by and of local Gamrie folk who had spent their entire lives in a northeast Scottish context dominated by revivalist Protestantism—indicates how complete this conflation was. I met men and women in their sixties and seventies who, having faithfully attended their church or meeting hall since childhood, would nonetheless tell me with grave seriousness that they were not Christian—"I haven't been converted" would come the explanation. The ontological implication was that conversion-as-being-in-the-world was simultaneously experienced both inwardly and outwardly through a relationship between a testifying speaker and a listening other.

Here, the 'form,' the 'structure,' the 'surface narrative,' and the 'cultural script' are indistinguishable from any posited 'inner reality'; there is nothing 'deeper' or more 'sincere' to be had when listening to someone's testimony because it is through the very act of retelling—through the standardized performance of rehearsing the self to the other—that one is known and made knowable as a sincere and committed Christian. I am in agreement with Stromberg when he argues that we must 'abandon the search for the reality beyond the convert's speech and...look instead at the speech itself,' but question his next assertion that 'it is through language that the conversion occurred in the first place and also through language that the conversion is now re-lived as the convert tells his tale' (Stromberg 1993: 3). This latter statement seems an insightful but partial observation, ignoring, as it does, the roles of both embodiment and emotion.

The work of Tanya Luhrmann (2004) on Christian intimacy has helped to redress this balance between language and the body by viewing religious testimony as akin to performing a dance, whereby emotions are carried within the body in a way that implicates both performer and observer (what Luhrmann calls 'metakinesis'). Yet, to the extent that Stromberg (1993) may be criticized for being somewhat logocentric, it seems that Luhrmann may be conversely criticized for overly emphasizing the psychological distinctiveness of the metakinetic as set against the linguistic (Luhrmann 2004: 519). In the Scottish context, neither word nor body is dominant; in 'giving testimony,' the relationship is one of inseparable co-constitution. What we see in Alasdair's conversion narrative is a verbal and bodily performance that operates in and through an emotional exchange between speaker and hearer—an exchange that can be viewed through the lens of Christian confession.

Foucault[1] is helpful in distinguishing two different but 'deeply and closely connected' forms of confession—the bodily renunciation of the self in *exomologesis* (1993: 213) and the analytical and continuous verbalization of the self in *exagoreusis* (1993: 220). More specifically, *exomologesis* is described as an episode of dramatic and penitent self-revelation that is undertaken in order to obtain reconciliation with the wider Christian community. Such acts are bodily punishments of the self, aiming at maximum theatricality to achieve somatic and symbolic expressions of the current state of defilement. As such, *exomologesis* does not aim to tell the truth about the sin, but aims to show the true being of the sinner and is thus not only a form of self-revelation, but is also said to be a form of self-destructive maceration (Foucault 1993: 215). Exagoreusis, on the other hand, centers not on the body but on a ceaseless examination of the 'nearly imperceptible movements of the thoughts [and] the permanent mobility of the soul' (Foucault 1993: 217). As with exomoloegesis, exagoreusis is still an act of explicit self-sacrifice because in continuously verbalizing the self, the self is obligated to renounce all evil of one's will in order to achieve complete (self-destructive) union with God's divine light (Foucault 1993: 220). The performance of 'giving testimony,' then, can be seen as a hybrid of the confessional methodologies of *exomologesis* and *exagoreusis*, uniting, as it does, both word and body through a 'tell all' performance of religious and somatic emotion.

'It's Emotional, You Ken'

Alasdair: In the area that I come from, everybody knows me and everybody knows the change in my life....Alasdair can now walk past every pub. I've never been [**voice breaks: turns in seat**]...since that day that I said I would never drink again to my wife, I've never put any alcohol of any kind to my lips and never will. All I drink now is water. When I got saved, I says [to my brother], "ken this, I never thought I'd see the day that I would be a saved man". And he says "but we all seen it coming" [**begins to weep. Silence. Covers face with hand**]. Praise the Lord for that, ken what I mean?...I would say I was a spiritual man...[break in recording as someone comes into the room].

JW: You just said you were a spiritual man...how would you describe to a non-Christian what you just said?

Alasdair: Well I'm just gonna tell you. When I came to the Lord and the night that I gave my heart to the Lord, and accepted him as my savior [**begins to weep**]...he put Jesus in my heart. He put Jesus in my heart, and he's still there, all this years...and I know what Jesus saved me from: he saved me from the drink, saved me from using bad language. He changed me and if you knew me 35 years ago you would see the change in my life....If there's no change, there's no change, if you don't see nothing, there's no change, but people know that I have changed because I've got Jesus in my heart. When I gave my life to the Lord I accepted him as my savior. He put Jesus in my heart and it's as fresh today as the day I was baptized and I'll tell you something: I could get baptized every week, that's how much it means to me [**begins to weep again. Wipes away tears. Smiles warmly**].

'Giving testimony' acts to make sense of the self by making sense of change. Alasdair stressed that he was a changed man and everybody knew him as such. By narrating the self in terms of transformation—being saved from drink and bad language and being given a new heart for Jesus—change wrought upon the self comes to be defined not only as essential ("if there's no change, there's no change") but also as social. Change is made intelligible by sharing it with the hearer, by providing what Foucault refers to in *exagoreusis* as an 'analytical and continuous verbalization of...thought' (Foucault 1993: 221). It is shared through the very act of giving testimony—by telling one's story to others, by confessing, by giving one's spiritual autobiography.

Yet it is important to note the wider context of more 'ordinary' and 'secular' reminiscence that these born-again testimonials are situated within. Strolling along the Gamrie seafront I would almost invariably meet some of the older men from the churches walking and talking together about the glories of days gone by. I remember on one particular occasion meeting a man from the Kirk who, walking alone, seemed glad of someone to 'muse awa to.' He very quickly settled on talking about how 'the village is a different world to what it used to be.' He spoke about his childhood—how he had spent his time outside playing with friends on the brae and at the beach. They were nearly always happy, 'nae like the bairns today; they're always inside, complaining about how bored they are!' He lamented the disappearance of certain kinds of local knowledge: 'the creel fishermen had names for every rock along the shore—all that's gone now. This was our *world*—we never left as bairns, maybe once a year for a trip to Fraserburgh, *but that was it!* Now people are fleein' aboot in cars all the time!' The results, I was told, were clear for all to see—the shops were gone, the school roll was down, and the churches were emptying. 'We was poor but we was happy!' he told me with a sad expression.

These 'secular' reminiscences of how village life had changed acted to invert the linguistic structure of local conversion narratives: where 'giving testimony' (like gospel preaching) was typically a story that moved from 'spiritual darkness' into 'God's glorious light,' reminiscing about Gamrie's past was almost exclusively focused on change for the worse (cf. Nadel-Klein 2003: 161). Even poverty was seen as a blessing of the past, and prosperity the curse of today: 'prosperity ruined this village—folk got money from the fishin' and noo they've nae needa God or so they *think*,' my friend told me, nodding almost angrily at the authority of his own analysis as we walked on at a funereal pace.

Importantly, the criticism that mammon had become the god of Gamrie's youth contained a specifically gendered inflection. It was young *men* earning high wages at sea—on the trawlers, oil rigs, and supply boats—who were said to be most at fault. Responsibility fell on men because, in local Christian imaginings, they were heads of their household; contrary to Eve's ruinously bad example in the

Garden, women (and, by extension, children) generally followed where their men led. Husbands and fathers—swollen with masculine pride and self-conceit—stood accused of leading their families away from God and his church in the hope of obtaining greater earthly riches purely by their own creaturely efforts. In doing so, the older generations of 'converted' fishermen accused them of denying their Creator and further hastening Gamrie's downward slide into godlessness.

Critical reminiscence—offered with particular force when a younger male audience such as myself was present—was explicitly directed at eliciting a response by calling the hearer to a kind of sacrificial reformation; to deny oneself the pleasures and conveniences of life in the town and to commit (or recommit) to a view of village life defined by an intimacy and continuity of people and place. As in testimony, then, these 'wider' reminiscences called for an experience of change. In the 'born-again' context, testifying to 'real' change involved a process of 'inner' rebirth ('He put Jesus in my *heart*') that coincided with, and was indistinguishable from, 'exterior' transformation ('I know what Jesus saved me *from*'). More than this, such a process of change—such a move toward discontinuity—was intelligible to the other (remember Alasdair's brother commenting 'but we all seen it coming') exactly because discontinuity is a shared experience with a shared history: everyone knew how Alasdair the man behaved in his 'bad old days,' just as everyone knew what Gamrie the village was like in the 'good old days.'

The trope of change is central, then, both in testimony and wider reminiscence. Alasdair mentions change no less than six times in three lines of transcript. By narrating change in one's own life, change is not only shared and therefore social, but also becomes an index of commitment: 'everybody knows me and everybody knows the change in my life....Alasdair can now walk past every pub.' In Scotland's Protestant northeast, a committed Christian man is a man who makes certain kinds of sacrifices, for example, by giving up certain kinds of (prototypically masculine) habits associated with a life at sea: drunkenness, promiscuity, smoking, and swearing. And as with 'wider' reminiscence, discussing such 'spiritual' change has an explicitly reformative aim: to call the listening other to recognize and react to social and moral transformation, in our case, by emulating Alasdair as a 'man of faith.'

Word and action, language and body exist here in a relationship of co-constitution, that is, they 'testify' to each other and about each other regarding the sincerity of moral change. Alasdair had stopped swearing and drinking, he had become a 'proper family man'; he talked differently; he spent his leisure time differently; he made the transition from the pub to the church. He was a new man, having experienced, in local terms, 'born-again' conversion by leaving the 'Kingdom of Darkness' to receive adoption into God's 'Kingdom of Light.' Yet simply *narrating* moralistic sacrificial change is not enough. Confession needs not only to be shared, but shared in a certain kind of way. As well as the need for the 'continuous verbalisation' of *exagoreusis* (Foucault 1993: 221), we also have, if the 'new man in Christ' is to be seen to be testifying with sincerity, the embodied performance of gendered emotion in *exomologesis* (Foucault 1993: 214):

> *Alasdair:* I couldna come out my bedroom this morning without speaking to my Lord. If I didnae have Jesus with me just noo I couldnae speak to you. But I know that's he's.... **[weeping]**...he made me into something else—took me back, took me into the church and used me....I always think back to my days in the Sunday school...it's a promise of the Lord's that he will never leave you...and its true **[pained expression: begins to weep again]**. Its emotional, you ken, with me, I mean, I'm a strong man, dinna get me wrong, I'm a powerful man, I stand up to anything, ken, but when I'm speaking about my Lord, I cry. But I look at the great men in the Bible: Jesus wept, David cried, you know what I mean, all the great men in the Bible all wept. Jesus...**[resumes weeping]**...The thing is, when I'm praying, I cry a lot, and it's Jesus, what he did for me. He went to that cross, he could have come down from that, but he didna bend...went to that cross lonely and he died for me and you and that blood spilled...**[crying: covers face]**. The cross was where it started and that blood was poured out for you and me, ken....I think the cross is the most important [thing]. That was the plan of God for my life...he knew us before we was born **[continues crying: hands trembling]**. Is that nae great? I think it's great....I dinna ken how I'd live my life without the Lord...he's been so much in my life this last years ken, its been a great comfort to me, a great comfort.

Note how Alasdair seems to be inverting, in a particular religious context, certain local expectations of what it means to be a man. Those who have seen any of the BBC television series *Trawlermen* will be well aware of the kind of masculinity that is dominant among the crews of the Fraserburgh fishing fleet. Words like 'arduous,' 'endurance,' 'bravery,' 'resilience,' and 'danger' (all of which are used to sell *Trawlermen Series 1* on DVD) seem to be more common than do words such as 'emotional,' 'wept,' 'cry,' and 'comfort' used by Alasdair when describing his love for Jesus. Having worked on two Fraserburgh prawn trawlers, I experienced firsthand the performance of hyper-masculinity among 'unsaved' crew onboard these vessels. Competitive displays of physical strength and endurance were common, as were conversations about drunkenness, bar fights, and sexual conquest. Swearing was a veritable art form, as was storytelling about raucous activities planned when onshore. Men's bunks were often decorated with cutouts from football magazines or, more frequently, with pinups from soft porn magazines. Lewd joking about masturbation was common, as were jokes with racist or misogynist punch lines. If the BBC's *Trawlermen* series is to be critiqued, then, it is not for sensationalizing, but for heavily editing such displays of masculinity.

Yet Alasdair was a fisherman all his life, and also describes himself as 'strong' and 'powerful.' While testimony is a highly ordered performance that exists to reproduce predictable forms of Christian narrative, it is also a gendered performance and one that seems to play with gendered expectations in interesting ways. Such 'play,' I suggest, is locally achieved by 'born-again' fishermen displaying emotional characteristics ideal-typically associated with 'good' Christian wives and children. Loving affection, submissive obedience, needy dependence, subservient gratitude, fond admiration, and willing indebtedness—such emotional states are performed, in word and body, through the giving of testimony. The key to understanding this context of gendered religious emotion has to do with the ways in which a Scots-Protestant preoccupation with the moral depravity of the human will combines with local expressions of what it means to be a properly masculine fisherman.

Pre-conversion, Alasdair described a life that fit well with the kind of hyper-masculinity I saw onboard the trawlers. As a child he rebelled; he would rather be outside with his pals than with his mother at home. Home, after all, was the locus of feminine activity; it was outside, on the football pitch, where masculinity first began to take shape. Church was also a place for womenfolk; Alasdair stopped going as soon as he was old enough to assert sufficient male independence. Laboring at sea soon filled this gap, with feminine piety giving way to the famously 'hard,' 'dirty,' and 'rough' life of a deep-sea fishermen. As a young man, weekdays at sea and weekends in the pub left little time (or desire) for church or family. Marriage and children heralded the arrival of a fully adult masculinity (cf. Almeida 1996: 138), but made little difference to a lifestyle of good money, bad language, and drink. But something changed, when, at an unexplained juncture, Alasdair returned home to proclaim 'this is nae a life.' The need Alasdair described was a need for family and for God—a need to return to the two things that demand his love and service. Alasdair cast himself as the wayward prodigal, who, upon realizing his transgression, returned home not just to his wife and children, but also, by extension, to his Heavenly Father.

Change comes about, then, in part because of the centrality of the concept of sin within Scottish expressions of Calvinism and Puritanism. The constellation of emotions surrounding 'born-again' conversion emerge here from a painful sense of Man's moral failure only resolvable by Christ's salvific redemption. Yet the soteriology of Arminianism was also present locally, emphasizing not God's irresistible predestination, but rather the centrality of human free will, and the imperative that every man 'choose Christ.' In this context, fishermen normally reliant on physical strength and a hardened determination to triumph at sea by 'doing battle with the elements' find themselves being asked to recognize that (spiritually at least), they cannot save themselves.

Indeed, Gamrie's Christian fishermen experience themselves as 'morally bankrupt,' who, being 'full of sin' should rightly 'fear the Lord.' Their only remaining act of volition—'to yield to Christ in the gospel'—was also said to be an act of 'surrender.' Descriptions of salvation, furthermore, drew heavily on Biblical notions of marriage, and mixed them with local notions of femininity. In Gamrie, salvation was often described as Christ arriving to 'woo' the sinner like a 'suitor.' Becoming a Christian was said to involve 'falling in love' with Jesus. The title of a locally popular hymn, 'Jesus, lover of my soul,' referred to the same God who, in the lyrics of another hymn, would 'pierce every heart'—an act of penetration that incorporated 'the saved' into the Church, his 'bride.'

For Alasdair and for the Christian fishermen I knew in Gamrie, becoming a Christian involved the sacrifice of masculine pride, whereby personal strength was replaced with abject weakness, feminine dependence, and childlike helplessness. The contrast here with expressions of masculinity found by Lima (2012) among Pentecostal men in Rio de Janeiro is striking. For Lima's informants, drawn from Brazil's largest denomination preaching prosperity theology, while becoming a born-again man entailed a similar sacrifice of drunkenness and promiscuity, and reengagement with domestic life, salvation had, far from softening their masculinity, actually 'strengthened' (Lima 2012: 4, 11, 17) them as men. Where these prosperity Pentecostalists shared with Alasdair a passion for work and for earning money to support a family, 'their narratives about themselves' had as their 'central axis,' variously, 'reason,' 'self-confidence,' 'perseverance,' and 'victory.' The result, Lima concludes, is the opposite of what I have been arguing for Alasdair and for the Scottish Protestant conversion experience: a transformation of 'vulnerability' and an attenuation of 'feeling[s] of fragility' (Lima 2012: 20, 22).

For Lima's informants, born-again conversion brought to them everything that Alasdair was trying to rid himself of: reliance on self, confidence in self, and sufficiency of self. Smilde, working with Pentecostal men in neighboring Venezuela also notes this importance of masculine self-reliance in the South American context: when 'a young man separates from his family of origin...being autonomous and self-sufficient can be an important aspect of self-esteem' (2007: 169). But for Alasdair and the Christian fishermen of Gamrie, attempts at such self-sufficiency were hopeless, dangerous, and immoral. Alasdair told me how he couldn't even leave his bedroom without speaking to his Lord. This was said to be so much more the case when leaving for the fishing grounds; despite advances in technology, deep-sea trawling was still difficult and dangerous work, requiring constant reliance on God for one's survival. Most importantly, self-reliance was said to emerge from the sin of pride—a sin that so many of Gamrie's 'unsaved' young men had fallen into, so my Christian friends told me, because of their recent financial prosperity.

Alasdair's salvation, far from attenuating his sense of fragility, actually created it. As Alasdair alludes to below, he had been drowning in his sin, and Christ had thrown him a lifebelt—all he could do was humble himself, embrace his 'Redeemer,' and hold on for dear life. Importantly, this experience of being rescued by Jesus is nothing like being plucked from the waves by a crewmember or lifeboat man—for one day these men might also need rescue, offering the possibility of the saved becoming the savior. With God's rescue, on the other hand, such status difference is experienced as impassable. For Alasdair and my other informants, all that was left to express in the light of such salvation was eternal love, ongoing dependence, and undying gratitude offered to his 'protector' and 'provider.' These last two attributes—commonly attributed to earthly husbands and fathers—indicate that, post-conversion, men like Alasdair learned not only to experience God as a kind of divine paternal breadwinner, but also adopted for themselves—in the local context of 'giving testimony'—the idealized emotional demeanor of dependent wives and children. A similar expression of being God's needy children is also found among the Sarakatsani shepherds of Greece:

> God not only provides, He protects. He is the father of men who are his children....God is concerned about His creatures and, because they are dependent on Him, He is disposed to have pity and compassion on them. (Campbell 1979: 323)

The result, for the Christian men of Gamrie, was an ability to embody, in word and gesture, the sincerity of their material and moral lowliness, and thus the unmaking of their masculinity. Such sentiments also echo Taylor's description of the rosary-carrying piety of the 'quiet, shy bachelors' of Catholic Donegal who stand in contrast to the minimal religiosity of their (presumably more overtly masculine) counterparts—the 'jokers and characters...found at the back of the church on a Sunday' (1995: 201). As in Donegal, some of Gamrie's menfolk were pious, others less so. Yet Protestant men like Alasdair who 'testified to God's saving grace' had other roles in their communities (many were 'gospel preachers' and almost all were fishermen) that required them to behave as 'strong' leaders and 'powerful' patriarchs. And like the Portuguese peasant farmers of Paço and Couto, men in Gamrie remained in charge of economic productivity away from the home while also (officially, but not always practically) remaining the household head, due to the 'weaker,' 'changeable,' 'fickleness,' of the morality and physicality of the women they ruled over (Pina-Cabral 1986: 87, 123). Unlike Catholic Ireland and Catholic Portugal, however, the daily religiosity of Protestant Gamrie was led not by Priests nor sustained by lay female piety, but was collectively controlled by all 'saved' men. So in what sense did testimony produce an 'unmaking' of masculinity?

The change was primarily located within the affective, emotional sphere of the home. The 'born again' fishermen who 'testified' to me did so with frequent reference to a transformation in their domestic life—they learned to love and appreciate their wives and care more tenderly for their children; time spent in the pub was now spent at home, talking more openly and sharing feelings more easily. Their hyper-masculinity had been *unmade*. While remaining the household 'head,' they now led 'properly,' by 'living out' the same kindness and grace that their Savior had shown them, *remaking* their masculinity and 'headship' to mirror the 'born-again' relationship they now had with Christ. Having experienced 'rescue' from his own sin, Alasdair sought to extend this rescue to those closest to him by becoming a loving husband, a good father, and, thereby, a 'proper' Christian man.

Gendered Emotion: Sick or Slick?

Alasdair: Ken this, I'll always remember my granny...me and her would be sitting there and my grandfather and father would be away to sea...[and] she would always say the same thing every night—"I'm praying for you the night". [**Breaks down in tears, unable to speak. Sits back and turns in seat. Wipes away tears. Long silence follows**]. It never leaves you, never leaves you....For all them that's heard the gospel and their parents has prayed for them and everything and them that has nae responded, where are they going? [Silence. Waiting for an answer]. Where are they going Joe?

JW: Well, they are lost.

Alasdair: They're *lost*. It's like somebody falling into the harbor, throwing them a life belt and they will na take....If you go to church every week of your life or ten times a day, read your Bible and everything, but there's no change, if you dinna have Jesus in your heart...[**starts to weep again**] you've got to have that Holy Spirit. Without that Holy Spirit we are lost, we are lost, I mean, the day I gave my life to Jesus I felt the Holy Spirit going into my heart, I really did, *in there* [**points to heart with trembling hand: crying**]: Great. Still there. Still there...[**continues crying**]. Will we have a word of prayer?

JW: I was just going to say...do you want me to turn this [dictaphone] off?

Alasdair: [**Nods, weeping. Bends forward, wiping away tears**]: Aye, turn it off.

[Interview ends]. [Alasdair begins to pray].

Among Gamrie's Christian fishermen, testimony sacrifices masculine self-reliance and pride through the public display of bodily emotion. This is especially true within the self revelatory *exomologesis* of testimony where giving a 'tell all' answer to the question, 'How did you become a Christian?' necessitates a renunciation of two key markers of a successful skipper: personal moral autonomy and total self-confidence. Thus, Alasdair's display of emotion was not so much telling some truth about the moment of his conversion (as a bounded event), but rather performed, in word and body, his 'general status in...existence' (Foucault 1993: 213) as a converted, born-again man. What Alasdair was offering was not a specific claim directed toward the truth concerning a specific salvific *act*, but was rather engaging in a simultaneously verbal and somatic reiteration of his converted *status*.

Alasdair performed, through his emotional testimony, that he was broken, needy, bankrupt, and penitent, and on this basis alone, he became nothing more (and nothing less) than 'a sinner saved by grace.' Casting down his gaze as he spoke—looking mostly at his feet—performed the same diminutive attitude to his Lord and Savior that women were expected to show to male leaders in church. Constantly shifting position in his seat—sometime bent forward, sometimes turned away—displayed a disquiet and lack of confidence deemed suitable for one so deeply indebted by God's grace. Wringing trembling hands communicated a 'godly fear' that was said to emerge from a proper understanding of the contrast between divine majesty and human inadequacy. Hands held to cover the face and to wipe away tears displayed the final death of masculine pride; Alasdair, though a man, was crying.

Such embodied revelations were not singular events but were achieved through repeated linguistic *and* metakinetic performances. By reiterating the 'conversion tale' through the act of 'giving testimony,' born-again masculinity was not just differently stated, but also differently enacted—in word and body—*through a relationship of co-constitution*. This was only partly achieved, then, through reiterative autobiographical statements: "I was born...," "I got married...," "I got saved...." Because reiteration was not simply undertaken by verbal statement or avowal, the redefining and remaking of Alasdair's masculinity was also achieved through bodily performance, in gaze, posture, trembling, covered face, and tears. Thus the death of masculine pride gave birth, in word and deed, to its opposite—needy, submissive humility.

In this refusal of the self, Alasdair remade his masculinity through the 'show-and-tell' of his exhaustive spiritual history. Weeping his way through his testimony, Alasdair defined his masculine Christian self as 'strong' and 'powerful' while simultaneously embodying gendered behaviors ideal-typically associated with women (cf. Almeida 1996: 123; Brusco 1995: 115) and children. Not only was Alasdair a 'born-again' Christian man, but also a fisherman and a family man. As a fisherman he undertook 'real men's work' by 'doing battle with the elements' in dangerous and dirty circumstances, all the while being 'upheld' by his 'protector' and 'provider.' As a husband and father he was head of household, but sought to lead with the same gentleness and grace he had received from his Savior. Emptying himself of self-reliance and self-sufficiency, all Alasdair could do was 'yield to Christ' and share his testimony of abnegation: 'it's *nothing* to do with me, it's the *Lord*, that's the way *He* works.'

But the ethnography presented so far might give rise to a sense that what we are dealing with in Alasdair's 'testimony' is not a generally coherent statement of confessional autobiography but a display of emotion that is actually rather pathological. Might Alasdair not just be sick? Two responses seem to be required. First, Alasdair's testimony is not a symptom of sickness but arises out of an established and locally coherent linguistic structure (cf. Stromberg 1993: 123–126) that seeks to make sense of the gendered self and other through the medium of emotional testimony. Second, the very fact that it occurs to us to ask the question, 'Is Alasdair, on the basis of his emotional testimony, sick?' is itself highly informative of the way in which the social sciences have had (at least in the past) a tendency to view Christianity not as an internally coherent cultural phenomena in its own right, but instead as a rather awkward addendum to the somehow more continuous particularities of other spheres of human culture and experience (Engelke 2004; Robbins 2007).

If we are happy to concede that Alasdair, in giving his testimony, was not straightforwardly deranged in his display of gendered emotion, could he perhaps be seen as theatrically slick rather than presenting as sick? Indeed, as another colleague in anthropology suggested to me, because the testifying self explicitly seeks to reform the listening other, might it not be the case that Alasdair's weeping represented little more than crocodile tears—a kind of emotional blackmail that had my conversion and not his confession as its design? How can we know that Alasdair wasn't being *insincere*? What is most striking here is not any answer that there might be to this question, but again, the very fact that some feel the need to ask the question in the first place. In its asking we again betray a typically Protestant interest in discovering the 'uniquely emergent' truth of the event that was Alasdair's conversion.

All I can do here is point the reader back to Foucault's (1993: 213) assertion that Christian confession (and thus 'giving testimony' as confessional autobiography) is *not* about eliciting the truth of a single event ('what's *really* going on, *deep down*, on the *inside*'), but about performing and thereby constituting the truth of a more general state of existence, in our case, of gendered experiences of 'born-again' conversion. Thus, rather than ask ourselves, 'Was Alasdair telling the truth about his past or was he rather demonstrating illness or perhaps even deception?' we might more profitably ask 'How is Alasdair's performance of testimony actually constituting the truth of his masculinity and his salvation in the present?' The answer lies in seeing the born-again conversion narrative as a kind of evangelism.

Testimony as Evangelism

Testimony, as a type of confession, is a fundamentally relational phenomenon that constitutes the truth of the experience of salvation in the present, not only for the speaking self, but also for the listening other. Ordinarily, making one's confession requires a priest, but in many cases (outside the strict limits set by the Church) it can involve a parent, a friend, a stranger, and so on. It can also, apparently, involve an anthropologist. What is important is that it ordinarily involves someone other than the person doing the confessing. It is through this 'other' (through the listening ears and watchful eyes of a crowd or individual) that the truth about the confessing, testifying self is made known. Alasdair's words and body co-constituted one another: his pained facial expression, his downward cast gaze, his shifting posture, his trembling hands, his covered face, and his teary eyes, these are the things that, when placed alongside his spoken narrative, produced a 'born-again' masculinity that was both powerful and diminutive. And it was this, as in confession, which revealed the 'truth' of Alasdair's selfhood.

But giving one's testimony, just as making one's confession, is not simply a revelation of the truth of oneself by the self, nor is it purely a free exchange with another (whoever that may be). Rather, it is an intentional (in a sense, *strategic*) interaction with that other. This is, I have argued, where I depart most clearly from Stromberg (1993). Where Stromberg argues that 'the only difference between the conversion and other forms of ritual is that the conversion is focused upon an individual rather than being an overtly communal action' (Stromberg 1993: 12), it has been my argument that 'giving testimony', understood through the lens of confession, is indeed, like all ritual, an overtly communal action.

Confessors and testifiers want not only a listening ear but also a responsive 'heart.' Where confessors of sin want to be met with a heart of forgiveness, those who testify to being 'born-again' want to be met with a heart of repentance—they want their testimony to move the listener in such a way so as to reform the state of their soul. Giving testimony (both in public and in private) was seen by these Scottish fishermen as a kind of 'Christian service'; Alasdair constantly sought to 'share something of his testimony' with those who were not locally recognized as being 'converted, born-again believers.' Through this communal act, Alasdair fulfilled his mission in life to 'speak to as much people as I can…[about] the Lord,' and in so doing, not only testified 'to the saving power of the Holy Spirit,' but actually enacted it—in word and body—in the presence of his audience.

Thus, testimonies are given with the intention of 'moving' the other (emotionally) with the aim of bringing about some kind of reformative effectual action. Reverend Melvin Campbell described to Harding how he was responsible for the tragic death of his own son; 'Now I'm saying that Susan because he is real…God is alive. And his Son lives in my heart' (Harding 2000: 52, 60). For Harding, the narrative intention was clear: 'Campbell created a space for me to take responsibility, and feel responsibility, for determining the meaning of his son's death.' But why? Campbell wanted, in the terms of our now familiar conflation, to *convert* Harding to '*born-again*' faith: 'Of all that I could give you.…I hope that what we've talked about today will help you make that decision, to let [Jesus] come into your heart' (2000: 57). What, then, was my responsibility toward Alasdair and his Lord? What did he want from me in return for sharing his testimony?

Alasdair, simply put, was trying to make me into the kind of Christian he wanted me to be. His performance was not only for himself—it was not an act of pure autobiography, spiritual solipsism, or self-transformation—but was also a deliberate act of evangelism; Alasdair was calling me to commit myself to the spiritual path that he himself had committed to. Yet, because during my fieldwork I was open about the fact that I was a practicing Christian, I had the sense that Alasdair was unsure not so much about my 'salvation' but of my personal 'commitment' to the faith that I claimed. My last encounter with Alasdair before leaving the field helps resolve this question, while also adding further clarification to what I have been saying about gendered emotion. It was a Sunday night in Fraserburgh, and the annual 'Harvest of the Sea' service at the Fishermen's Mission had just come to an end. I was speaking to an older lady who sat beside me, when Alasdair, having heard of my soon departure, came to say goodbye. He hovered for a while, flush faced and teary eyed, looking unsure how to interject. When it became clear that my elderly conversation partner was not to be deterred, he leant over to me, and, with breathy intensity, whispered in my ear '*just remember what a great Savior we have!*' And blinking away tears, he smiled warmly, turned, and was gone.

This final exchange again placed Alasdair as speaker and me as listener. In switching from an inferred second person singular (*you* 'remember') to an explicit first person plural ('*we* have'), Alasdair was able to tacitly imply that he and I were the same—being, in local terms, 'saved'—while also alluding to the fact that we were different. This difference was expressed in terms of memory; whereas he remained ever mindful of his needy dependence upon his Heavenly Father as 'protector' and 'provider,' I, in the folly of male pride, had forgotten, or was at risk of forgetting, the greatness of our shared Savior. And it was his job, as a 'soundly saved, born-again believer,' as a 'man in Christ,' and as my elder, to remind, challenge, and encourage me by performing the words and embodied emotions that constituted his testimony-as-evangelism.

Such is the somatic and discursive complexity of 'giving testimony' that we can (and must) point to several things going on at once in any given performance. Alasdair was 'moved,' then, not only by himself and for himself; he was also moved on my behalf, and this, out of a desire to see me (that is, my *soul*) renewed and reformed by being brought to a fuller life of faith, repentance, and humility. Alasdair was moved on my behalf and sought, in turn, to move me through the emotional retelling of his testimony. He had wept *in front of me* and *for me*—but was I willing to sacrifice any pretence of masculinity and join him in his tears? Hence his pointed question right at the end of the interview: 'For all them that's heard the gospel and…has nae responded, where are they going? Where are they going Joe?' In the awkward silence that followed, Alasdair was not simply sharing his testimony; he was also calling me to greater Christian commitment.

My own experience of that moment in the interview, told us both, to my discredit I think, that I was unwilling and unable to follow Alasdair into his tears. 'Well, they are lost,' I said finally, offering the answer I knew was expected, and only after a delay in realizing that the question was not rhetorical. Having undergone a kind of reverse 'Hawthorne effect,' I am still not sure as to what extent my reply was 'insincere.' Alasdair seemed less troubled by this possibility than I was—'they're *lost*,' he nodded through tears. 'It's like somebody falling into the harbor, throwing them a life belt and they will na take it.…If you go to church…ten times a day, read your Bible and everything, but there's no change, if you dinna have Jesus in your heart…we are lost.' And after just a few more words, Alasdair finished his giving his testimony, the tape recorder was off and he was praying through yet more tears that I would receive God's guidance and blessing.

Conclusions

In giving a close 'reading' of one man's testimony I have argued for four main points. First, the 'born-again' religious experience represents real discontinuous moral change. This is the case insofar as Alasdair and my other informants described their 'born-again' experience as inseparable from 'conversion' understood not as a *'religious'* transition but as an *ontological* one; a transition from the 'Kingdom of Darkness' to 'God's Kingdom of Light.' Yet, conversion narratives defined by discontinuity also complement the language of continuity (Engelke 2004: 106) insofar as the 'born-again' life, while defined by newness, transition, and transformation (Stromberg 1993), was also characterized, in the lives of Gamrie's Christian fishermen, by the ongoing (pre and post-conversion) struggle against the sins of male pride: self-reliance, self-sufficiency, and self-confidence.

Second, then, while the performance of conversion is part of a global evangelical-Christian tradition, Alasdair's born-again experience also needs to be understood within its local context of conservative Protestantism in northeast Scotland. 'Giving testimony' is a gendered performance, that, through a theological emphasis upon moral failure, personal weakness, and the need to 'yield to Christ' and his salvific rescue, inverts and thereby redefines certain local expectations about what it means to be a masculine fisherman. Assumptions about physical strength, independent spiritedness, and emotional control are *unmade*, leaving men like Alasdair to learn (in word and body) how to experience and share their conversion in ways that are ideal-typically associated with women and children. A new type of 'born-again masculinity' is thereby *remade*, centering on male work and leadership—at sea, at home, and in church. Here, being a 'real man' is experienced not as a rebellious, foul-mouthed, and drunken seaman, but as a 'strong' and 'powerful' skipper, husband, father, and church member.

Third, 'born-again' conversion narratives are not, contra to Stromberg (1993), entirely or even predominantly a project of *self-transformation* but are only properly comprehended as part of a wider project of witness and evangelism that explicitly seeks to transform the hearing *other*. In this sense, to view the ritual of giving testimony as 'focused upon an individual rather being an overtly communal action' (Stromberg 1993: 12) is a serious error. Thus, among the Scottish Christian fishermen I lived alongside, the act of 'giving testimony'—indeed the very act of living one's life as a *'man in Christ'*—was defined by an evangelistic 'calling,' which, for Alasdair and my other friends, was a calling to 'speak to as much people as I can...[about] the Lord.'

Forth, 'born-again' conversion narratives in the Scottish context need to be understood anthropologically, not only as overtly communal, but also as a specific kind of communal religious performance akin to confession. Testimony as confession, viewed through the lens of Foucauldian ethics, helps us to see how the linguistic and metakinetic, far from 'imply[ing] quite different learning processes' that are 'psychologically distinct' from each other (Luhrmann 2004: 519)— are in fact sociologically inseparable. Having discussed the life of one particular retired fisherman, let us move to consider the lives of those who still work at sea—not only in terms of the material labor of trawling for prawns, but also in terms of the spiritual labor that surrounds being a 'fisher of men.'

Chapter 5

Fishing

The fishermen inhabiting the eastern coasts of the north of Scotland have ever had peculiarities of social life belonging to their own class... [with] the habits of one generation fall[ing] naturally upon that of the succeeding. [...] The man who ventures from day to day on the briny deep must have mental courage combined with physical strength. [...] A thorough-bred fisherman is distinguished by attributes—moral, mental, and physical.

(Thomson 1849: 173–174)

This chapter, like the two preceding it, is about the enchanting power of words. Insofar as it takes as its frame the life and work of two different deep-sea fishing crews in northeast Scotland, it is also about boats, bodies, prawns, and water—after all, as Thomson tells us, a 'thorough-bred fishermen' is knowable not only in 'moral' and 'mental' terms, but also with regard to the physicality of their own 'strength' and that of the 'briny deep' (Thomson 1849: 173–174). The ethnography presented below is based on two trips to sea during my last winter in the field. This involved working (and being paid) as a trainee deckhand on two different trawlers that fished for prawns in the North Sea, one hundred miles east of Fraserburgh, half way between the shores of Scotland and Norway.

Both trips were arranged informally with skippers local to Gamrie and at very short notice. Both skippers were committed Christians and organized their entire working life around never being at sea on Sunday (traditionally leaving Sunday midnight and returning Saturday dawn). The skipper of the *Flourish*, called Kenneth, was a member of Gamrie's FPCU. The skipper of the *Celestial Dawn*, Jackie Sr., was a member of Gamrie's OB. Both boats usually had six of a crew, some of whom called themselves ('born-again') Christians and some of whom pointedly did not.

The crew would typically earn around £1000 a week, sometimes more, sometimes less, and were paid on a share basis as opposed to a straight wage. Skippers, (who were usually also boat owners) earned considerably more; the vast majority were reputed to be millionaires. The *Flourish* had an entirely Scottish crew whereas the *Celestial Dawn* employed two Filipinos through an agency in Manila. These men lived on board the boat and told me they were paid about £100 a week plus discretionary bonuses. The hours for both skipper and crew were long (sometimes upwards of one hundred hours in six days) and the holidays few, with some men taking only two or three weeks off in a year.

The Flourish

Kenneth, the skipper of the *Flourish* (figure 5.1), picked me up in his jeep at 'the bog' (the bottom of the village) at ten o'clock on Sunday night. With me I had a sleeping bag and pillow, a few changes of clothes, my Nikon D40, and two packets of 'Stugeron' anti-sickness tablets. I was standing in an old pair of trainers, a cheap pair of jogging bottoms, a synthetic fleece jumper, and an old terracotta orange

Figure 5.1 *Flourish* BF 340

rain coat that was several sizes too big. I looked (and felt) not like a fisherman, but like a total fraud. And I could not stop thinking about being sea sick.

We left at 11 p.m. It was a pitch-black night. It was slightly choppy as we moved through the harbor but the boat started to roll an awful lot more as soon as we left the harbor walls. A few minutes before we set off, Kenneth's father smiled wryly and told me to take a plastic bag to bed. Once onboard, I was shown my bed and told how to wedge myself between my bag and the bunk to stop my body bouncing off the walls as I tried to sleep. I was told where the life jackets were—stuffed into an unused bunk—in case we ever needed them. Next I was taken up into the wheel house to have a look around. Despite the fact that total blackness surrounded the boat, the wheel house itself was lit up like a Christmas tree—panel after panel of switches and buttons, as well as six lit up monitors giving information about the location of the vessel in relationship to the oil rigs and other boats, the water depth, wind speed and direction, the plots of past trawls, and so on. What struck me as odd was the fact that the wheel-house also had Sky TV—a little bit of luxury in the midst of so much bewildering technology.

Kenneth was radioing other boats when I climbed the ladder through the hatch into the wheelhouse. He was trying to find out 'fit likes the fishin?' by getting important information from other skippers about 'where the bonnie prawns is at' and 'fit size and weight of haul' they were getting. He knew all the boats by name and they all knew him. The Fraserburgh fleet was fairly small, further broken down into cliques that, at times, shared information about catch sizes and locations. Soon enough Kenneth and I were chatting about 'all the rules that the EU had recently brought in'—about the problems with the quota system and the new CCTV scheme designed to document (and eventually reduce) 'throwbacks.'[1]

As we chatted, dots of light began to appear in the distance. Kenneth explained he could tell how far ahead the boats were and which direction they were steaming in just by looking at their configuration of lights. To me they looked like blobs of light in a mass of darkness. After a while Kenneth went to his bed and his brother Mark took watch. The conversation quickly turned to Christian things. Mark told me he worshiped at the AoG in Fraserburgh and was soon to go on a mission trip to Ghana. He spoke of a man at his church who had received a vision from God of an African girl reading a children's Bible to her illiterate mother; since receiving this vision, the man had gone on to distribute thousands of children's Bibles across

Africa. Mark then turned to me and said, 'I think God sent you here this week for me.' Noting my surprise, he began to explain. He himself was a skipper and was waiting for his own boat to be built. His family had been teasing him all week: "You're just a deckie,[2] you're just a deckie!" saying that he wouldn't survive the physical labor, which, he admitted, he had been dreading. Yet he was encouraged, he said, because of the difference it would make to have me—a fellow Christian—on board while working at the tray.

No sooner had Mark finished describing how I had been sent to him by God to help him get through the week-long trip than he flicked on the Sky TV and started surfing through the Christian channels, coming to an abrupt stop when he reached UCB[3] that was showing an 'Answers in Genesis' programme on scientific creationism. A cartoon picture of a mammoth flashed on screen. Seconds later another hand-drawn diagram popped up, this time of the earth, suggesting what the tectonic configuration of the planet would have looked like when they were all united as one mass. We chatted over the commentary provided for each picture and Mark quizzed me about my own beliefs on creationism and evolution. I was struck, as the conversation drifted from scientific creationism to denominational distinctives to beliefs about the end of the world, that I could have just as easily been having the same conversation in Gamrie as opposed to a hundred miles east, half way to Norway. We spoke until 4 a.m. I really did not want to go to my bed because the conversation was so interesting. I was also worried about lying down in case it made me feel sick, but eventually I had to retire because I could not keep my eyes open. I was in bed until about 8 a.m., when the call came to get up and shoot the gear. Not being used to sleeping flat on my back—a necessity to stop myself shifting around with the roll of the boat—I got almost no sleep. While I was worried about exhaustion, I was comforted by the fact that I did not feel sick, so I kept taking the pills and told myself they must be working.

Throwing myself into the routine of work, I quickly lost track of time. Hauling the gear, dumping the catch in the hopper, and shooting the gear out to sea happened four times a day, round the clock (figure 5.2). Apart from Kenneth, Mark, and I, there were three other men on the boat—Brice, the engineer; Max the cook; and Todd, an experienced deckhand, none of whom were Christians. While we all stood in a line along the tray tailing the prawns (figure 5.3), Brice and Max kept trying to get Mark to sing us a hymn, which seemed odd at the time, but I later learned was simply an attempt at killing the boredom of work. At one point Brice asked Mark what he thought about

Figure 5.2 Preparing to shoot the gear

Figure 5.3 The crew and author working at the tray

churches having gay ministers and Mark said he didn't think it was right. What about if one of his sons was gay—would he throw him out the house? No he wouldn't. Would he be devastated? Yes, probably. 'There you go!' cried Brice triumphantly in a mock show of victory, having established that, yes, Christians were all secret bigots.

Mark and Brice continued the religious banter, with Brice mostly playing offence and Mark stuck in defense. This verbal battle usually involved Brice throwing the occasional grenade Mark's way in between long silences of tailing prawns. Did he believe in evolution? No. Did he believe in dinosaurs? Yes. But did he believe that the bones were millions of years old? No. Why was there so much suffering in the world? Because of human sinfulness. And so it went on. At one point Kenneth came down from the wheel house to see how quickly we were clearing a backlog of prawns and immediately got drawn into the conversation. He leant over to Brice, Todd, and I to explain how before sin entered the Garden of Eden there was no death— death, he said, was a product of the Fall. He went on to follow the logic through for us. If there was no sin in the garden before the fall, then there must have been no death, and if there was no death then all animals must have been herbivores. He went on to describe how scientists had recently discovered the skull of a monkey with massive fangs. If you were to look at the skull, you would immediately think that the monkey was a meat eater, but this wasn't the case: research had shown that those large fangs were actually used to break into hard skinned fruit. Kenneth looked triumphant. Brice looked unconvinced. Todd looked uninterested. I felt a bit embarrassed. Eventually we all fell back to tailing prawns.

About halfway through a 10 p.m. haul that was mostly full of useless herring, I climbed into the hopper to push out some more of the fish and prawns into the tray. As I raked away at another layer of live creatures packed into the solid wall of fish stacked up beside me, a large brown crab, legs flailing, tumbled out and landed at my feet. I had been warned about these animals during our first haul—their claws are incredibly powerful; if they got hold of a finger, they could do serious damage. Without stopping to think I smashed its body with the flat end of the rake and pushed it onto the tray with the rest of the catch to be sorted, jumping down to continue tailing. Todd, who was working opposite me, held up the sorry looking creature in front of me and said, 'Huh! Jesus Saves!' before throwing it down a dump shoot, shaking his head, and getting back to work. Suddenly Max struck up a merry little Sunday school tune: 'All things bright and beautiful, Joe will kill them all' as an ironic comment on my unnecessary cruelty.

Seeing my embarrassment, Mark came to my rescue: 'Ah, but when he goes to bed tonight, he'll be *saved*.' I later realized that the crab and I were actually rather unimportant window dressing in a wider religious debate that had been going on between Mark on one side and Brice, Todd, and Max on the other. The debate—about who went to heaven, who went to hell, and why—had been going on for years between the men in one form or another. The crab and I were just good to think with. As it turned out, it was a debate that would continue for the entire trip.

The next haul, we had what Max dubbed a 'Bible study' while sorting the catch. Mark told Brice how the Holy Spirit spoke to him personally as he prayed, read the Bible, and went through daily life. Brice responded by asking—assuming the Adam and Eve story was true— how was the world populated without resorting to the sin of incest. It looked like Mark was going to crumble. Feeling the need to repay him for his earlier rescue, I came to his aid. I had heard it preached, I said, that it wasn't a sin in those days because the genetic line was pure enough for incest not to cause deformities; God only decreed that incest was sinful when it became dangerous. This seemed to do the trick and Mark looked relieved.

Later that night, at around 8 p.m., we had a full roast dinner and watched *The Ten Commandments* film on UCB. The situation struck me as altogether surreal: we were bobbing up and down in a small prawn trawler in the middle of the North Sea, eating a full roast dinner while watching Charlton Heston lead the Israelites out of the desert and into the Promised Land. During a lull in the action, Brice declared that he had been reading his Bible in between hauls (the fact that as an 'unbeliever' he had a Bible and took it with him to sea I found surprising), opening it at random, and finding himself in the book of *Leviticus*. The passage he read was all about the Mosaic sexual purity laws. He said that the Holy Spirit had not spoken to him in the way that Mark had experienced. Brice waited for a response but Mark did not say much.

Toward the end of the trip I was physically tired and struggled to do the work. My arms felt like lead and were very weak; my hands were stiff and slow; my feet were aching badly from standing on the grill, tailing for hours; and my knees felt all bashed from climbing in and out of the hopper. During a breakfast of fried herring, in the middle of a conversation about how many boxes of prawns and fish we had stored away in the hold, a news clip about the discovery of a fossil that was 150 million years old flashed across the TV. Brice immediately turned to Mark to see his reaction: he didn't believe it, saying how carbon dating wasn't accurate. Somehow, this led to an argument about a Christian skipper who kept the fridge in the mess locked: 'Why does he go all the way to Africa to build darkies hooses and won't even feed his *crew*?' Brice demanded angrily, going on: 'It's just for show: "Look at me, I'm a Christian,"' at which point Mark got up from the table and walked out in protest. After a while, once Mark had come back into the mess and everyone had calmed down, we watched a bit more TV and then headed to our beds.

After a mid morning haul, we began cleaning the boat to prepare for landing the fish at market the next day. After a cup of tea in the mess, Mark and I went down to the cabins to compare Bible translations. He showed me his NLT,[4] and I showed him my ESV.[5] After he quizzed me on why I had chosen this version he decided he wanted an ESV too and said he would buy one when we got back onshore. Just as I was about to head to my bunk to get some sleep, Mark began to speak about his anxiety about going on the mission trip to Ghana; a couple of nights ago he was feeling scared and could not sleep so he opened his Bible at a random page and began to read. The passage was Deuteronomy chapter one. As he read, he said that verses 29 and 31 really leapt out at him:

> But I say to you, don't be shocked or afraid of them!...And you saw how the Lord God cared for you all along the way as you travelled through the wilderness, just as a father cares for his child. Now he has brought you to this place.

Mark then went on to describe how 'comforting' those words were and how he felt 'blessed' by them. No sooner had we finished our conversation were we back in the mess debating with Brice, Max, and Todd about whether or not Christians should be allowed to gamble. If a Christian were to be a contestant on 'Who Wants to be a Millionaire?' would they have to quit as soon as they were guaranteed a win of £1000 because anything beyond this would be gambling? I was exhausted, and the religious debating did not look like it was going to stop. Eventually I excused myself and went to bed, leaving the others to their verbal jousting.

Our last haul of the trip was long and slow. Max and Todd came into their own, dominating the conversation with really foul chat about 'the turtle club.'[6] At one point they directed their attention to me and started to quiz me about my own sex life, leading to endless innuendo about both my landlady and my girlfriend. Later, Max looked at me almost apologetically and, referring to his earlier conversation with no double meaning intended, said 'we really are wading through a stream of shit aren't we?' and excused himself by saying that dirty talk was the only way to pass the time. 'Mark, sing us a hymn!' he suddenly shouted, and before long we were singing along to our various 'favorites.'

We arrived to land our catch in Fraserburgh around 5:30 a.m. on Saturday. We unloaded the boxes of prawns onto the pier and into a truck that would take them to a market inland. The fish went straight to the market at the harbor. Fresh boxes were loaded, the boat refueled, and the nets spread out on the pier and mended. As soon as I stepped back onto the pier, the ground started swaying beneath my feet to the point where I actually had to hold onto a stack of boxes to stop myself from falling over. Kenneth gave the crew lifts back home, dropping me off last at the bottom of the Gamrie brae before finally heading home himself.

When I got back I put my washing on, had a very long shower, and went straight to bed. It was about 2 in the afternoon. I got a few hours sleep and, in the hope of sleeping through the night as well, set my alarm to get up for the evening prayer meeting at the Kirk. When I arrived at the church I was met by several of the older folk who were bursting to hear how I had got on at sea, particularly because the weather on shore had been awful. When they heard that I had not been sick they were all immensely relieved and assured me that they had been praying for me all week. 'Someone was looking after you!' they exclaimed, beaming from ear to ear; 'the Lord has answered our prayers!' After answering lots of questions and telling a few stories we bowed our heads and began to pray.

Fishing and Witness as Competitive Labor

In an ethnographic account of conflict management in a Portuguese fishing village, Johnson (1979) argues:

> The fishery can...be seen as a zero-sum game in which the success or failure of any one boat may affect the prospects of all the other boats. [...] It would be unreasonable for an individual boat to limit its effort; what it doesn't catch will be left to others. [...] Thus it is not only to the advantage of individual boats to catch as much fish as they can, but there is some temptation to diminish the amount caught by others. Inter-boat conflict is...inevitable. (Johnson 1979: 246)

The result, Johnson tells us, is 'a social climate rife with secretiveness, lying, avoidance, and general suspicion' (1979: 246) between boats in the same fleet. Similarly, Pina-Cabral (1986: 125) describes how Portuguese peasant farmers' strong attachment to the household 'leads to a divisive tendency and to social conflict':

> In a situation of conflicting interests, the peasant may be quite ruth-less in attempting to advance his own household. Parish society is fairly restricted in numbers; competition, therefore, both for economic and for prestige goals, can be very intense. One household's success is far too often another household's failure. (Pina-Cabral 1986: 125)

As in the 'parish society' of the Alto Minho, so too among the Fraserburgh fishing fleet, numbers are small and competition—financial and reputational—is severe, often expressed in terms of winners and losers. Yet, whilst the 'parish' and 'fleet' undergo simi-lar processes of conflict, the experience of competiveness is evaluated very differently. Where for Pina-Cabral's peasant informants,

> the existence of this divisive proclivity is acknowledged but regret-ted...as a serious failure to achieve the accepted ideals of parish and hamlet life, [namely communal 'belonging' and 'egalitarianism.'] (Pina-Cabral 1986: 125, 129–130)

Gamrie's fishermen showed no such regret in either their evalu-ations of economic or religious life. To explain this difference, it is helpful to note how nautical anthropologists Stiles (1972) and Prattis (1973)—writing on Newfoundland and the Isle of Lewis respectively—have both suggested that competition *between* boats leads to solidarity *within* individual crews. Their argument, con-cerned with the functional role of social conflict, can be broadly summarized as follows:

> Inter-boat conflict functions to *minimize incongruence* by creating *social solidarity* via *occupational status equivalence*.[7]

The example of Gamrie, especially when an examination of fishing is conducted alongside that of religion, shows a more complex picture. Where Johnson (1979), Stiles (1972), and Prattis (1973) assume that inter-boat conflict leads to intra-boat harmony, the ethnography pre-sented above suggests a different set of social relationships. My focus will not be on inter-boat conflict but upon intra-crew verbal jousting and its connection to religion. It will be my argument that

> intra-crew verbal jousting functions to *maximize incongruence* by creating *social separation* via *salvific status differentiation*.

This approach is insightful insofar as inter-boat contact was limited and intra-crew verbal jousting was considerable. What is more, the subject of such banter was explicitly religious with participants divided on religious grounds that were rarely—if ever—crossed. The Christians 'taught' each other and 'preached' to their 'unsaved' crew members; the 'non-Christians' joked with each other and argued with their 'saved' crew members. Brice's questions seemed incessant. What was wrong with gay ministers? Why couldn't the earth be millions of years old? Why couldn't Christians gamble? It was obvious to Mark and those who watched him that the questions he was responding to were meant not purely to elicit information about Christian theology but (insofar as Brice's questions emerged with an unmistakably mischievous grin) were designed to cause a ruckus. 'There you go!!' cried Brice as Mark admitted he would be uneasy with having a son who was gay, as if a prosecution lawyer had finally caught the accused in a self-condemning lie. Such was the competitive and almost pugilistic nature of emotionally enskiled witness (and counter witness) at sea.

The debates that ensued on the *Flourish* (about the authenticity of fossils or the authority of the Bible), while partially undertaken as an antidote to the boredom of tailing prawns, also had a socially constitutive effect—that of maximizing the felt incongruence between Christian and 'non-Christian' crew members. These two camps were not compatible, because, according to both Mark and Brice, Christians and 'non-Christians' lived and believed in very different ways. Brice played the lottery and Mark did not. Mark believed in divine creation and Brice in evolution. Mark voiced strong opposition to homosexuality and Brice said he wasn't bothered. Their verbal jousting circled around the same point time and again: Mark and Brice were both fishermen, but were fundamentally not the same. Incongruence was not an end in itself; when it came to the verbal joust, it was necessary but not sufficient. The initial goal of the game was to establish status differentiation on the basis of who was and was not 'saved.' Only latterly, once this status differentiation had been established, could the real work begin through the 'testimony' of preaching and teaching and the 'anti-testimony' of joking and arguing. This 'work' went beyond the verbal joust, addressing the more substantive matter of one's future after death.

When I was in the hopper raking prawns onto the tray I smashed and killed a crab. Todd and Max reacted by jokingly pointing out what they saw as my blatant hypocrisy—claiming to be a Christian while being needlessly cruel to one of God's creatures. But they were not really talking to me—they were arguing with Mark. Hence Mark's leaping to my defense: 'Ah, but when he goes to bed tonight he'll be *saved*,' said with the unmistakable tone of a preacher in his pulpit. From Mark's point of view the difference in status could scarcely be greater; I had been 'saved' and was going to heaven regardless of my cruelty to crabs; Todd and Max however had not been saved and were presently en route to hell. They needed to be told so—and in the same manner as at a gospel preaching in Gamrie on a Sunday night.

While this status difference was expressed first and foremost in salvific terms and thus held to be ultimate, it was also made knowable spatially and thus experienced in the present. To give a commonly deployed local example, Mark might be found in a prayer meeting on a Saturday night whereas Brice might well be in the pub. Max and Todd went on to stretch this social distance as far as fantasy permitted, describing binge drinking, gorging on Indian food, and sex acts involving defecation. The goal was not intra-crew solidarity via status equivalence but rather intra-crew separation via salvific status differentiation, symbolized, at its most extreme, in the utter incongruence between hymn singing and coprophilia.

The 'unholy alliance' that seemed to exist between Max, Todd, and Brice found its inverted mirror image in the conversations that occurred between Kenneth, Mark, and myself. Christian crew were expected to 'preach the gospel' to the 'unsaved' on deck and 'teach the Bible' to each other, through discussions of theology, Biblical history, creationist science, and so on. Mark asserted this relational expectation early on by telling me that God had sent me to him to help him get through the week. Later on, monkey fangs were used by Kenneth to teach us about the account of the 'Fall of Man' in the Book of Genesis. I played my part by rising to defend Mark against a thorny question from Brice about creationism by repeating a sermon excerpt that asserted the innocence of incest in the Garden of Eden. It was this teamwork that acted to socially construct the 'zero-sum game' of the verbal joust; evangelistic witness countered by pugnacious rebuttal followed by evangelistic witness and so on.

Such verbal exchanges can be construed as competitive labor, involving the back-and-forth point scoring of religious debate and banter. Unlike Inupiat whale hunters (Turner 1996) the efforts of Gamrie's fishermen, then, cannot be described as egalitarian, either spiritually or economically. As with fish, the stocks of human souls available for harvest were limited and constantly attempting to elude capture. Where the whales of the Arctic Circle 'give themselves' to their Inupiat sea-hunters, neither fish nor souls gave themselves up willingly to Gamrie's trawlermen, but had to be struggled for if they were to be brought on deck or 'under the sound of the gospel.' This struggle was both human and divine: while the crews of the *Flourish* and the *Celestial Dawn* personified the Protestant work ethic by fulfilling their dutiful calling to labor at sea, it was their God, as 'protector' and 'provider,' who ultimately filled the nets.

Without a hint of paradox, North Sea trawling continued to operate on an industrial scale in every sense: competitively organized, resource intensive, technology reliant, credit dependent, and profit driven. Where the zero-sum game of trawling for prawns was largely one of capitalist economics, the zero-sum game of trawling for souls was experienced not as a competition between rival boats but between rival spiritual kingdoms. The incongruence within the churches between 'teaching the Bible' to the 'saved' and 'preaching the gospel' to the 'unsaved' also existed on the boats; the 'saved' witnessed and the 'unsaved' pushed back. Yet it would be wrong to give the impression that the 'game' of evangelism neatly placed those who witnessed in offence and those who were objects of witness, in defense—as Brice made clear, the opposite was often the case.

How might evangelistic verbal jousting be 'read' as a kind of labor? 'Witness' is labor insofar as local people described it as such, referring to their evangelistic efforts—their prayers, their preaching, and their teaching—as a 'spiritual toil,' a 'labor for the Lord,' and a 'work of faith.' Local fishermen described how labor at sea (both the physical work of trawling for prawns and the 'spiritual' work of evangelism), was not primarily a product of sin or a mode of atonement (Mayblin 2010: 100, 109), but a 'calling' placed upon the lives of the already saved. The zero-sum game of fishing for prawns and being 'fishers of men' simply *had* to be engaged in. 'It's all we've ever known,' these fishermen would tell me—a phrase that was also used to describe the 'spiritual privilege' of growing up in a Christian village. Fishing and witness were held to be mutual imperatives, materially and religiously. Theirs was a double kind of fishing, fulfilling the 'scriptural mandate' for a man to 'provide for his family' (cf. Mayblin 2010: 112) and 'fulfill the Great Commission' by evangelizing the whole world.

Putting fish on the table and bottoms on the pews involved real sacrificial toil. Fishing for prawns was dangerous, dirty, and exhausting work. According to many of my Christian informants, so was a life of 'teaching' and 'preaching,' littered, as it was, with discouragement, rejection, and ridicule. Mark was adamant that God had sent me to him during our week at sea—he wasn't so much nervous about coping with the physical labor of trawling for prawns as the spiritual toil of witnessing to fellow crew members. As with preaching, fishing, and evangelism were said to require a kind of sacrifice—of self, time, comfort, and worldly pleasures. Witness required this same 'sacrificial suffering' (Mayblin 2010: 90)—through loss of privacy and dignity—as the soul of the Christian was laid bare in self-destructive confessional avowal before those being evangelized.

The Village in Miniature

At the heart of the competitive 'zero-sum game' of fishing and witness is a picture of the village in miniature, bringing Gamrics' socio-spiritual coalitions and divisions into uniquely sharp relief through enforced intimacy on the trawler, forming its own 'triple pinch' at sea.

Money shapes much of life in Gamrie, and residence and religion are no exception. Historically, money has tended to move up the brae, with the fishermen initially living in tiny cottages by the shore in the Seatown. In the two decades following the Second World War, these dwellings were vacated in favor of more modern, spacious, and prestigious housing, some private and some local authority. Since the 1990s, newly custom built 'fisher mansions' have been commissioned by wealthy skippers at the very top of the brae with the old fisher cottages now almost exclusively the preserve of retired English 'incomers.' A strikingly similar spatial division exists onboard the trawlers. At the very top of the boat is the wheelhouse, largely the domain of the skipper, generally the best paid and most wealthy person on board. One deck below is usually the skipper's private quarters. Below this were the crews' shared quarters and below this the engine room and below this the hold for the catch.

Such (often specialized) income and wealth inequalities were a source of latent tensions onboard the boat, emerging—as they did onshore—in boasting and jealousy, over, among other things, cars, clothing, and holiday destinations. Those with the strongest religious commitment were widely recognized as having the most money—a (strikingly Weberian) sign of God's blessing according to local Christians and an aggravating puzzle to those without this salvific status. Gamrie's Christian fishermen—men in their forties and fifties—asserted that their success was due, among other things, to their faithfulness in 'keeping the Lord's Day.' Their 'unsaved' contemporaries, on the other hand, grumbled that 'Gamrie folk' banded together in a mafia-like Christian cabal, protecting each others interests while never sharing resources or information with outsiders. It is difficult to generalize as to the extent to which Gamrie's younger fishermen were convinced by either of these competing accounts.

What was abundantly clear was that they did not, by and large, show the same religious commitments as their fathers and grandfathers, with some choosing to leave the local fishing industry and its Christian heritage behind, in favor of easier money on the oil rigs and supply boats.

Inequalities between 'insiders' and 'outsiders' were made more visible and extreme by the fact that some boats contracted Filipino workers. This migrant labor (the nautical equivalent of an 'incomer,' but without their wealth), slept on the boat even when ashore, earning a small fixed wage—about £100 a week or £1/hr if the fishing was exceptionally heavy—as opposed to a share. Despite having no costs of food or board, these Filipino laborers were paid badly by local standards, receiving about a tenth of what their Scottish counterparts earned by way of the share system. Skippers justified this by calculating the wages they paid migrant labor in the relative terms of foreign purchasing power, commenting that Filipino fishermen were 'building mansions back home' with wages earned in Scotland. Some of the Filipino men I met in Fraserburgh were less convinced—being on the wrong side of an enormous pay gap caused a resentment, which, because of their weak structural position, was rarely openly voiced.

Demographic power inequalities were also noticeable, extending beyond the Scots-Filipino divide. Familial proximity to the skipper was key. As described below, Jackie Jr. (the skipper's teenage son) slept more and worked less than the crew who were not the skipper's kin. Such power dynamics carried over into the churches, with more than one retired fisherman complaining to me that being a successful (and wealthy) skipper often transferred into undue influence over the running of religious affairs onshore. As again was the case onshore— age remained a factor onboard the boats with regard to one's level of religious commitment. Max and Brice, in their late thirties or early forties (the age group most strikingly absent from church) were also the most vocally hostile to Mark's efforts to preach to them. Mark, on the other hand, was the youngest and most committed Christian crewman onboard, and, by virtue of being a skipper awaiting the construction of a new boat, was also very likely the wealthiest. It was this economic and demographic power base that combined to form the sociological backdrop to the competitive 'zero-sum game' of evangelistic witness.

But what of the eschatological pinch? How did the impending end of the world color this game of 'witness' and 'counter-witness'? It did so in the same way it did onshore, by creating, reinforcing, and reproducing the (urgent and imperative) socio-spiritual boundaries of 'saved' and 'unsaved' personhood. Hence Brice, Max, and Todd forming a team to play one side of the 'game' and Mark, Kenneth, and myself forming a (albeit more tacit and uneasy) team on the other. Salvific status thus becomes the key indicator of who is said to be what type of person. And it is this that frames who says what at the tray and with what effects. Evangelistic conversations between Christian fishermen about Biblical creationism—spoken not only to edify the 'saved' but to challenge the 'unsaved'—led to just as obviously sideways conversations between non-Christian crew about drunken sex. 'Teaching' and 'preaching,' then, are not discrete categories performed in isolation from each other, but, as with 'saved' and 'unsaved,' are mutually interdependent categories that are only intelligible insofar as they stand in (linguistic and material) relation to their eschatological opposite. And so it goes on, round the clock, for six days—or as long as there are prawns to tail—along the short steel tray that comprises the working universe of Gamrie's trawlermen, played out as the village in miniature.

The *Celestial Dawn*

It was Sunday night and I was packing my bags to get ready for another week at sea, this time on the Celestial Dawn (figure 5.4), a trawler owned by a Brethren skipper who had come out of the Closed

Figure 5.4   *Celestial Dawn* BF 109

movement to join Gamrie's OB. It was a month after my first trip on the *Flourish* and the weather, being October, was growing worse. What's more, I was sailing on a full stomach having just feasted upon two plates of rich food at a 'goodbye' bring-and-share meal for a Romanian couple who had been living with an OB couple for the year. I took my anti-sickness tablets, made a few rushed phone calls to say goodbye to family, and headed over to meet the skipper, Jackie Sr., and his son, Jackie Jr., at the Bog.

We were on our way to Fraserburgh by 9 p.m. When we got to the harbor I was introduced to the other crew: Jonathan, Jackie Sr.'s nephew, Ross the cook, and two Filipino fishermen, Leon and Jay, neither of whom spoke much English. As soon as the boat left the harbor it started heaving from side to side. I was standing at the back of the boat with Jackie Jr. watching the harbor disappear out of sight. After the lights of Fraserburgh were no longer visible, we headed through to the mess and joked about how sick we felt. Jackie Jr. went to his bed and I went up to chat to the guys in the wheel house but spent most of my time concentrating hard on not vomiting. Jonathan discovered a book of comical Doric[8] poems and read a couple out to Ross and myself. They all laughed at the punch line but I was left none the wiser. As my nausea rose, I headed for bed, remembering to take a bag with me. Laying flat seemed to make things worse. I must have been drifting in and out of sleep; all I can remember is being in a cold sweat and saying, 'Jesus have mercy' over and over again in my head, this being the only anti-sickness prayer I could muster. Unfortunately it didn't work—I vomited three times that night.

We were rudely awoken by Jackie Sr. making strange screeching noises over the loudspeaker that then gave way to the even more bizarre wake-up call: 'ALL NATIONS RISE!! ALL NATIONS RISE!!' that, I learned later, was the signal to shoot the gear. I was told to help, and, having never done so on the *Flourish*, was nervous at the prospect. It was my job to move the poles that directed the nets into their right position and then climb to the upper deck to feed a steel cable over the front of the trawl door and down to the lower deck to allow the catch to be hoisted aboard and dumped into the hopper. After a couple of corrective instructions I got the hang of the process and only had to watch that the trawl door (a huge 2 m squared piece of steel) did not crush my arms when I was feeding the cable to the men below. After we shot the gear we went to the mess for breakfast. Not feeling overly revived by the freezing sea air, I picked my way through a bowl of cornflakes and headed below deck with the others for a few hours sleep before our first haul.

Figure 5.5   Winching aboard a huge haul of prawns

Having eaten little, by the end of the first haul I was listless. The second haul was huge (figure 5.5) and took seven hours to clear with only a two minute break in the middle for Pepsi and biscuits that we had at the tray. As we cleared the backlog Ross (the oldest and most experienced crewmember) was constantly barking at us to speed up, which, after several hours, became wearing. At one point I lost my temper and dragged far too many prawns onto the tray at too great a speed causing some to spill out onto the deck. Ross just smiled and kept tailing. Jackie Jr. was by far the slowest worker, but at only 16 years old, this was hardly surprising.

As on the *Flourish*, much of the conversation around the tray was about religion. Leon and Jay didn't speak much, especially because Ross demanded, when working at the tray, that they spoke English or not at all. Jonathan said he was brought up in the AoG but had since married into a (hugely wealthy) OB family in Peterhead. Ross said he was raised as a nominal CofS goer but no longer attended any place of worship. Leon, who read the Bible in his bunk at the end of each haul, was Protestant (from a Baptist and Pentecostal background), and seemed very committed to his faith. Jay said he was raised Catholic, but was no longer practicing. Neither man said much, nor did the others make any real attempt to draw them into our discussions.

The conversation moved from churches to evolution and back again. Jonathan asked me what I thought about creationism and I told him that while I did not believe in literal six-day creationism, I actually thought it did not matter much—what mattered for me was not how the world was created but who created it. Jonathan said that while he could see what I was saying, he did not agree—for him, sub-scribing to literal six-day creationism was important if the authority of the Bible was to be upheld. Jonathan then asked me about my own church background—what did the Free Church of Scotland believe? Why did they not have music? Why did they only sing psalms? What were the key differences between the Free Church, the AoG, and the OB? Much of this conversation was being pushed by Jonathan, not for my benefit, but for Ross's—as an act of witness. Jonathan told us about his own conversion experience—how he had realized that he needed a savior, how he had responded to the gospel, how he had come to the OB, and how he had been baptized as an adult and entered into mem-bership. Jonathan then turned to me and asked when I had become a Christian. Aware that my Christian life lacked the temporally specific and personally dramatic rupture of most 'born-again' conversion nar-ratives, I stuttered something vague about not really knowing when I was 'saved' but that I had started to take the faith my parents raised me in more seriously when I first went to university.

This clearly was not the response Jonathan had been looking for. To try and partially meet his expectation I changed tack by speaking about how what mattered most in the Christian life was not church but Jesus. I emphasized that from my experience, all churches—and all Christians—were full of faults and problems. As I talked (that is, as I *testified*), I grew increasingly uncomfortable with the implications of what I was saying. Had I stepped over an invisible intellectual line and transformed myself from an anthropologist into a missionary? It was clear that Jonathan did not share my hesitation, enthusiastically agreeing with all of my most Christocentric comments.

Eventually we cleared the hopper and went through to the mess. Jackie Sr. said a prayer to give thanks for the food (spicy fajitas) in exactly the same way as he always did, in a low, almost completely inaudible tone, with head bowed and hands folded. We all had to wait for this grace to be said before we could eat, even if Jackie Sr. was last to the table by several minutes. These prayers felt very much like a ritual: what seemed to matter was not any conveyed linguistic meaning—for the words Jackie Sr. prayed were not intended to be audible—but rather the simple fact that 'the grace' had been said, thereby allowing us to eat.

The conversation returned to religion. Jackie Sr. began to quiz me on how I had found going to the other places of worship in the village, eventually steering the conversation around to the two most recent splits at Braehead—the CB fellowship that he and his family had been attending until 1999. What reasons had I been given for the splits? I responded vaguely by outlining a few commonly voiced complaints. 'Maybe its better that you only ken half the story,' Jackie said tantalizingly. I assured him it wouldn't be, hoping he would fill in some blanks, but he only repeated what I had heard elsewhere— accusations of secret meetings and keys being intentionally broken off in locks. In a strange twist, Jackie then began to criticize the fellowship he currently attended—the OB—and specifically their view of adult-believers baptism; how they ignored passages in the Bible where entire households were baptized, and how Moses leading the ancient Israelites through the Red Sea was also a 'type' of baptism.

I was struggling with physical exhaustion after clearing the previous hauls of prawns so went straight to bed after we had finished eating. As the days went on, it was this rhythm of work followed by food followed by sleep that framed much of my experience of living on the *Celestial Dawn*.

On Tuesday afternoon we cleared two huge hauls—a 50 stone and a 70 stone. We each ate a pie on deck halfway through the first haul, then a cheese roll when it was clear, only to haul again immediately. The religious talk persisted with Jonathan instigating an intense conversation about salvation. Did Ross ever think about death? Did he have assurance about where he would go when he died? If God were to ask him, what reason would he give to be allowed into heaven? Jonathan's questions to Ross were largely rhetorical, designed to elicit, in the words of many a gospel preacher, a 'silent response of the heart.' At one point, Jonathan turned to me and said 'Ross kens it all, he kens it *all*, don't you Ross? He kens the gospel—I've told him *loads* of times.'

Later on I found myself backing Jonathan up by repeating what I had heard in an OB meeting where the preacher spoke about the difference between actively rejecting and passively neglecting salvation. Ross seemed to be listening hard to what we were saying. As Jonathan and I talked, I began to feel that same sense of unease about having 'overstepped' some kind of boundary—was I a participant observer or a preacher? I seemed to be losing purchase on the difference, as my words and presence became appropriated into Jonathan's program of evangelism. When we finally had the hopper emptied and it was time for dinner, I felt as relieved as Ross looked.

By Thursday I was becoming increasingly exhausted, too tired to text many notes on my phone before I fell asleep after hauls. The hauls had been enormous and full of small prawns. The work was slow and my 'moon boots' (huge thick steel capped wellington boots) had next to no padding and my feet were in agony—a common problem—making the work miserable. During one haul I was reduced to standing on a bit of scrap carpet that came up in the nets that I cut to double thickness to try and take some of the pain away. Later, Leon offered to use his reflexology technique to relieve the pain. Out of sheer desperation, I agreed. We sat at the bottom of my bunk and he carefully identified various areas of my feet and lower legs by gently pressing on them with his thumb. At first the pain was severe, causing me to moan through gritted teeth. Slowly he rotated around various 'pressure points.' Eventually the pain subsided, until, as if by magic, my feet no longer hurt at all. I thanked him and collapsed into bed; Leon smiled kindly, and, returning to his bunk, opened his Bible and began to read.

We returned to Fraserburgh harbor by 3 a.m. on Saturday morning. My feet were hurting again but we still needed to unload the fish and load new boxes onto the boat. Lee (Jackie Sr.'s twin brother, a member of the Seatown CB) came to the harbor to help us land. As we worked he asked how I had gotten on at Braehead when Carol, a mutual friend, was preaching (the one and only time I heard a woman preach in Gamrie). What did she speak on? Was she any good? Lee explained that one of his main reasons for leaving Braehead was that he didn't feel that 'wifey preachers' were 'scriptural': 'You see Joe, we believe in head coverings for women. If you let that go, there's always something else. You can tell if a place is right or not by if the women wear head coverings.'

During the conversation we had a dangerous moment when two huge stacks of fish boxes came loose and fell onto the boat. Once the boat was unloaded and reloaded, I power washed the top deck while the other crew mended the nets. A problem with fixing a chain resulted in a long delay and we eventually headed home by midday. I had a long shower when I arrived and then slept before heading back out—totally exhausted—to do my normal Saturday night shift at the Fraserburgh Fishermen's Mission.

Verbal Enskilment: Learning to be Fishers of Men

The ethnography above shows us that religious talk, like other forms of labor, exist as a kind of learned emotional and material practice. By examining this practice we can develop an understanding of the relationship between words, objects, and emotions. In a seminal reconfiguration of practice theory, Gísli Pálsson argues that 'getting one's sea legs' is a type of enskilment; skills such as fishing are not only bodily dispositions but also 'a necessarily collective enterprise—involving whole persons, social relations, and communities of practice' (1994: 902). Such skills are themselves located within a 'social and natural environment' (1994: 901). In applying Pálsson's comments to the 'zero-sum game' of evangelistic witness, I consider how the verbal content of a social environment is itself apprehendable in and through the deployment of words. Traversing this environment (like learning a language or catching a fish) requires skill in connecting person, place, and thing, which, in the religious context of Gamrie's prawn trawlers, involves the meeting of fishermen, the North Sea, and words of witness.

While it might seem strange to try and speak of 'getting one's evangelistic legs,' this is essentially what I want to argue. Such sentiments were familiar to my informants who not only delighted in the Biblical language of being 'fishers of men,' but also associated evangelistic preaching with the walking of feet. As with the physical skill of hunting prawns, Gamrie's Christian fishermen also needed to learn how to become fishers of men. We see here the emergence of a kind of enskilment—the deploying of a skill within its proper environmental (in this case linguistic and emotional) context. Such skill can be seen in Jonathan's careful steering of our early conversations at the tray from discussion of church backgrounds (to establish where we stood ecclesiastically), to discussions of creation and evolution (to establish where we stood theologically), to a more personal and emotional account of his own 'conversion experience' (his primary act of witness) and finally to questions about my own salvation, requiring me to testify as he himself had done. The aim was clear as far as Jonathan was concerned—he and I were to evangelize Ross.

But, we were not, apparently, to strive the same way for Jay's soul. As a nonpracticing Catholic, he seemed an obvious target. I met Christian skippers volunteering at the Fishermen's Mission, who, on Sunday mornings, would drive to Fraserburgh Harbor in a minibus, roundup Filipino fishermen, and cajole them into attending church. Why were these extraordinary efforts not replicated among the Filipino crew on the *Celestial Dawn*? Assuming that Leon's Bible studying piety convinced Jonathan that he was 'saved,' why ignore Jay (albeit tacitly) as an object of witness? Neither Jonathan nor Jay had the required skills to foster a viable evangelistic encounter because their language barrier was simply too great.

Thus verbal evangelistic success was not said to be commensurate with a specific salvific change (what fishermen call a 'catch') in the soul of the *hearer*, but was rather rendered in terms of the *speaker's* ability to continually and effectively discharge their lifelong duty of witness. 'He kens it all, don't you Ross? He kens the gospel—*I've told him loads of times*,' came the explanation from Jonathan; a telling that came from Jonathan to Ross, but—ever since God's confounding of speech at the Tower of Babel—simply could not, in this context, be passed onto Jay. Evangelistic success was about 'speaking a word in season'—the right words at the right time in the right context. Which is why Jonathan was so enthused by Ross's reflective mood and so unconcerned by Jay's lack of interest.

Evangelistic witness, like fishing, is an enskiled practice that must be learned in a certain way and in a certain place (cf. Luhrmann 2012: 226). Witnessing is like getting one's sea legs; it is achieved when one's evangelistic commitment is deployed in a contextually appropriate manner by using the verbally and emotionally appropriate tools of preaching and testimony. But anthropology can claim no monopoly over this attentiveness to context. Austin (1962), for example, in his now classic statement on linguistic philosophy *How to Do Things With Words*, shows language as both action and circumstance.

> It seems clear that to utter the sentence [I name this ship the *Queen Elizabeth*] (in, of course, the appropriate circumstances) is not to *describe* my doing...or to state that I am doing it: it is to do it. (Austin 1962: 6)

Austin goes on to spell out these 'appropriate circumstances,' listing several conditions that must be met for any 'performative sentence' (Austin 1962: 6) to be 'happy,' (that is, successful). The first and most important of these for our discussion here is:

> There must exist an accepted conventional procedure having a certain conventional effect, that procedure to include the uttering of certain words by certain persons in certain circumstances. (Austin 1962: 14)

This requires a holistic approach to the study of language: 'we must consider the *total* situation in which the utterance is issued—the *total* speech-act' (Austin 1962: 52. Emphasis added). Austin's anthropological tone here is notable, closely mirroring not only Pálsson's (1994) practice theory but also Tambiah's (1968) call for ethnographers of language to recognize that

> ritual words cannot be treated as an undifferentiated category. Rituals exploit a number of verbal forms which we loosely refer to as prayers,

songs, spells, addresses, blessings, etc. It is necessary to study...their
distinctive features in terms of their internal form and their sequence.
(Tambiah 1968: 176)

The point, for Pálsson, Austin, and Tambiah, is that our view of
language needs to be sufficiently *broad* to encompass words and practical actions (and words-as-practical-actions), while also sufficiently
finely grained to distinguish different 'performatives' (Austin 1962:
6), 'verbal forms' (Tambiah 1968: 176), and 'communities of practice' (Pálsson 1994: 902). Where Pálsson's answer to this double
bind is a theory of enskilment, Austin and Tambiah offer different
solutions. Tambiah, in analyzing religious language, poses a distinction between 'semantics' (the 'inner frame' of ritual in 'word and
deed, language and action') and 'pragmatics' ('how ritual relates to
other activities, in what contexts and situations it is practiced and
what consequences it may produce for various segments of society')
(1968: 188–189). Austin, in his famous typology that seeks to show
how words can indeed be actions, defines 'locutionary,' 'illocutionary,' and 'perlocutionary' acts, as, respectively, an utterance which has
'a *meaning*'; has 'a certain *force* in saying something'; and has achieved
'certain *effects* by saying something' (1962: 121). While there is much
in Tambiah's work that is useful, Austin's account of the performative
nature of language, as that which is not only forceful but also directly
efficacious, gives a more compelling account of the 'utterances' spoken on board the *Flourish* and *Celestial Dawn*.

Preaching and testimony *do* have both an 'inner' and 'outer' frame,
that is, both an internal logic of relating language to action and an
external setting of context, situation, and consequence (Tambiah
1968: 188–189). But words in Gamrie have an even greater capacity for
magic than attributed to Trobriand spellcraft by Tambiah. Trobriand
garden magic, for Tambiah, functions by 'metaphorical equivalence'
and 'verbal substitution' whereby 'an attribute is transferred to the
recipient via a material symbol' (Tambiah 1968: 194). Soil from a
large bush hen's nest rubbed on garden tools whilst reciting magical
incantations makes my yams grow large not by 'mystical contagion'
but by 'substitution' and 'imitation' that 'ingeniously conjoins the
expressive and metaphorical properties of language with the operational and empirical properties of technical activity' (Tambiah 1968:
202). In this sense, magical language 'gains its realism by clothing a
metaphorical procedure in the operational or manipulative mode of
practical action.' The consequence, for Tambiah, is that the magical words of the Trobriand islanders can hold 'an air of operational

reality' (Tambiah 1968: 194), but not, (as I have defined it), any genuine experience of enchantment.

Even where we concede, as Csordas does in his analysis of
Tambiah's theory, 'that the performance of metaphors carries illocutionary force' (Csordas 1996: 93), it remains the case that something more seems to be happening among Gamrie's Christians.
While Tambiah's 'general statement about the widespread belief
in the magical power of sacred words' (1968: 182) rightly includes
the proposition that 'language…has an independent existence and
has the power to influence reality' (1968: 184), his assertion that
this functions not literally but metaphorically would be rejected by
Gamrie's Christians as blasphemy. In Gamrie, the 'magic' of preaching and testimony are not produced by metaphorical equivalence or
metonymic transference (Tambiah 1968: 194), but by a real, literal
force that seeks literal effects (cf. Laderman 1996). In Austin and
Pálsson's terms, the religious conversations onboard Gamrie's trawlers were illocutionary acts (Austin 1962: 121), that, when delivered
with 'enskilment' (Pálsson 1994), became 'perlocutionary' acts,
marked, as they were, by a certain force that achieved certain effects
within a certain context.

As among American Catholic Charismatics, then, for the Christians
of Gamrie, 'experiences of efficacy are…a prototype for experiencing
the force of divine power' (Csordas 1996: 108). Csordas' conclusions
are striking in their applicability to our own discussion of preaching
and testimony: 'For Charismatics, efficacious healing is predicated not
only on a cultural legitimacy that says healing is possible, but on an
existential immediacy that constitutes healing as real' (ibid.). Where
Csordas argues that the 'causal efficacy' of the 'ritual performance'
of healing, when occurring through embodiment becomes 'uniquely
realistic' (ibid.), a similar process can be seen at work among Gamrie's
Christian fishermen as they preach and testify while venturing from
day to day on the briny deep.

Indeed, Mark and Jonathan were preaching all week. These 'illocutionary acts' were delivered not from pulpits or platforms, but by
standing at the tray while tailing prawns, extolling the miracle of
divine creation, and the imperative of spiritual salvation. Both men
'gave testimony,' seen in Jonathan's emotional retelling of his first
response to hearing the gospel and Mark's 'heartfelt' description
of the work of the Holy Spirit in personally illuminating the scriptures. The importance of using these evangelistic tools in the right
way mirrors the importance of properly using the right gear when
trawling for prawns, a practice that involves its own kind of skilful

'in-gathering' of God's creaturely kingdom, not through the verbal and emotive practice of sermonizing and witness but through the (no more and no less material) deployment of boats and nets. Enskilment requires learning to use the body—one's arms, legs and inner ear; one's tongue; one's eyes; and one's heart—in conjunction with the entire 'social and natural environment' (Pálsson 1994: 901) of the fisherman to deliver an utterance marked not only by illocutionary *force* but also by perlocutionary *effects*. And this must be done in its proper context, that is, in a sufficiently enskiled way so as to avoid stumbling and catching neither prawns nor men, but only worthless herring and the scornful rebuttal of the 'unsaved' other.

Enchanted Labor

Because fishing for prawns and being fishers of men are broadly analogous practices, what makes a good ('enskiled') skipper is also what makes a good evangelist. What unites both vocations is an enchanted view of labor. This can be seen by looking to another example of enchanted labor found in a different ethnographic context—to 'direct selling' in Mexico and to the work of Peter Cahn (2006).

Cahn conducted fieldwork among 'direct' (unsolicited, door-to-door) salesmen and women in Morelia working for Omnilife, a multilevel marketer of powdered nutritional supplements who fused their profit motive with explicitly spiritual aspirations. Omnilife is said to be shot through with an 'evangelical fervour' for sales assisted by 'annual pilgrimages' to large quasi-religious events at company headquarters. The founders of such (usually American) firms claim God as a business partner with the result that 'Protestant Christian beliefs in salvation through individual born-again experiences mingled with the demands of profit making' (Cahn 2006: 132). Because multilevel marketing firms achieve sales through an extended network of regular consumer/vendors, this 'pursuit of recruits...lends itself to the intense Protestant-style proselytizing that characterizes contemporary direct selling' (Cahn 2006: 132); Omnilife is said to preach a 'spiritual message of rebirth through self-empowerment' (Cahn 2006: 133). The similarity here with what it means to be an enskiled Christian onboard Gamrie's trawlers is striking:

> Selling in Omnilife does not require either training in nutrition or knowledge of marketing. *The sole requirement is a personal testimony* of self-transformation that compels listeners to want to try the products for themselves. (Cahn 2006: 133. Emphasis added)

What matters is being 'born-again'—either through the selling of nutritional supplements, or by evangelizing the unconverted. Both the method (testimony) and the effect (self-transformation) remain the same. It is in 'witnessing', variously, to the power of 'Omni-life' and the 'Holy Spirit' (which, semantically at the very least, are not so different) that other 'listeners' (customers/congregants) are compelled to 'try the products for themselves' (Cahn 2006: 133) be it 'Thermogen Coffee' or 'the blood of Jesus.' It is not education or training or knowledge that matters, but rather the ability to skillfully engage in the zero-sum game of competitive evangelism by winning converts to a cause—a 'perlocutionary act' if there ever was one. Such converts will themselves not only become consumers, but also, in a literal sense, both 'street preachers' and 'door-to-door' direct sellers of the gospel of rebirth and self-transformation.

Omnilife and evangelistic witness are both examples of enchanted labor. Cahn argues the case for Omnilife by suggesting that direct selling is not straightforwardly a precursor to the full-blown adoption of neoliberal economics but rather a kind of spirituality:

Instead of aligning people's mental frameworks with the conditions of capitalist work, *direct selling brings concordance between their work lives and their spiritual beliefs.* (Cahn 2006: 138. Emphasis added)

Which is why, at a rally Cahn attended, one of his informants 'called' other Omnilife converts to a life of full commitment to the company:

Don't count the amount of money you've earned; count the number of people you've helped.... We've received so many blessings. It's beautiful to know I'm the carrier of something that helps people. The grace is his who created us. (Cahn 2006: 136)

Consider this quote again, slightly amended, to better fit the concerns of Gamrie's Christians:

Don't count the amount of money you've earned; count the number of people you've [saved].... We've received so many blessings. It's beautiful to know I'm the carrier of something that [saves] people. The grace is his who created us. (Cahn 2006: 136. Quote amended)

By replacing the word 'help' with the word 'save,' we obtain a near perfect statement of the local folk theology of being a fisher of both prawns and men. The message I heard preached in pulpits and witnessed to at the tray was that, for 'the man who ventures from day to day on the briny deep' (Thomson 1849: 174), such a calling did not finish with the accumulation of wealth (even where it started with it) but was also fundamentally concerned with the (perlocutionary) saving of souls. It was this that constituted the enchantment of labor—the concordance between a life of work and a life of religion. For the Christians of Gamrie, such an enchanted state of affairs—a work-life animated by the magical possibility of catching not only prawns but also the bodies and souls of men—was not a 'bringing back'; it was not, despite wider economic and demographic pressures, a *new* process of *re*-enchantment, but rather the continuation of an enchantment that always was. The enskiled, zero-sum game of competitive evangelistic witness was never anything but an enchanted religious enterprise.

What is it, then, that made a good skipper? It was the same thing that made a good door-to-door salesman of health promoting powders, and the same thing that made a good evangelist, or any good (modern Weberian) Protestant for that matter: a competitive, all-or-nothing, self-made, workaholic who relied not upon nautical or theological or business qualifications, but 'merely [upon] a testimonial of personal transformation' (Cahn 2006: 136) from a uselessly seasick deckhand to a properly enskiled fisher of prawns and men. Like the direct salesman, the 'calling' of the fisherman (whatever their religion) can be seen as a kind of Protestantism par excellence, that is, without the need (or even the option) of a human-divine mediator (Jorion 1982: 280). Where every man is said to be his own *skipper*, he is also—through a kind of elective affinity—his own *Priest*, fulfilling his own individual quest to undertake his own enchanted labor. Having considered the enchanting power of words, let us now turn to signs, and specifically in the next chapter, to the enchanting power of the immanence of God and the devil.

Part III

Signs

Chapter 6

Providence and Attack

Sitting in Robert's car in Macduff, something caught my eye. I saw his Bible had a glossy yellow plastic bookmark poking out of it. I picked it up to see it was actually a reading schedule. Printed on top was the following:

> The Goal: To read one chapter of the New Testament each weekday. . This will take us through the New Testament in one year. As you read, remember to be expectant, God wants to fellowship with you and speak to you every day.

When Robert got back he explained he was given it when visiting a local Charismatic church. Seemingly baffled by my interest in a card he was using for a bookmark, Robert simply stated that the congregation intended to read the Bible together—so I let the matter go.

What does it mean to read the Bible expectantly? How do Christians like Robert come to know this fellowship with the Divine? Is God the only one who speaks, or are other spiritual forces involved, and in what ways?

God in the Gutter

One winter evening I was invited to an informant's house for dinner. Our time of fellowship started with a lengthy conversation about the strengths and weakness of a variety of Bible translations. Both the husband (Gregor) and wife (Carol) went to different rooms in the house to find and flick through numerous Bibles of various versions, sizes, and ages. In the process, Carol unearthed a long forgotten, wrinkled and grubby scrap of paper, folded over and inserted into the pages of a personal devotional Bible. Her eyes lit up and she moved to my side saying, 'Look at this Joe—I want to show you something.' Delicately removing the scrap of paper, she slowly opened it. As Carol silently read it over, it was obvious she was struggling to hold back tears. Having regained her composure, she told me the story that lay behind it.

Gregor and the family were facing bankruptcy because he was failing to repay the mortgage on his trawler. She was frequently by herself in the house because her husband was constantly away at sea, fishing. God, too, felt very distant. One morning, she could not stand the thought of being in the house alone, so she walked down the brae to the harbor, her mind full of troubles, silently calling to Jesus for help in prayer. As she turned along the path, something caught her attention; a small piece of paper flapping in the gutter. Strangely, she felt a strong desire to investigate. Upon inspection she saw it was a page from a 'Choice Gleanings' day-by-day scripture calendar used by some of Gamrie's Christians. On it was printed a verse from the Psalms: 'God is our refuge and our strength, a very present help in trouble.' Carol looked at me, lowering the page, eyes moist with tears: 'Now wasn't that amazing!' Having showed me the page, she reverently returned it to its home, placing the Bible with the others, and started to make the dinner.

If Carol's encounter can tell us anything, it is that her God is a God of immanence and providence. Similar stories from my other friends would lead us to comparable conclusions. Boyd accepted a posting to the Fishermen's Mission having experienced what he (and others) referred to as a series of 'Godincidences'[1] (Webster 2012)—'Some people write these things off as a coincidence,' he told me, 'but as a Christian…God has His hand on these things.' Gavin was given direct signs from God about where to pitch his tent and precisely how much fuel to buy when touring Europe. When Doug was 'born-again' he disposed of £750 of Harry Potter merchandise[2] in his bookshop, then, after inspecting his financial records, found profits were exactly £750 up from the previous year. Robert ought to read expectantly on the same grounds that Carol, Boyd, and my other informants did so—because, as Boyd told me, 'God has His hand on these things' (career changes, financial accounts, fuel tanks, and pieces of paper) in ways that are 'too significant just to be able to write off completely.'

God was not merely experienced as immanent through providentialism; this initial experience of providence was conditional on the abolition of coincidence and its substitution for the local category of 'Godincidence.' Carol's story summarizes this religious world view. Her encounter was amazing because it came to her as an incontestable act of divine providence. God placed that particular piece of paper with that particular verse in that particular location at that particular time so that she would discover it and have her soul revived. But why was Carol's discovery not purely serendipitous?

'Semiotic Ideology' and 'Representational Economy'

If, in Gamrie, being a fisher of both prawns and men rendered life as modern and enchanted, how was this enchanted modernity inflected locally? Keane's (1997b, 2007) concepts of 'semiotic ideology' and 'representational economy' are helpful here. Semiotic ideology refers (in deliberately broad terms), to what one accepts about 'the world within which signifying practices take place' (Keane 2007: 18). As related to representational economy, it considers the concepts and actions that place words alongside objects and causation.

> [Semiotic ideology] is predicated on some capacity to take language as an object within experience. That is, it involves at least some incipient form of objectification....This emphasis on materiality means...that ideas and the practices they invoke have not only logical but also causal effects....They are part of what we could call a *representational economy* [which] situates[s] words, things and persons...dynamically within the same world with one another. [...] [In this sense] Semiotic ideology is a reflection upon, and an attempt to organize, people's experiences of the materiality of semiotic form...[that] exist[s] as much within a representational economy of causes and effects as within a realm of logics and meanings. (Keane 2007: 17–19, 21)

Significantly, 'the power and effects...of semiotic form...are not fully determinate'; they thus 'have quite different implications in different contexts' (Keane 2007: 17). Carol's and other similar encounters that orbited a specific set of assumptions regarding providence only made sense contextually insofar as they rejected outright the possibility of coincidence. The representational economy of 'providence' eliminated 'coincidence' (cf. Luhrmann 1989: 151) by establishing the new semiotic ideology of 'Godincidence.' Thus each detail in everyday life could be transformed into an individual experience of the divine. The *specificity* of Carol's encounter was significant because it granted her a greatly heightened sense of the immanence of God's transcendence. To echo Wagner (1986: 8), for Carol, the 'as if" had become the' is"[3]: God (or, perhaps God's *providence*) was near enough to hold in the palm of her hands, read, and then fold and place back inside the pages of a Bible.

But are all objects equal bearers of divine immanence? Because the representational economy of providence includes the semiotics of gutters and scraps of paper, *in potentiality*, all materiality functions equally well as indexes of God's presence. This is partly because, in Gamrie, expressions of nonconformist theology tend to refuse external regulation and imposed hierarchy in favor of decentralized management and personal autonomy (cf. Bauman 1983: 35–36). The splendor, power, or affective qualities of a religious object was not, in Gamrie's representational economy, produced by compliance with a catalogue of prescribed ecclesiastical measures but surfaced through lay Bible reading, prayer, and spiritual conversations—such was the post hoc character of the semiotic ideology of 'Godincidence' as an objectified linguistic practice.

Comparable anecdotes were told to those attending prayer meetings: prophetic revelations via scripture, remarkable answers to prayer, and fruitful evangelistic conversations—these were all appropriated into the representational economy via the sharing of experience (cf. Taylor 1995: 238). The categorization of Carol's textual encounter as providential was recognized as such *afterward*, in telling and retelling, (what some evangelicals refer to as 'gossiping the gospel'), thus giving the semiotics of 'Godincidence' a normative, collectively legitimated character. In the same way that millenarian expectations about what it meant to be living in 'the last of the last days' were shared and widely agreed upon across all six churches, so too were expectations of providence a source of theological (and thus social) agreement.

Material Providentialism

The washing machine where I was lodging had broken down, and Sarah knew she could not easily pay for a replacement. On Sunday, Robert picked me up to visit friends in between church services. As we talked, Robert, completely out of the blue asked: 'You don't know anyone that needs a washing machine do you? Because my new flat came with one and I don't have anywhere to put my own.' Having recovered from the surprise I described how Sarah urgently needed one as her own machine had just broken. 'Well, there you go then,' said Robert with no hint of surprise 'she can have my one,' suggesting that the entire incident was obviously a 'Godincidence.' I telephoned Sarah to give her the news. She was thrilled and said what an answer to her prayer it was.

Providence was frequently much more mundane—meeting someone on the street whom you needed to talk to, having a car exhaust repaired more quickly than anticipated, receiving a telephone call just before you planned to leave home—all these could be (and were) 'read' as 'Godincidences'; as God sovereignly providing. 'There's no such thing as coincidence, only Godincidence!' my Christian friends would say. But what representational economy does Godincidence occupy in conjunction with the material world? Even 'quintessentially spiritual' experiences of providence are unavoidably embedded in the semiotics of materiality, and this, because of the verbosity of social affairs in everyday life. For Keane,

> The realism and intuitive power of objects often derives from indexicality, their apparent connection to the things they signify by virtue of a real relation of causality or conjunction. That is, they point to the presence of something. (Keane 2006: 311)

Indexicality[4] points to the materially immanent presence of the divine. God's omnipresence is not bounded by a religious doctrine, an embodied emotion (Csordas 1994) or 'absorption' into the 'inner worlds' of 'imaginations' (Luhrmann 2010) but is knowable *existentially* (Keane 1997b: 20, Wagner 1978: 34) in and through the objectified semiotics of household appliances, pieces of paper, discarded merchandise, and precise quantities of fuel. As McDannell's (1995) study of objects within American Christianity shows so convincingly, the importance of religious objects is incontestable because of how human activity is tied to the world of materiality

> Christian material culture does not simply reflect an existing reality. Experiencing the physical dimension of religion helps *bring about* values, norms, behaviors, and attitudes. (McDannell 1995: 2)

What is true of the American context seems equally true of the Christians of Gamrie:

> In spite of Protestant concerns about idolatry and image worship, many Protestants have intimate and powerful relationships with objects. [...] Christians use religious goods to tell themselves and the world around them that they are Christians.... Religious objects also signal who is in the group and who is not. They teach people how to think and act like Christians.... Religious goods not only bind people to the sacred, they bind people to each other. (McDannell 1995: 26, 45)

As the American Protestants documented by McDannell wore clothing displaying slogans such as 'MARANATHA!' and 'In case of RAPTURE this T-Shirt will be empty' (1995: 252), so too did the Christians of Gamrie embody the gospel message by donning jackets with 'Jesus Saves' written on the back, or, more frequently, by wearing their 'Sunday Best,' complete with Christian tie pins for men and head coverings for women. But how do washing machines, scraps of paper, tie pins, and hats differ from ritually segregated and sanctified objects of immense religious and monetary value?

In a significant functional sense, there is no difference. The resemblance here with Orthodox Christian perspectives on ritual objects is conspicuous. By examining the agentive force of the rainmaking icon of Saint Ana in Romania, Hanganu (2010) shows how the effectiveness of such objects is inextricably linked to the individual and material biographies that surround them. Those sharing the name Ana—personally or via kin—become uniquely drawn into the ritual procession of the icon through this relatedness, which acts as a 'divine prototype' for this-worldly enchanted activity. The material power of the icon did not emanate from its beautifully preserved precious gems or metals. It was rather the severely discolored paintwork of other rainmaking icons— 'allegedly the result of the countless rainfalls endured' (Hanganu 2010: 41)—that proved their efficacy. Thus the power of iconism is its ability to form 'an existential connection between sign and signified' (Keane 1997b: 20). The same is the case for indexicality.

> Indexical signs are linked to what they signify by existential connections: they show causal effects...or actual proximity....By their very character, they also forge bonds between causal and logical meanings. (Keane 1997b: 79)

Carol's scrap of paper, then, can be viewed not only as words on a page, but as a type of icon; a 'divine prototype' (Engelhardt 2010) of providentialism. In signifying a real ('existential') association between her personal biography and God's material presence, Carol's piece of paper becomes an object of amazement because of the *time* at which it came into her life and the *form* it had as it did so; a private 'crisis of faith' prevented by a calendar page that could (and should) have been whisked away by the smallest breeze of wind. Just as a water-damaged, rainmaking icon testifies to its own effectiveness, so too did Carol's piece of paper present a self-referential testimony to its own providentialism and divine willfulness. It became 'an "icon" of itself' (Wagner 1978: 32). Thus

> Christianity in whatever form it takes is embedded in ordinary practices...[and] creates recurrent practical means by which these concepts can be lived in concrete terms. (Keane 2006: 310)

This is also how divine providence functions in Gamrie ontology, being embedded in the 'ordinary practices' of everyday life; in the semiotics of washing clothes or refueling a car. Providence, as a representational economy, is 'lived in concrete terms' in an attitude of expectancy to the point that

> material things...are enmeshed in causality, registered in and induced by their forms [and] as forms...remain objects of experience. (Keane 2008: 124)

But what kind of a universe did my informants dwell in for the semiotic ideology of Godincidences to be so taken for granted? Their universe was enchanted by providence, being made alive with a kind of magic that restored (or preserved) the 'inwardly genuine plasticity' (Weber 1978c: 148) of their modern lives. Crucially, enchantment was not simply the effect that providence imposed upon the world—it was also the cause. Understanding the agentive force of enchantment, requires us to look only as far as coincidence. What does the cosmos have to be for it to be completely lacking in chance? It must be saturated by divine intentionality and enchanted by a sense of cosmological rootedness[5]—otherwise the denial of coincidence would be an absurdity.

In struggling to operationalize coincidence—despite strong ontological disagreements—my Christian informants and Luhrmann's (1989) occult magicians seem here to share a central 'hermeneutic challenge':

> When a magician is struck by a remarkable coincidence, it is hard for them to blame contingency rather than cause....Magicians begin to pay attention in different ways....The desire to find ritual presents a hermeneutic challenge: magicians become skilled interpreters of symbolic association and learn to anticipate these unfolding patterns in their lives. (Luhrmann 1989: 152–153)

Whether we speak of hermeneutics or semiotics, witches, or Christians, the result is essentially the same: enchantment works its 'magic' by etching divine action upon the cosmos (cf. Evans-Pritchard 1976: 22–32) through the elimination of coincidence, thereby bypassing the requirement that symbols (of providence) act as secondary indexes of a primary reality. The 'magic' of enchantment works as a semiotic short circuit, releasing symbols from the need to do anything more than simply point *to themselves* as the real object of God's immanence. Indeed

> a metaphor or other tropic usage assimilates symbol and referent into one expression [whereby] a metaphor is a *symbol that stands for itself*...[and] assimilates that which it "symbolizes" within a distinct, unitary expression (collapsing the distinction between symbol and symbolized). (Wagner 1978: 25)

A number of conclusions about Gamrie's representational economy may be drawn. First, such an 'economy' is ruled by providence where 'the people of God' live with a strong expectation of encountering the divine. Second, this creates a world where coincidence is eliminated, being replaced by Godincidence; where divine foreordination renders the intimate details of everyday life as a uniquely personal experience of (micro) predestination and (macro) cosmological rootedness. Third, in this representational economy, God is close at hand, not only in the rituals of reading scripture, preaching, and praying, but in a way that allows God to be experienced as present—materially immanent—through the semiotics of household appliances and so on. Finally, the 'causal effect' of this is that the universe is 'made alive with a kind of magic,' charging life with a deeply rooted spiritual significance, magically restoring 'plasticity' to human experience by presenting the world as entirely free from serendipity and the unintended. It is a world defined by enchantment.

The gap between received anthropological ideas concerning Christianity as defined by transcendence—wherein 'God withdraws from man' (Cannell 2006: 39)—and the experiences of my friends is striking. Carol and my other informants inhabit a representational economy where divine transcendence and material immanence are essentially the same thing: as God was known to be materially present in seemingly mundane objects, so too could materiality index the presence of God. Thus

> artifacts become particularly important in the lives of average Christians because objects can be exchanged, gifted, reinterpreted and manipulated....We can no longer accept that the "appearance" of religion is inconsequential to the "experience" of religion. The sensual elements of Christianity are not merely decorations that mask serious belief; it is through the visible world that the invisible becomes known and felt. (McDannell 1995: 272)

What troubled my friends was that God held no monopoly over enchanted materiality. The devil was also known to be a material reality that had to be lived with and battled against.

Material Demonism

Euan's earliest encounter with demonic possession was while working with a church in Aberdeenshire. A local woman called Moira came to a church service and began to 'manifest' that she was filled with evil spirits by shrieking, shaking, and falling to the ground. She became so out of control that evening that a neighbor took her home. The next day Euan phoned Moira's neighbor to announce that God had 'given him the key' to helping her demon tormented friend. When they met again, Euan prayed over Moira with spectacular results, counting 47 separate evil spirits as having been cast out of her. As they were exorcised, Moira vomited what Euan called 'slime' from inside her body: 'She was actually bringing it up into a bucket,' he said. Moira described how the spirits were crawling up her back like worms, struggling to get outside her body. They were gone in minutes, and Moira was free.

In this and many other accounts I heard, the immanence of the devil was understood as corporeally present in the chaotic disordering of 'demonic attack.' Such attacks inverted the representational economy of divine providence; rather than gifting an intimate experience of God that the Christian takes pleasure in, demonic attack inflicts a frighteningly personal and hideously abusive experience of the devil that the Christian fears. Such a standpoint is not distinctive to Gamrie. Campbell (1979) describes how the Sarakatsani shepherds of northwestern Greece live in a world similarly divided between the goodness of God and the evil of the devil, with humans placed in between

> God is the creator of the universe and all things in it.... Over and against God stands the Devil, the agent and first cause of evil.... God and the Devil fight a pitiless and continuing battle for the souls of men in which the three elements are the grace of God, the cunning and subtlety of the Devil, and the will of man. (Campbell 1979: 322, 331, 335)

Where it is the human *will*, particularly regarding the avoidance of sensuality and envy, which is decisive for the Christian Orthodox Sarakatsani in this divine-demonic battle, for Ewe Pentecostals in Ghana, it is ritual *action*—most especially rites of deliverance and exorcism—that define this-worldly struggles between God and the devil.

> Most Christians, especially women, did not share the [German Presbyterian] missionaries' proclaimed rejection of ritual at the expense of belief, and retained an understanding of religion as a practical affair.... People affected by sickness or other problems had to conclude that missionary Pietism, with its claimed anti-ritualistic attitude, could not really satisfy their needs, for just like non-Christians they still felt that evil could be removed through ritual.... [For Agbelengor Pentecostalists] real problem solving has to be achieved in the spiritual realm...by defeating Satan and his agents, and this is expected to have consequences in the physical realm. (Meyer 1999: 105, 157)

Through fasting, prayer, laying on of hands, and the interpretation of embodied signs and prophetic dreams, the names of evil sprits are discerned, allowing them—usually after some struggle—to be exorcised. As among Pentecostal Christians in Ghana, many of Gamrie's Christians view deliverance from demons as requiring practical action within the 'physical realm.' Yet, as with the Christian Orthodox Sarakatsani, the human will—located in the spiritual dispositions of the heart—was also fundamental to the struggle against demonic temptations toward sensuality. In Gamrie, neither disposition nor action was prioritized when waging war against the demonic realm. Where it may be easy to envisage the ways in which God and the devil are said to differ, it nonetheless seems that the ways in which these supernatural entities operate as a semiotic ideology remain strikingly similar.

Demonic attack, an informant explained to me, 'is part of the cost of trying to break through into the kingdom of darkness; it's just one of the things to expect when you are engaging in spiritual warfare.' In summarizing the life of the Christian as a 'spiritual battle,' demonic attack, like providence, was not merely marked by the intentions of spiritual forces, but was to be anticipated (cf. La Fontaine 1998). As with anticipation of sickness or death, these experiences were generally found to inhabit the body. Demonic attack, as with providentialism, was marked by conspicuously 'ordinary' qualities. While understood to be like 'warfare'—acute and episodic—it was also said to be a 'daily struggle'; a chronic and remorseless undermining of the Christian 'life of faith.'

It was a summer morning, a Sunday, and I was in the Kirk with Gavin waiting for the first service of the day to begin. As the preacher stood to speak, introducing all eight of his main points (it was clearly

going to be a rather long sermon), I saw out of the corner of my
eye that Gavin began to sway slightly. The preacher was already in
full flow: 'they devoted themselves to the apostles' teaching!' Gavin
leaned and then jolted his head upright. 'They devoted themselves to
fellowship and the breaking of bread!' Gavin's eyes slid shut and he
snored quietly. 'And they were filled with joy!' I gave Gavin a nudge
with my elbow. As if in slow motion, his eyes opened slightly and he
righted his Bible in his hands. But soon enough his head began to
drift downward once again.

Gavin came for lunch after church and we talked as I prepared the
meat and vegetables. When the meal was ready, I asked Gavin to say
grace. Rather than pray a brief blessing over the food, he prayed a
lengthy and meandering prayer asking God to pardon him for continually falling asleep during the service. When the 'amen' came,
food had not even been referred to. As we ate, Gavin described how
he believed his drowsiness was caused by demonic attack. He never
usually fell asleep in church, he explained, but in recent weeks had
repeatedly done so. He did not even feel sleepy before church or during the opening time of worship. He only ever felt drowsy when the
sermon began; as soon as he was outdoors all feelings of tiredness dis-
appeared. The pattern, Gavin described with real unease, was recur-
ring; he fell asleep specifically when the Bible was preached. This,
he stated, was indisputable proof that the devil was assaulting him.
Looking to me for comment, I somewhat tentatively proposed that
he might 'pray against' tiredness prior to attending services in future.
Gavin thought this could work, so we left it at that.

Gavin's drowsiness was not a chain of unfortunate coincidences,
because, in Gamrie's representational economy, mischance had been
eradicated by my friends' declarations that 'there's no such thing.'
This left two possible explanations—'divine testing' or 'demonic
attack.' God *did* cause bad things to take place 'in order to bring
his people back to himself,' my informants told me. Amy was especially mindful of such happenings, in her own biography and in
world affairs, describing how swine flu, the global financial crisis,
the British MPs' expense scandal, and countless other trials had been
orchestrated by God. 'I think God is ruffling up the waters to bring
people down to their knees in prayer. Yes, I think God is laying the
foundations for revival,' Amy would muse to me as we sat beside her
electric heater drinking cups of tea. 'Divine testing,' then, referred
to the outworking of God-ordained affliction intended to reveal to
humankind their defenselessness without the protection and provision
He granted them.

The notion that God was 'protector' and 'provider' was especially strong among fisher families. I heard stories of Christian skippers, who, having made the unusual decision to go against their consciences by fishing on a Sunday, experienced God's judgment by catching nothing and ripping open their nets on the seabed. The devil, however, was also implicated in fishing catastrophes. Violent storms were occasionally said to be caused by demonic powers: poor weather on Friday and Saturday followed by ideal fishing conditions on Sunday, returning to gales on Monday (maximizing economic disincentive to Sabbath keeping) was a frequently occurring pattern one friend maintained was demonic in origin. Other informants explained how these patterns were the result of God testing one's dedication to 'remembering the Lord's Day.'

Things were seldom clear-cut: one fisherman described how his father and three crewmembers were lost in a storm that he managed to survive—a disaster that led, that very hour, to his 'born-again' conversion. My friends often discussed the spiritual authorship of such happenings. Some asserted that God Himself had sent the crisis regarding gay ministers to the Church of Scotland to bring his 'faithful remnant' out of an 'apostate' denomination as a way of preserving their moral and ecclesiastical purity. Other informants argued this calamity was stoked by the devil, to 'spoil the witness' of 'Bible believers' in Scotland's national Kirk. These debates, whilst frequently unresolved, did not undermine the foundational ontological supposition that the origins of such trials were spiritual. As far as I am aware, I was the only person to suggest that any given event might be a *coincidence*. The replies my comments elicited were informative. Usually I would be given a knowing smile and reminded that there was 'no such thing!' On other occasions the response was stronger and I would be admonished. Whatever the reaction, the point my informants were making to me was plain: in Gamrie's semiotic ideology, suggestions of coincidence were synonymous with a rejection of God's sovereignty and the devil's schemes, and thus sacrilegious or spiritually foolhardy.

Demonically appointed trial was frequently mundane—a husband and wife squabbling, paraphrasing scripture instead of translating it literally, restricting EU fishing quotas—these were all experienced by my Christian friends as calculated attacks of the devil.[6] Here we see how the enchantment of the world had a totalizing effect—serendipity was eradicated insofar as the agentive power of God and the devil were constantly at work. Nevertheless, this representational economy in no way stripped my informants of their agency. The 'gospel message' pleaded with those who heard it to 'make a decision for Christ' rather than 'deciding to reject Him.' Choosing which happenings were to be categorized (post hoc) as divine testing and which as demonic attack was an additional outworking of this agency. Simple logic was often deployed; God would not cause one of his children to slumber during a sermon, so such tiredness was sent by the devil. Where no clear reasoning could be presented (regarding the economic crisis, for example), the deployment of words—in prayer, scripture reading, and Christian conversation—established such authorship.

But what role did *things* play in demonic attack? Building upon Cannell's critique of received anthropological wisdom that Christianity is essentially a religion of transcendence allows us to see that objects played a key role in local experiences of demonism. Consider, for example, how this sermon stirred a friend to decisive action.

> When we become Christians, what sorta *wicked stuff* do we still hang onto? What sorta *things* do we meditate upon which is going to open up our minds to the enemy?...If you have been in the Freemasons, do you destroy all your artifacts: your robes, your books, your medallions? If you have been involved in witchcraft do you take all your paraphernalia and your *stuff* and burn it, according to what the scripture teaches? Or do you put it in a box and put it up the loft somewhere, and then you wonder why you can't get any blessing?

At the end of the service, Gregor urged me to come back with him to his house. As we went he explained how a friend had given him a box sermons on video cassettes from a religious group he was not familiar with. After several disturbing spiritual discussions with this friend, Gregor had become unconvinced of their orthodoxy. He was adamant that he did not want the videos in his house if they were 'full of false teaching,' particularly because they might cause demonic attack to befall his family as the preacher had suggested. Having ascertained that the videos were Seventh Day Adventist, Gregor told me he wanted them burned. I suggested it might be best to throw them away. He shook his head explaining that someone might discover them. We could easily pull out and cut up the magnetic tape, I offered, which would make them unwatchable while saving the need to burn them, which would create a dreadful stench that his neighbors might complain about. But Gregor was determined. He must burn them that very night.

Gregor told me the next morning how the videos had 'burned for hours.' 'What an amount of smoke they made!' he said with a smile. '*Still*,' Gregor commented with a darker tone, 'there gone now.' Such an urgent, literal destruction warns me against Tambiah's (1968) steer toward a metaphorical interpretation of Gregor's actions. Gregor did not seem anxious to destroy a set of demonic *metaphysical relationships* that might have unwittingly developed between himself and the devil. Rather, he sought to eliminate an evil *physical presence*. Thus, what Taylor attributes to the enchantment of the premodern world, seems very much alive in modern Gamrie.

> In the enchanted world, the meaning is already there is in the object/ agent, it is there quite independently of us... it can take us over, we can fall into its field of force. It comes on us from the outside [and]...can impose meanings, and bring about physical outcomes. (Taylor 2007: 33–35)

Equally, as with providence, local experiences of demonic attack confront us with the materiality of bodies (cf. Bialecki 2011). The devil possessed Moira, threatening to kill her by hurling her down the stairs. She could feel the evil spirits crawling up her back, eventually vomiting them into a bucket. The devil controlled Gavin's body with tiredness. His eyes slid closed, his head drooped, and his breathing slowed to a quiet snore—he fell asleep. These embodied events were not supplementary to demonic attack; they were not fleshy window dressing for an otherworldly encounter—these experiences of 'the flesh' *were* the demonic attack.

Symbolic obviation is therefore eminently material. Indeed, 'an obviation sequence...does not *say* things but *makes* them, and then disappears into its results' (Wagner 1978: 252). Demonic attack disappears into the material body in the same way that divine providence disappears into a scrap of paper, only to then reemerge in lived experiences of the immanence of transcendence. Not only does the devil take over people's bodies with evil spirits, he is also indexed (*existentially*) in Masonic robes and video cassettes. Therefore, a box of witchcraft paraphernalia in the loft still exercises powers over the owner's household—it prevents God's 'blessing.' It is not enough, therefore, to renounce such *practices* and consign their *materiality* to a box. The 'inwardly genuine plasticity' (Weber 1978c: 148) of Gamrics' Christian lives makes any 'easy' division between self, body, and object impossible. The box of 'wicked stuff' must be burned 'according to what the scripture teaches.' This is surely because objects are cosmologically rooted (powerfully connected) to 'porous' selves (Taylor 2007: 38) and bodies. Such connectedness resides in their semiotic materiality, that is, inside their 'thingness' *as objects*. Objects, then, have an agentive capacity outwith human intentionality, that is, they have indexical effects that fall outside their *usage* by people whilst still impinging upon the experiences of those people (cf. Gell 1992). The only resolution is to destroy their materiality, thereby removing them from the representational economy of wider human experience.

These happenings require us to pay serious attention to Cannell's (2006: 14) assertion that Christianity is not fully definable in terms of transcendence. Local experiences of the materiality of both 'providence' and 'attack' display not the 'radical discontinuity' of an 'impossible religion' (Cannell 2006: 39) but a radical *continuity* (and 'plasticity') between spirit and flesh, words and objects, the seen and unseen, the transcendent and immanent. So strong is this continuity that it develops into an enchanted conflation. Gregor's videos had to be burned not only because they pointed to the external material immanence of a transcendent devil (even though they did do that) but also because they were themselves the immanence of satan—an existential 'icon' of demonic attack.

We see, here, not satan in flesh, but in plastic. This is possible due to the way in which the semiotic ideology of everyday objects becomes enchanted by the immanence of transcendence. As in providentialism, not only is demonic attack rooted in materiality, but so is its capacity to confer a sense of spiritual immanence. Thus, where God's omnipresence came to be experienced existentially through household appliances and pieces of paper, so too did the omnipresence of satan come to be experienced existentially through video cassettes and Masonic regalia. We see here the clearest convergence between Keane's view of materiality and Cannell's view of the immanence of Christianity. For Keane,

> Religions may not always demand beliefs…[but] will always invoke material forms. It is in this materiality that they are part of experience…provoke responses…have public lives and enter into ongoing chains of causes and consequences. (Keane 2008: 124)

As with providentialism and experiences of Godincidence, demonic attacks have a life outside linguistic utterances insofar as the *things* that compose these experiences themselves have an independent (and immanent) material existence. Thus,

> even in its most abstracted and transcendent, the human subject cannot free itself from objectification. It retains a body, it continues to work on, transact and possess objects. (Keane 2006: 321)

It could only be this way in so far as the devil and his demons— just like Christ and His people—have a real substantive existence, both corporeally (demonic possession and crucified flesh) and in objects (witchcraft paraphernalia and scraps of paper). Demonic attack, as with providentialism, not only 'retains a body' but also 'work[s] on...objects' (Keane 2006: 321) with the effect (again, as with providence) that spiritual immanence is made an irrefutably real and startlingly everyday occurrence. Where God was brought close through Godincidence, the devil was brought close through demonic attack, by making one vomit slime, sleep through sermons, or cause evil to befall one's household because of a box of videos in the basement. The work of symbolic obviation—the collapsing of one existential modality...to produce another' (Wagner 1978: 34)—enchanted the world of my friends by transforming material *signs* of providentialism and demonic attack into material *referents* of the immanence of transcendence. Taking seriously this enchanted obviation provides one way to act upon Cannell's challenge to the anthropology of religion that

> if transcendence is not necessarily exclusively Christian, then it is even more clearly true to say that Christianity is not exclusively a religion of transcendence. (Cannell 2006: 41)

Demonic attack secures existential experiences of immanence—it makes the devil a material and embodied reality that is so close that demonic encounters are eminently expected as part of living in a village defined not by disenchantment but by the cosmological rootedness and plasticity of enchantment.

Conclusions

While 'providence' and 'attack' *are* about the transcendent (concerning both the divine and the demonic), in Gamrie, these religious experiences are also vitally taken up with religious immanence. Viewed through Keane's (2006) theory of indexicality and Wagner's (1978) theory of symbolic obviation, immanence comes to be experienced as a kind of transcendence and transcendence as a kind of immanence. This observation is made only by examining in detail the 'semiotic ideology' of a local 'representational economy' (Keane 1997a, 2007). Among the Christians of Gamrie, this necessitates studying how objects, words, and bodies move around within a wider economy of divine provision, protection, testing, and judgment as set against demonic deception, temptation, and attack. Experiences of 'spiritual battle' are 'real' insofar as they forge *existential* connections (Keane

1997b: 20; Wagner 1978: 34) between materiality and divine presence, thereby bringing about *causal* effects (Keane 1997b: 240) in everyday life—stormy seas, clean laundry, bouts of fatigue, and such. Crucially, this is all the result of how particular ontologies, like obviation sequences, function, as Robert's bookmark told us, through the 'eminently expected,' not by *saying* things but by *making* them, and disappearing into their results (Wagner 1978: 252).

As in providentialism, local experiences of demonic attack show how the life of the Christian, glossed as a 'spiritual battle,' resembles an enchanted struggle against the devil. Where my Christian friends expected to experience the perfect ordering of divine providence through *God's* immanence, they also expected to experience the disordering of spiritual attack on the basis of their expectation of the experience of *demonic* immanence. The devil was brought so near that everyday encounters—feeling drowsy during a sermon— were folded back into the realm of the supernatural and consubstantiated into material experiences of spiritual reality in one's everyday life. Each struggle, each disturbance, each misfortune became a probable source of intense religious consequence; a bearer of the immanent transcendence of God and the devil. Because 'there is no such thing as coincidence,' only two categories remained: divine providence and demonic attack. The effect was essentially the same—life became enchanted. Having considered the *immanence* of God and the devil as experienced through the daily expectation of providence and spiritual attack, let us now turn our attention to the *imminence* of God and the devil as experienced through the daily expectation of the end of the world.

Chapter 7

Eschatology

I am waiting for the dawning
of the bright and blessèd day, [...]
I am waiting for the coming
of the Lord who died for me;
O His words have thrilled my spirit,
'I will come again for Thee.'
I can almost hear his footfall,
on the threshold of the door,
and my heart, my heart is longing
to be with Him evermore

(Popular hymn, Gamrie, S. T. Francis, 1873)

God and the Devil Are 'soon'

Walking down Gamrie brae early one afternoon, I met Hazel, a woman in her sixties who attended the Braehead Hall with her husband Keith. She invited me in to see Keith who was ill—he would be glad of the visit, she told me, so in I went. The afternoon passed with Keith chatting to me about his failing health and his past working life. As he finished recounting his story, he turned to me and said:

> What is it exactly that you would...? [Stops himself] Now, we all ken that we're living in the last days, but if you get to, ken, if the Lord doesna come back, what is it that you would like to do eventually [after you finish your studies]?

Keith's comments—more than his actual question—express the widely held belief that we are living 'in the last days' (frequently expressed as 'the last of the last days') and that as such, all questions about the future, no matter how mundane, need to be qualified eschatologically. This chapter, unlike the previous one, does not concern the way that the self relates to the world (asking 'how does my religious experience constitute the world I live in?'), but the opposite, that is, how the world relates to the self (asking 'how does the world constitute my religious experience?'). My discussion takes as its primary ethnographic object conversations I had with my informants about all those multifarious 'signs of the times' that made Keith's qualification to his question about my future plans make sense to him and those he worshipped alongside. A great many of these 'signs' were found in the realm of the political, and most commonly concerned both Israel and the EU. It is these wider geopolitical forces, that go well beyond Weber's 'brotherliness' (1978c: 155), which provides much of the substance for my analysis. For Weber

> The fate of our time is characterized by rationalization and intellectualization and, above all, by the 'disenchantment of the world'. Precisely the ultimate and most sublime values have retreated from public life either into the transcendental realm of mystic life or into the brotherliness of direct and personal human relations. (Weber 1978c: 155)

Yet these geopolitical forces were not divorced from 'the transcendental realm of mystic life' (Weber 1978c: 155) in quite the way that Weber imagined they would be as a result of capitalism taking root across much of Europe. What follows is inevitably less cut-and-dried than a public/private or personal/political dichotomy. The two questions mentioned above overlap, requiring the sociological truism that the world and I co-constitute each other to be constantly borne in mind. My separation of the material here is based on something of an oversimplification, namely that the public and private are in some senses discrete entities that can be discussed in isolation from each other. Yet, it is an oversimplification that clarifies more than it obscures, inasmuch as any Weberian 'ideal type' would seek to do. The analysis hinges on maintaining a distinction between 'immanence' and 'imminence' as typified by the distinction between 'near' and 'soon.' Where immanence is fundamentally spatial, with God and the devil being experienced as materially and corporeally near, imminence is temporal with God and the devil being experienced as soon. While I am aware that the phrase 'God and the devil are soon' may sound, if not obtuse, then certainly a little awkward, I retain its use for reasons that will become clear later.

The 'Near Future'?

In an important piece entitled 'Prophecy and the near future,' Guyer, commenting on macroeconomic and evangelical understandings of time, describes what she refers to as 'a strange evacuation of the temporal frame of the 'near future' (2007: 409). All that matters, according to this relationship to time, is the now and the ultimate end—what Guyer refers to in another context as 'enforced presentism' and 'fantasy futurism' (2007: 410). The effects are stark: a 'shift in temporal framing [that] has involved a double move, towards both very short and very long sightedness, with a symmetrical evacuation of the near past and the near future' (2007: 410). 'What one sees now,' Guyer continues, 'is not so much a break as a major shift composed of a multitude of small ruptures' (2007: 410). As a result of these ruptures, 'the world itself falls increasingly into the disciplines of a punctuated time that fills the gap between an instantaneous present and an altogether different distant future' (2007: 417).

Time is both utterly polarized and radically compressed in the same breath; all that exists with any certainty, in the rhetoric of many an evangelical preacher, is 'tonight!' and 'eternity!' These two temporalities, which, in salvific and eschatological terms could not be further apart (think of the incommensurability of 'worldly' suffering and heavenly deliverance), are, in another sense, actually next in line to each other. As the epigraph to this chapter describes, Gamrie's Christians are still forced to inhabit something of the near future (which, Guyer states, 'cannot disappear altogether' [2007: 411]) if simply as a matter of 'waiting for the coming' of the Messiah whose 'footfall' can be heard 'on the threshold of the door.' The near future, inasmuch as it exists at all, exists as a time of waiting.

During one of my many pre-fieldwork visits to Gamrie, my father and I attended a gospel service at the OB hall one winter evening. I don't remember a thing about what the preacher said, yet one small moment I observed that night persuaded me that Gamrie was the village in which I would conduct research. The moment happened at the start of the service, when a man (who I later came to know as Lachlan) stood up to announce the meetings that were planned for the week ahead. There would be a prayer meeting on Wednesday evening, a Bible reading on Friday evening, a breaking of bread service on Sunday morning, a ministry meeting on Sunday afternoon, and the gospel service on Sunday night. What happened next struck me at the time as strange, but now, I realize, sounded entirely mundane to most of those present: 'Now brethren,' Lachlan said, 'we make these announcements every week, but of course it's only if the Lord will. We might not be here next week because the Lord might have returned to take us home.' And with that said, he took his seat.

The similarity here with what Guyer speaks of in her own analysis of 'evangelical time,' while striking, is perhaps not surprising given the degree to which evangelical Protestantism is shaped by and reliant upon globalized processes. Indeed, Guyer could just as well be speaking about the Christians of Gamrie as American evangelicals when she states,

> For evangelical Christians, the interim between the first and second coming of the Messiah is the time in which present life is lived.... Current church leadership works out the implications for life in the present, in an enduring attitude of expectant waiting. (Guyer 2007: 414. Emphasis added)

Clearly, evangelicalism is itself a globalizing process—all a Protestant missionary really needs is words, that is, a Bible and an ability to speak the local language. As Coleman (2000) has shown, such a highly portable religion carries with it (not only in space, but also across time) the ability to transform 'local' perspectives and practices by conforming them (albeit in part) to a global-evangelical view of 'The Word.' It is this common denominator of (prophetic) 'expectant waiting' that characterizes much of my Christian informants' experience of the near future. But how does this relate to other expressions of millennialism? It was the Presbyterians of Gamrie, and not their more strictly dispensationalist Brethren neighbors, who most readily subscribed to the kind of 'historic' premillennialist innovation described by Harding (2000) as the 'little tribulation.' In essence, this theology suggests that the Tribulation—a season of divinely permitted demonic rule on earth—is occurring now rather than being restricted to a future post-Rapture period. This is important in the American context, Harding tells us, because it casts the present in a very different light:

> The period before the rapture, the end-time, was now understood to be a time in which God would judge Christians, as opposed to Jews. And his judgment was not fixed by biblical prophecies. It was, in other words, reversible. If Christians responded to God's call through holy living and moral action, God would spare them and the American nation. Thus, with this little tribulation, Bible prophecy teachers opened a small window of progressive history in the last days, a brief moment in time when Christians could, and must be, agents of political and social change. (Harding 2000: 241)

'God would spare them and the American nation.' Amy and many of my other Presbyterian friends hoped the same would occur in Scotland. Amy herself read the signs with little difficulty—homosexual ministers in the Kirk, the Scottish banking crisis, the spread of Islam—all these things told her that God's judgment was upon Scotland, a nation once known as 'the Land of the Book' but now infamous for its love affair with strong drink. Yet a key difference separated Gamrie's Christians from Harding's informants: where Falwell's Moral Majority sought to bring about political change through direct lobbying of governmental powerhouses, my own informants tended to be politically active in a more roundabout way, with many choosing to limit their interventions to the medium of prayer.

Perhaps tellingly, I never met a Member of the Scottish Parliament during my fieldwork in Gamrie, nor could any of my informants be described as political activists, apart from one man whose involvements were restricted to two local campaigns, one to protest abortion and another to improve safety on school buses. The Christian Institute—a pressure group campaigning on a range of policy issues—found some supporters among those attending the Kirk, who discussed and prayed about the various religious liberty cases the Institute defended in the Scottish courts. Other avenues for Christian politics found conspicuously little support. The Scottish Christian Party, for example, was regarded with suspicion by my Kirk informants; many felt that such overt entry into the political domain was 'going too far' by inviting moral compromise and 'risking' one's testimony. The irony of supporting a 'secular' party instead (such as the Scottish Nationalists) was not lost on my friends and contributed to their strong sense of ambivalence toward (and general disengagement with) party politics. Even the alternative—supporting narrowly focused (and ostensibly nonpartisan) causes championed by groups like the Christian Institute—garnered little excitement.

My friends in the Brethren and the FPCU felt greater clarity on the question of Christian engagement with politics, but provided opposing answers. The Brethren, who generally do not vote as a matter of conscience, shunned politics and political activity as 'worldly' at best and demonic at worst. This was felt strongest among the CB who assured me that a 'special judgment' would fall on 'so called' Christians who had 'courted earthly powers' to 'get their own way in this world,' effectively doing a deal with the devil in the process. Protesting against abortion in the street was regarded as dangerously polluting; voting in elections for a party that took the name of Christ for itself was abhorrent.

One local target of such comments was the FPCU, whose founder, the Rev. Ian Paisley, being both a 'minister of the gospel' and an elected member of the British and Northern Irish parliaments, was said by the Brethren to personify much of what was wrong with the mixing of politics and religion. He was too willful, he had a violent temper, and he orchestrated political events in a way that obfuscated God's agency, my friends explained. William and the expatriate Northern Irish farming congregants he led as part of the Gamrie FPCU vehemently disagreed, accusing those in the Brethren of abdicating all responsibility to defend hard won civil-religious liberties whilst continuing to enjoy those same liberties as a result of the labors of Christians engaged in politics. The (usually unspoken) context—the 'Troubles' in Northern Ireland—was an experience none local to Gamrie were ever touched by. Gamrics attending the FPCU did not share this politicized Christianity as a result; when the Christian Institute held a meeting in the church, inviting all in the village to attend, less than 20 people came; when William travelled to Edinburgh to protest the Pope's visit to Scotland, none from Gamrie joined him.

This combination of separatism and political rejectionism within the Brethren, the provincialism of sign searching within the Kirk, and the history of political activism within the FPCU leaves us with a picture of dispensational politics in Scotland that is messier than that painted of Baptist fundamentalists by Harding (1994, 2000). The Christians of Gamrie are split between and within the village's six churches. William, whose Northern Irish Protestant background seems to place him squarely within the historic premillennialist camp, sought to redeem the nation through Christian morality and politics, by preaching the gospel, supporting the Christian Institute, protesting the Pope, and, since returning to Northern Ireland, by supporting the Unionist political cause. Others, like Amy, seem to fit only partially with Harding's 'historic' premillennialist typology. For these Christians, the 'little tribulation' is being experienced now, but as a precursor to Scotland's deliverance ('God is laying the foundations for revival'), transitioned not by politics but by prayer ('bringing people down to their knees').

Still others, including friends in the CB, were dogmatic 'futurist' premillennialists (Harding 1994: 58), flatly denying that end-times prophecy could be fulfilled until the (post-Rapture) tribulation period had begun. While their outlook partially fits Bloch's (1992) theorization of the politics of millenarianism, other aspects of his theory sit uneasily with the Brethren experience. The CB did seek to be free of this-worldly sinfulness, personified by the wicked politics of Scotland's 'failed earthly leaders' (Bloch 1992: 92). They also sought—along with all of Gamrie's Christians—the 'incorruptible transcendental' (Bloch 1992: 92) rule of Christ in the new millennium as that which would conquer today's politics (cf. Faubion 2001). Yet they did not envisage the end times as 'a world-wide funeral' (Bloch 1992: 90), nor did they seek 'a communal death which will bring an end to all forms of practical processes in human life' (Bloch 1992: 92).

Where for Bloch

> there is nothing more characteristic of millenarian movements than their refusal of reproduction, [that is]...the refusal to engage in such activities as sowing for the next harvest and producing children, since to continue earthly life would belie the commitment to total universal earthly death. (Bloch 1992: 91)

It seems that for my Christian informants, a daily waiting for the apocalypse in no way precluded fishing for prawns or bearing children. To the contrary, for Brethren believers like Jackie Sr., a productive life at sea was that which rendered the eschaton immanent and imminent. Even more fundamentally, these Christians waited not for 'total universal earthly death' (Bloch 1992: 91) but for total (earthly and heavenly) new life. The only persons who were said to wait for death were the 'unsaved,' and these, despite being repeatedly offered 'new life in Christ.' My Christian informants, on the other hand, as the 'saved,' waited to enter into eternal life, imagined as an Edenic 'new heavens and new earth,' which, in yet another enchanted conflation, would be drawn together by God and rendered gloriously indistinguishable. For the Christians of Gamrie, this-worldly life existed as a shadow of the life to come—free from sin and death, populated by new bodies, youthful vigor, feasting, singing, and celebration—defined not by the 'non-vital' (Bloch 1992: 90) but by the vital. As Cannell (2007) points out, Bloch's morbid reading of ritual (1986) and millenarianism (1992) as can be seen as

> incorporating a view of religion as a radical split between human and non-human powers that is, in itself, a view which developed historically in Judeo-Christianity [with the effect that]...transcendence becomes intimately associated with an ascetic, anti-physical thinking that elevates the things of the 'spirit' and devalues those of the 'body.' (Cannell 2007: 123)

In contrast to Bloch, then, I argue that asserting a 'radical split' between life and death is unable to capture the essence of Gamrie religion, which, far from dichotomizing immanence and transcendence, actually conflates them, and enchants the world as a result. Crucially, this conflation occurs not only through spatial 'immanence' but also through temporal 'imminence,' and specifically through the imminence of millenarian politics.

But in what sense is the near future inhabited as part of one's daily experience of the present? Lachlan talked not only about a potential withdrawal from the near future ('we might not be here next week'), but also a denial of the definitiveness of future orientated human agency ('it's only if the Lord will'). The effect was that human purposes were rendered null unless occurring in the immediate present. However, even where human future-making was denied in the near term ('we make these announcements every week, but'), the near future nonetheless remained an essential part of my friends' eschatological experience. Far from being 'evacuated' (Guyer 2007: 409) or 'devalued' (Crapanzano 2007: 424), the near future was seen as holding the key to unlocking the ('yet to be revealed') eschaton and thus the entire timetable of the cosmos.

Unlike the category of coincidence, the near future was not abolished but rather addressed directly as the experiential bridge between Guyer's 'enforced presentism' and 'fantasy futurism' (2007: 410). *Waiting* existed as only half of the spiritual equation; the Christians of Gamrie were not eschatologically idle during what they referred to as 'the waiting time' but were also engaged in the busy task of *watching*. Where this 'watching' was crucial in establishing an attitude of expectancy that shaped much of Gamrie's providentialism, so too was watching central to eschatology:

> The "end" ends earthly time, that singular gap that stretches, as evangelicals put it, between eternity past and eternity future....Although progression is evident in God's dispensations, in dispensational Christianity, it is centered on a wholly exceptional event, Christ's coming, which marks the beginning of the final dispensation...and offers the possibility of salvation. It is this point that conjoins cosmic and individual history, but before salvation and world ending can occur, Christ must reappear. His second coming is at once anticipated and expected. (Crapanzano 2007: 423. Emphasis added)

Crapanzano's observation begs the question: 'How does this [eschatological] picture...color their everyday experiences of time?' (2007: 423). The answer I offered regarding providentialism—that the world became enchanted—is also the answer I offer here. Where

Crapanzano agrees, arguing: 'Doubtless...believers are enchanted by a transcending temporal orientation' (2007: 423), the reason he gives for how this comes about differs from my own account. For Crapanzano, it is soteriology that forges the relationship between eschatology and enchantment: 'enchantment...is facilitated by the promise, the certainty, of personal salvation' (2007: 423). In Gamrie, however, it is not soteriology but sign searching that enchanted my friends' theology of eschatology.

One August Sunday morning, during a breaking of bread service at Braehead, Gregor stood to end the meeting in prayer:

> We think of the next great event that this world is going to experience, when you're going to come into the air with all your archangels and your power and the glorious coming of yourself. Lord, we are waiting for you! As we scan the skies day by day, we can say "Is it today?" Lord, your coming is near! Everything's pointing to it Lord, and we are waiting upon it. This may be the last occasion [we meet to break bread], we do not know.

After Gregor prayed, some of the ladies stood up and prepared the tea and cakes we always had during the interval between the breaking of bread and Bible reading service. As we sipped our cups of tea an interesting conversation about wartime rationing arose, leading me to ask why even during this period there was so much wastage of fish when people in urban areas were going hungry. Why did the government not step in and send the excess fish to the big cities? Without answering my question at all, Euan, another man present that day, started to speak about how tight government control over the fishing industry was today. He and several others present agreed that increasing EU regulation was a sure sign of the end times, indicating a definite move toward fulfilling Biblical prophecy about the establishment of a one-world government. The Euro was offered as another sure sign, this time with regard to the prophetic establishment of a one-world currency. Rhoda agreed, mentioning that she had been watching a program on Genesis TV, a popular Christian broadcaster, in which George Hargreaves (leader of the Scottish Christian Party) was being interviewed about how Christians in America view British society; 'abortion, gays, drunkenness, Islam,' came the list, with a sense of alarm, 'and it's all true! It's all true!' she said, shaking her head with a grave expression.

The Christians of Gamrie are watching—literally 'scanning the skies' in Gregor's terms—for the Second Coming of Christ. More than this, they are looking for the signs that indicate the imminence of such a return—'everything's pointing to it Lord, and we are waiting upon it,' Gregor prayed. Rhoda was equally clear; 'abortion, gays, drunkenness, Islam'—these were the signs that constituted the eagerly anticipated 'soon return' as an enchanted certainty. To Gamrie's Christians, it was indeed 'the next great event that this world is going to experience.' The question was not 'if' but 'when,' of that they were convinced. Yet the question as to exactly when produced less certainty. 'This may be the last occasion [we meet to break bread], we do not know,' Gregor ended. But how was this 'not knowing' experienced? What role did it play in watching for 'signs of the times'? And how did it impact the eschatological shape of the near future?

Signs of the Times

Driving along the road to Macduff one morning in late February, Doug, a key informant, started to tell Robert and I about the unfolding of certain spiritual 'signs' that indicated to him that we were living in 'the last of the last days.' When I asked what kinds of signs he was referring to, what he said next I still find difficult to fully comprehend. He told us how the devil was preparing the unsaved population of the world to be tricked into worshipping the soon to appear Antichrist, and in so doing, to condemn themselves to an eternity in hell. The early stages of this trickery were clearly visible, he told us, in certain aspects of popular culture. The television show *Star Trek* was an important example. The handheld 'tricorders' used by the crew of the Starship Enterprise as 'scanning' devices had, he argued, seen their satanic real-world fulfillment in the advent of flip-phone mobiles.

Such technology—once a thing of science fiction—was now reality, Doug told us. This was sinister, he alleged, because when the 'signs and wonders' of the fast approaching apocalypse took place, far from falling on their faces in terror and calling upon God for salvation, people would explain away such genuinely miraculous occurrences as simply yet another leap in technology. The same evil intent, he told us, was behind the *Star Trek* 'transporters'; the concept of being able to 'beam someone up' from one place and transport them millions of miles away in an instant was clearly a demonic counterfeit of the soon-to-occur 'rapture,' when all the world's born-again Christians (living and dead) would disappear 'into the air' at the point of Christ's Second Coming to earth.

Applying similar logic, the Harry Potter books were also said to be a demonic plot, with children becoming desensitized to the evil realities of witchcraft and thereby being prepared to welcome (and later worship) the Antichrist and his satanic magic during the 'end times.' The conversation grew stranger still when Doug went on to describe how he also believed in alien abductions. He explained to us how accounts of alien abduction were remarkably similar to each other, with many involving descriptions of various sorts of (usually anal) 'probing.' This latter detail, consistently provided by those who claim to have been abducted by aliens was crucial, Doug said, because it suggested that the devil himself was responsible for these extra terrestrial activities. This was so, he elaborated, insofar as it provided clear evidence of demonic attempts to genetically resurrect the Nephelim (a race of giants that emerged, according to the Jewish-Christian tradition, when fallen angels mated with women), via alien probing in order to build up satan's kingdom on earth.

Doug further explained that the current global economic recession would slowly move humanity toward accepting a one-world government and single world currency that would be instated by the (as yet unrevealed) Antichrist, who would rise to godlike status having solved the credit crisis, only to then financially enslave the human race under a rule of demonic tyranny. As for the actual identity of the Antichrist, Doug was uncharacteristically coy. He explained that where the Old Testament had different Christ-like figures (such as Noah and Joseph) that prophetically pointed toward the eventual arrival of the Savior, in our day we could see different world leaders who closely resembled the Antichrist to come, such as Mikhail Gorbachev and Tony Blair. Such world leaders had a dual spiritual purpose as far as Doug was concerned—they existed to warn and thus sensitize Christians, and precondition and thus desensitize 'unbelievers' to the spiritual dangers to come. Having sat in the car listening, I arrived in Macduff with my head spinning. I turned over in my mind what Doug had been saying as we walked to a Kirk coffee morning, but, before long, we were sitting at a table, eating 'home bakes', drinking tea, and chatting about plans for the rest of the weekend.

The answer that was given to me on dozens of occasions in response to questions about how my informants knew with such certainty that we were living in the 'last of the last days' was, predictably enough, a quotation from the Bible:

> This know also, that in the last days perilous times shall come. For men shall be lovers of their own selves, covetous, boasters, proud,

blasphemers, disobedient to parents, unthankful, unholy, without natural affection, trucebreakers, false accusers, incontinent, fierce, despisers of those that are good, traitors, heady, high-minded, lovers of pleasures more than lovers of God; having a form of godliness, but denying the power thereof: from such turn away. Yea, and all that will live godly in Christ Jesus shall suffer persecution. But evil men and seducers shall wax worse and worse, deceiving, and being deceived. (Second Timothy 3:1–5, 12–13)

Not only was this a well remembered and much discussed passage of scripture, but it was also the 'key text' of many a sermon. A frequently offered refrain in such sermons was 'we're not living in first Timothy days; we're living in second Timothy days!' Judging by the solemn agreement of much of the congregation, I came to realize this temporal placement of Second Timothy alongside the present was deeply significant for my informants. Biblical time had been conflated with the present via these prophetic texts—but what effect did this have on the ways in which the Christians of Gamrie related to the past, present, and, 'near' and 'distant' future? How did my friends' belief that they were living in the 'perilous times' of the 'last days' become experientially and materially real to them?

It became real (in an existential sense) in the same way that divine providence and demonic attack became real, that is, via a certain 'reading' of their own 'semiotic ideology' (Keane 1997b). The signs were everywhere: Star Trek, mobile phones, Harry Potter, emptying Sunday schools, Mikhail Gorbachev, Tony Blair, the recession, swine flu, the MPs expense scandal, unusually heavy snow falls, homosexual ministers, the perceived spread of militant Islam, abortion, earthquakes, and public drunkenness, to name only a few. Because of the radically multifarious nature of these 'signs of the times,' in an attempt to give as nuanced an analysis of the workings of this representational economy (Keane 2007) as possible, I only want to focus on one 'type' of sign, the political, and only on two formulations of it—that of Israel and the EU.

The Indexicality of Eschatology

One of the last things [Rev] John Robertson said to us before leaving Gamrie to become a minister in Edinburgh was: "Watch Israel! She's God's signpost in the world!" I always remembered that and took an interest in Israel ever since.

(Amy, elderly Christian, Gamrie)

What does it mean for a geopolitical entity like Israel to be a signpost—God's signpost no less—and one that is to direct and guide the entire world? The answer is not only temporal and eschatological, but also eminently material.

I was introduced to local people's fascination with Israel a few days after moving to Gamrie, during my first meeting with Rev Murdo McKinnon, the Kirk minister. Murdo spoke to me about his 'passion for the Jewish people' and described his most recent trip to Israel, showing me some items he had purchased—a replica crown of thorns and a Star of David key fob. As we talked, I found myself wondering why, being a Christian minister, Murdo did not feel inclined to support the cause of Palestinian Christians over that of Israeli Jews. When I summoned the courage to ask he looked mildly affronted and replied that most Palestinians who claimed to be Christians were not 'committed,' 'born-again' evangelicals but saw their faith primarily as a marker of political affiliation. This turned the conversation to the conflict in the Middle East, with Murdo specifically mentioning the 'Six-Day War' where, he said, Israel experienced God's divine deliverance as when Moses led the Ancient Israelites to safety through the miraculous parting of the Red Sea. He went on to decry what he called the 'anti-Israel stance in the British media' that he said was tantamount to 'propaganda.' Murdo also predicted all out war in the Middle East, especially in view of the fact that Israel would attack Iran if it persisted in its nuclear program.

Two days later I had another chance to make some sense of all that Murdo had been saying, and why this conversational foray into the realm of politics was coming from a man who represented a Protestant tradition generally resistant to 'worldly' politics. As we chatted again, Murdo told me that he believed the Bible made it clear that Christians could expect to receive spiritual blessing from God only if they loved and prayed for Israel. On still other occasions, Murdo spoke about how the land Israel currently inhabited was theirs by divine right, and as such, the world could be certain that the Jews would reclaim the entirety of the Promised Land before Christ's Second Coming:

> The people of God will be back in the Land. God has a plan. I think the next big thing is Iran. I think Israel is like the Christian—always under persecution. The Bible tells us to pray for the peace of Jerusalem. True Christian believers stand up for the fundamentals of Scripture and stand up for Israel.

While I could grasp most of what Murdo was saying on a theological level, it was only after many months, when attending a Christian
Zionist conference with Murdo, that I began to understand what
'stand[ing] up for Israel' meant to local Christians, particularly with
regard to the ways in which they experienced politics. The conference, in Perth, was led by a group calling itself 'Yachad[1] Scotland.' In
amongst discussions about their fears of infiltration, how evangelical beliefs were being criminalized, the need for a mobile Christian
Zionist library, how 9/11 was a watershed moment for the fortunes of
Israel, and prophetic warnings about 'the coming storm' of Islam, it
was something one particular woman said to the assembled group of
ageing but enthusiastic Christian Zionists that struck me as particularly insightful: 'We've all got a burden for Israel—it's so that Jesus
comes back!' It was then that I realized that Christian support and
concern for Israel was, in essence, eschatological.

Christians were to offer prayers for Israel, Murdo told me, if they
wanted to experience God's blessing. What I did not fully appreciate at the time was that while some of these blessings could legiti-
mately be thought to occur in the present, their dominant focus was
transposed onto the future—to the return of Christ at the point of
the Second Coming. This was the case because the majority of my
Christian informants believed that the Second Coming would not
occur until all the Jewish peoples of the world had been gathered into
the borders of Israel and then converted, en masse, to Christianity.
'We've all got a burden for Israel—it's so that Jesus comes back!' the
woman proclaimed to a room full of people nodding in agreement.

Evangelical support for the Jews was (in a strange turn of phrase
I heard while listening to a sermon recording with Amy) about 'pro-
voking Israel to jealousy.' The ethno-theological logic was as follows:
Christians, in praying for Jews, would receive a blessedly close relationship with God—a relationship that Jews would observe, covet, and seek
after, only to discover that the true object of this blessing was Jesus. This
discovery would lead to their conversion and salvation and thus usher
in the end of the world. The results were experienced by my Christian
friends as a win-win situation—temporal blessing on earth in the near
future, giving way to eternal blessing in heaven, all brought about by the
prayers of 'true Christian believers [who] stand up for Israel.'

The Materiality of Eschatology

While the 'politics of eschatology' overlapped with 'the transcendental
realm of mystic life' (Weber 1978c: 155) in prayer and missionization,

other aspects of my informants' Christian Zionism were more nakedly political. During the Yachad conference in Perth there was a time of discussion and prayer during which very strong support for Benjamin Netanyahu and the Likud Party was voiced. Delegates prayed that Netanyahu would continue in power, not being forced to enter into coalition with opposition parties who might push for the halting of settlement construction. Fears that the 2009 water crisis in Israel might play into the hands of liberal political opponents willing to negotiate with neighboring Islamic states on key policy issues was also the subject of much discussion and prayer. Such topics, far from being seen as the exclusive remit of secular politics and thus 'off limits' at religious gatherings, were actually deemed to be central to the aims and purposes of the conference. Support for Israel as a geopolitical entity was seen as inseparable from the wider concerns that local Christians had about faithful adherence to scripture in general and to Biblical 'end times' prophecy in particular.

As a result, Israel became a temporal marker in the near future of the eschatological calendar. What mattered for my informants were 'real' political events: Likud's electoral fortunes; the handling of the water crisis; and negotiations with neighboring States; these political issues were God's politics because they addressed the future fortunes of God's chosen people. These issues concerned Israel (and by extension Gamrie's Christian Zionists) not just in the present or the distant future, but also in the near future, over the next decade. The drought of 2009 did not simply represent the problems of the past; as demand for water rose, the problem was transposed onto the spiritual and civic happenings of the near future. Elections fought today concerned the political complexion of, for a minimum, the next four years. So too with Israeli settlements—UN resolutions to halt their construction clashed with Likud's policy of 'natural growth,' with such conflicts being played out not only in the newspapers of today and the next day, but also in the months and years to come. The near future is not only unavoidable as Guyer points out, but, contrary to her wider argument, actively engaged with as a vital platform on which the drama of the eschatological calendar is soon to culminate.

Where Israel being a signpost meant inhabiting the political eschatology of the near future, this habitation was by no means purely an example of the overlap between folk theology and political ideology. I am not simply referring to what Weber might well have readily identified as 'the transcendental realm of mystic life,' nor am I limiting myself to 'direct and personal human relations' (Weber 1978c: 155), but include inanimate objects that exert a kind of agency upon the world through their material properties. This is made abundantly visible by attending to those objects that make up the physicality of the signpost, which, just like all signs, are able to 'point the way' not because they communicate ethereal impressions but because they are themselves material indexes.

The material nature of Israel's indexicality has already been discussed through an analysis of land and water, that is, through settlement construction and problems with drought. Of course, the 'Land Issue' is central not only to the identity of many in Israel but also to Christian Zionists. During the Yachad conference I remember one particular woman who prayed with a heavy, almost angry tone that 'Netanyahu would not have to give away one inch of land! Not one inch!' her zeal firmly based upon an insistence that the land Israel currently occupied was theirs by divine right. Theirs was the 'Promised Land,' another delegate insisted to me, 'and God *doesn't* break His promises.' So too with the water issue—where Israeli settlement expansion was seen as a prophetic fulfillment of the Jewish peoples returning to reclaim the entirety of the Biblical promised land (a process Gamrics said would be completed in the near future), material provision of adequate supplies of water was seen as eschatologically essential.

In another conversation with Robert and Doug, Robert said that he was amazed to learn that much of present day Israel was built on what had previously been swamp land. Doug agreed further adding that Israel was also partially built on desert ground, which, he told us, was a prophetic fulfillment of the Biblical prophecy that 'the desert would blossom,'[2] made a reality, he said, by various tree planning programs set up by different Christian organizations, such as God TV. I was vaguely familiar with this particular scheme, as other friends in the village had mentioned their support for the 'Million Trees' campaign at God TV, but had never explained to me what it involved or why they were taking part. Later that day, with my interest renewed, I went to God TV (god.tv/israeltrees) for more information. What I discovered was an entirely different imagining of the 'born-again' Christian's temporal relationship to eschatology to that which I had previously assumed:

JOIN US TO MAKE PROPHETIC HISTORY...in this apostolic prophetic act as we prepare the Holy Land for the return of the King....GOD TV is planting over ONE MILLION TREES across the Holy Land as a miraculous sign to Israel and to the world that Jesus is coming soon. This is a unique opportunity to make your mark on the land of Israel. We're not going to stop doing this until, I believe, the Lord comes back.... [A]s you read Isaiah 41, you find out about how passionate God is about turning deserts into a blooming garden.... He Himself says He will do it. Of course, how will he do that? He will do it through you and I!

The Lord challenged us to prepare the land for the return of... the Messiah. And I tell you I feel like we are in the last days, in fact, I know we're in the last days! No man knows the hour. No man knows the day. But we do know the season and this here is the last days. And the Lord said, 'Prepare the land Rory, Wendy—challenge my people across the earth'. And that's what we've done.... This little [tree] because of your generosity has been put in the soil of the Holy Land! So dear partner, this is an extraordinary hour we are living in! We are fulfilling, literally, the Word of the Lord through Isaiah chapter 41 and we are doing it as his body! His hands and his feet and his body; we are literally fulfilling the Word of the Lord! This is so exciting! The instruction from our heavenly father, Abba, said 'A million trees!' [...] So for us as a Christian family around the world to put in a million trees in this land is a profound prophetic statement and I believe will touch this land, will touch the heart of the people, of the nation. (God TV 2011)

Where religion, because of its inherent materiality, 'provokes responses' (Keane 2008: 124), the response of some of Gamrie's Christians to the eschatological statement 'I know we're in the last days!' was not simply a material one, but one that played out in the near future. Indeed, the planning and execution of a £15 million tree planting project seems to fit with each element of Guyer's typification of the near future as:

The reach of thought and imagination, of planning and hoping, of tracing out mutual influence, of engaging in struggles for specific goals, in short, of the process of implicating oneself in the ongoing life of the social and material world. (Guyer 2007: 409)

That God TV's 'Million Trees' campaign is an act that engages in a struggle for a specific goal and thereby implicates one's self in the social and material world seems clear. This ethnographic observation also contradicts much of what Bloch (1992) assumes characterizes millenarianism; the struggle is eschatological—to 'prepare the Holy Land for the return of the Messiah'—but it is also fully vital and this-worldly. The campaign is implicated, furthermore, in the social and material insofar as it sets up a (simultaneously real and imagined) social relationship between Israeli Jews and Christian Zionists via the materiality of trees.

That this should be occurring semiotically in the way that it is, is unsurprising, for, as Braverman (2009) points out, the cultural and political salience of trees in this part of the Middle East is deeply embedded. Yet, where Braverman examines the ways in which the 'ostensibly apolitical' planting of pine trees and olive groves (by Israelis and Palestinians respectively) fuels 'a brutal yet clandestine war…over the natural landscape' (2009: 3), my concern is not with the politics of military conflict, but with the ways in which the materiality of this representational economy is able to instantiate a specific kind of relationship between eschatology and human agency.

Notice how Rory Alec—cofounder of God TV with his wife, Wendy Alec—appears to be asking a similar (if differently worded) question to the one I am asking here, namely how will these eschatological 'signs of the times' come to pass in the near future? We have already both provided our own response: where Rory proclaims 'a million trees!' as his answer, I have answered in a not totally dissimilar way by discussing the central importance of the way in which materiality 'provoke[s] responses' (Keane 2008: 124). But how do objects provoke responses? And to what end? Rory's answer again sounds familiar: 'He will do it through you and I!' that is, through those who give $25 or £15 or €20 to plant a tree in the Negev desert. Remember, after all, how Rory's supporters are told that they are 'fulfilling, literally, the Word of the Lord through Isaiah chapter 41….[W]e are doing it as his body! His hands and his feet.' My answer, although certainly not an apologetic for Rory's afforesting missionary zeal, takes much the same tack insofar as I too turn to human agency as providing the solution.

What we see in my friends' support for the 'Million Trees' campaign is what I want to call 'eschatological agency.' By this I simply mean to refer to the way in which Christians can and do appropriate the eschatological narrative contained within the prophetic texts of the Bible by directly inserting themselves into the actual unfolding of 'end times' events. This is crucial insofar as it turns a (strictly theological and therefore ideational) conversation about Biblical texts and Biblical events into a conversation about texts and events that take as their stage 'the ongoing life of the social and material world' (Guyer 2007: 409). Where these texts and events occur not only in the present but also in the near future, we can see that the objects under discussion (trees for planting, land for construction, and water for drinking) granted my informants some ownership (or perhaps authorship) over the unfolding of the eschaton.

They were the ones who were ushering in the Second Coming, not only through their prayers, but also through their political support for Israel, and, as we now see, through their 'literal' (that is, material) fulfillment of the prophetic scriptures: 'We are fulfilling, literally, the Word of the Lord through Isaiah chapter 41.' As previously noted, the materiality of the body is central: 'We are doing it as his body! His hands and his feet.' Eschatology is fulfilled, then, not through the unknowable, inscrutable will of God, but through the words and objects that humans and their bodies bring to bear upon the world—through prayers that Benjamin Netanyahu would not have to form a coalition government with opposition parties and through the planting of trees in the Negev desert.[3]

Being a signpost means being a temporal marker in the near future of the eschatological calendar. The 'representational economy' (of end-times signs) brings its indexicality (Keane 2002) to bear upon the world in and through materiality—through settlement construction, water provision, and the planting of trees. 'The afforesting of the Promised Land' (Braverman 2009: 3) shows us how the Christians of Gamrie became agents of eschatological change as they engaged in an 'apostolic [and] prophetic act [to]...prepare the Holy Land for the return of the...Messiah.' In this context, all those who participated in the Million Trees campaign became what Harding refers to as 'historic' premillennialists.

Signs, as indexes, function successfully (that is, they point convincingly) not only by virtue of the immutability of their nonhuman material properties (think here of security walls and tree trunks), but also because of their ability to draw human agents into their 'field of force' (Taylor 2007: 34) allowing for the possibility that the sign may be changed, reworked and given, if not an entirely new meaning, then undoubtedly an altered temporality. While this altered temporality obviously concerns bringing the Biblical narrative of the ancient Israelites into the daily lived experience of twenty-first century Gamrics (the past brought into the present), it also concerns the compressing of the eschatological timetable from two polar extremes—the utterly imminent and eternally distant—into a newly populated near future (today and eternity brought into the 'soon to occur'). The signs of the endtimes that my informants sought out, then, were those that pointed to politics—particularly to political happenings in Israel, and, as we shall see below, within the EU. Politics provided particularly 'convincing' indexes because of the fluidity of the political realm, offering near endless chances for end-times prophecy to be fulfilled 'in our day and generation.' But it was not only God who was experienced as being temporally imminent and who was said to materially inhabit the near future—the devil too was regarded as a key player in the unfolding of the politics of the eschaton.

Is Brussels the Antichrist?

It was the day of the annual Kirk Sunday school picnic. In between sack races and rounds of tea and hot meat pies, a woman in her late sixties sat down beside me and struck up a brief but arresting conversation about the Antichrist. Without any introductory small talk she turned to me and said, 'Homosexuality is now protected by law you know. Yes, it's this European Union thing. It's a sign of the end times. I sometimes wonder if Brussels is the Antichrist.' And with that said, she turned to greet her grandchildren who were clamoring to show her the prizes they had won during the morning competitions.

What is insightful here is not so much the way in which a person might initiate a casual conversation about the end of the world with a relative stranger (although I do think this is interesting and relevant) but rather, in this specific instance, the matter-of-fact identification of 'Brussels' (the EU) as the Antichrist—a counterfeit savior controlled by the devil to inspire blasphemous and thus soul ruining devotion. The woman's comments also touched on another key area of eschatological sign searching—the politics of sexual morality. Stories were constantly circulating in the village about legislation 'from Europe' that 'would soon force ministers to marry gay couples' and required 'homosexuality to be taught in primary schools these days.' Licensing laws were another key sign: 'The Scottish Government couldn't even shut the pubs if they wanted to because the EU keeps them open!' one retired fisherman told me, shaking his head in disbelief. Having already examined spiritual imminence through the political eschatology of Israel, we now consider spiritual imminence through the political (and economic) eschatology of the EU. I want again to concentrate on two specific 'signs of the times'—the global recession and Scottish fisheries regulation—by attending to the imminence of the devil and his Antichrists.

A key 'sign of the times' my Christian informants identified as indicative of the soon-to-occur apocalypse was the global economic recession. This was not so much due to the direct problems associated with the present financial climate, but rather imaginings about what possible future solutions to the crisis might entail. In explaining this, it will be helpful to recount two ethnographic encounters. The first comes from a series of conversations with Leslie, a CB friend of mine from Gamrie; the second is taken from two sermons given by Roland, a visiting Christian Zionist preacher from South Africa who worked as a missionary in Israel.

This new EU President fulfils the [Biblical] prophecy about a one world government. Israel will be led by a false prophet to make a pact with the EU [...]. 2nd Thessalonians tells us that after three and a half years the [EU] President will break the pact and the Lord will return in judgment. That's why we dinna vote; politics is nae for Christians Joe; democracy is nae God's way [...]. [In the New Testament] Israel is in the yoke of Rome, but nowadays it's the same: if you are working, you feel the political yoke of Rome [the imagined evil alliance between the Roman Catholic Church and the EU]. The world is looking for a man [a human savior]. This Beast...the Antichrist, is going to come out of the EU and will crush all religion, especially those who lobby government to get their own way. [...] This man is going to rise up out of the EU. He will be a financial wizard and he's going to solve all this economic crisis, the recession, just like that [in an instant] and the world is going to totally go after him [worship him]. And then he will reveal himself to be the Man of Sin [the Antichrist]. They [the unsaved] don't realize that their time is almost up; the thing about the EU is it's a leopard—it moves fast!

* * *

We are living in the end times! Where do we stand at the end of time? The shaking of the American economy is the beginning of that big shaking. The nations are in perplexity. It's not going to be fixed. This is just the beginning! I believe we are standing at the door of the failure of Western society! [...] In the end times God says we will call good evil and evil good—abortion is not sin, it is reproductive health; an alcoholic is not a sinner, but sick...I believe the time of testing is going to come and it's not going to be easy! This world is in the most polluted state it's ever been in because of greed! We're never going to have enough! [...] We must be alert...There will be no peace in this world until Jesus comes back. [...] Credit is an evil trap from satan! America is addicted to debt! By using credit cards you are aligning yourself to the Antichrist! Do not serve the world! Do not run the rat race! This world is in a mess but when the time comes we will be able to stand. [...] The UN will unite against Jerusalem and Jesus will defeat them!

Eschatology establishes the near future by identifying 'signs of the end times.' A central feature here concerns the issue of financial debt as an index of future change—a theme that is explicit in

Roland's sermons and implicit in much of what Leslie and I spoke about. 'America is addicted to debt! By using credit cards you are aligning yourself to the Antichrist! Do not serve the world!' was the rallying call from the pulpit that Sunday night at the Kirk. 'The Antichrist...will be a financial wizard and he's going to solve all this economic crisis,' Leslie told me, predicting how the grim events of the Tribulation would see the vast majority of the population of the planet enslaved to this 'Beast' who would rule via his control over world debt. What is important about debt is the temporal relationship it establishes with the eschaton. Debt is fundamentally concerned with the near future, being inextricably linked to 'the process of implicating oneself in the ongoing life of the social and material world' (Guyer 2007: 409). This matters for the eschatological projects of people like Roland and Leslie because being implicated with the world financially means being implicated with the politics of the devil. Credit cards, after all, align oneself to the Antichrist.

Note the double bind in which this view of debt places local fishermen reliant upon credit to maintain their businesses. With the cost of trawlers ranging from £2 million to £25 million, no one in this family run industry can purchase a vessel without taking out an enormous mortgage. Does this mean that the material and ideational experiences of being a millenarian Christian and a fisherman are somehow incompatible, as Bloch (1992) might argue? I want to suggest not. This is because debt *per se* was not seen as demonic or even particularly significant. What gave it eschatological significance was not even the fact that (personal) debt and (global) recession caused financial pressures and problems. Rather, debt and recession were eschatologically significant for my informants because of the nature of the solutions that these financial problems would seemingly demand.

What were these solutions? According to Roland and Leslie, they were demonic ones: 'The Beast...will be a financial wizard and he's going to solve all this economic crisis, the recession, just like that [in an instant] and the world is going to totally go after him,' Leslie explained. Roland agreed, describing how credit cards were an evil trap from satan, tantamount to slavery; a kind of economic bondage, which, by wreaking havoc in people's lives, would cause them to reach out for financial deliverance from any quarter. Their monetary savior, emerging from the EU, would come as a 'wizard,' sweeping their (and the world's) fiscal problems away—'just like that'—as if by magic. Economic salvation, would, according to this view, lead to idolatrous spiritual devotion. At the point where this wizard reveals himself to be the Antichrist, the situation would be irretrievable; all those who had bowed the knee to the 'Beast' would be cast into hell forever.

By holding that the recession was an eschatologically significant index by virtue of the fact that it pointed forward, into the near future, to the soon arrival of him who was known variously as the 'Man of Sin,' the 'Beast' and the 'Antichrist,' the political eschatology of economics—as revealed by the current financial crisis—was, for Roland, Leslie and many others in Gamrie, a crucial sign of the soon-to-occur apocalypse. Politics and economics, far from being 'secular' concerns, acted as prophetic barometers, which, just like all forecasting devices, had as their primary temporal object, not present happenings or eternal states, but that which falls in between— the near future. The near future was invoked in and through the medium-term consequences of the unfolding of the eschaton. While the crisis was being experienced presently (and also had eternal consequences), what really mattered was the watching and waiting that had to be done during this 'in between' period. Remember, after all, how the temporal focus of Gregor's prayer during a breaking of bread service was not focused upon the past death of Christ, but upon his future return: 'As we scan the skies day by day, we can say "Is it today?" Lord, your coming is near! Everything's pointing to it Lord, and we are waiting upon it.'

In Gamrie's representational economy, this temporal nearness is indexed, not by the imminence of God, but of the devil and the Antichrist. The Christians of Gamrie experienced the 'ongoing chains of causes and consequences' (Keane 2008: 124) of the eschatology of the devil in and through politics and economics. The recession would lead to the stellar rise of the Antichrist, who, in receiving the worship of the world, would condemn it to a 'lost eternity.' The consequences of his 'wizard-like' fiscal solutions—to appear in the near future— would instantiate a demonic one-world government held together by a totally unified economy and single world currency. The ultimate material consequence would be all out war against Israel and the eventual (bodily) return of Christ to rescue his chosen people.

Causes cannot be neatly separated from each other; as with the 'Million Trees' project, both human and supernatural agency are said to be at work. The consequences, likewise, do not cast the Christians of Gamrie in a role of passive observation; 'scanning the skies' in Gregor's terms, is not an inert task, but rather one that actively shapes the unfolding of 'end times' events. It is precisely because of the constantly fluctuating makeup of political and economic events that these spheres of human life functioned so well as eschatological indexes. The result was a compressing of the temporal experience of local Christians, with imminence and the near future co-constituting each other without losing any of what made them distinct. The Second Coming was experienced as utterly imminent, in an apparent paradox, exactly because of the ways in which these 'signs' were said to prophetically apply to the medium term of the near future. The imminence of eschatological agency occurred in the present while also being pushed forward into the political and economic happenings of the years to come. Debt repayments, political conflict in the Middle East, the establishment of an EU president, and, as we shall see below, international management of fisheries were all said to be occurring in the present, culminating in the near future, and, eventually, achieving their eternal fulfillment at the end of time.

Food Sovereignty and the Mark of the Beast

My first visit to the Fraserburgh Fish Market was exhilarating. The mounting smell of fish as boxes were dragged across the concrete floor by deckhands gripping long metal hooks; the quick, intense movements of merchants as they dove their hands into mounds of ice to pull up and inspect random specimens; the shout of an auctioneer signaling the start of a sale; the gathering groups of men jostling for position around a row of boxes; the furious pace of auctions in a language even more indecipherable than the local Doric; the occasional sudden silence as a coin was discreetly tossed (ostensibly out of sight of the auctioneer) to determine who won a box if two bidders had the same maximum price in mind; the scribbling of final prices into notebooks; the scattering of paper tickets bearing the merchant's name to mark a sale. As exciting as that first trip to photograph the market was, I left feeling discouraged by the fact that, because my research concerned 'religion,' I would be unable to find a link, no matter how tenuous, to justify the inclusion of such material into the book. As it turned out, I had no need to worry.

My discouragement stemmed from an assumption that the fish market was an altogether too 'secular' place to be written into a book about Protestantism in Scotland. The fish market was noisy, smelly, colorful, and full of life and youth and had nothing to do with the quiet, reserved, and elderly world of the churches of Gamrie. Not only was I mistaken, but my error was revealed to me in the very place where I assumed the divide between market and church was strongest: at a Gamrie Brethren hall. It was a Monday night in February and I was attending a Bible Reading with half a dozen other people at the Braehead Hall. The passage we were studying was all about the Second Coming. With the meeting lasting over two hours, we covered a wide range of eschatological topics. At one point, Gregor spoke about how a prophecy in the Old Testament book of Daniel was being fulfilled in our own times as a result of the 'crushing...bear like hug' that the EU was inflicting upon the Scottish Fishing Industry:

> *Gregor*: This day we're living in, we're living in the power of Rome, ken, the Roman Empire...and this small horn [in the prophecy of Daniel] had a crushing effect and we can see that in the day that we're living in. Our prospects as fishermen...we've seen in the EEC [now the EU]....We see the bear like hug, as the bear crushes its prey....We see this coming in steady in the fishing industry...because there's more rules and regulations and they're trying to crush the life outta the fishing industry, ken [...] We're in the end times and this is a process that we're going through and it's a crushing effect. We are seeing it continually, and it will go on and things will get more difficult and more difficult. And to fight against it—it's very near impossible now to be a Christian skipper of a boat and to tow the line that they're seeking you to tow. Making up your log books without falsifying them...it's very near impossible. The signs is all there.
>
> *Mitchell*: And we can see the Mark of the Beast: you're nay allowed to buy or sell fish without the Mark of the Beast.
>
> *Carol*: It's the same with the cattle. Unless your cattle is marked you canna sell it.
>
> *Mitchell*: It's the Mark of the Beast at the end of days.

At various points during fieldwork, Gregor, Carol, Mitchell, and others described how the EU was the 'new' Roman Empire, that is, the dominant global superpower that, imagined as a new world order that failed to submit to a totalizing theology of Christian 'exceptionalism' (Cannell 2006), also existed as a new evil empire. For Gamrics, fishing was a key 'sign of the times' that plainly displayed this fact. Fishing boats out at sea and fish markets on shore were spiritual battle grounds. As with providence and spiritual attack, God and the devil were experienced as being at loggerheads, with the Christian (fisherman) in the middle. 'It's very near impossible now to be a Christian skipper of a boat,' Gregor complained.

This eschatological conflict did not only concern the vagaries of global politics but also the lived material experience of the everyday lives of local fishermen. Detailed log sheets itemizing the quantities of each species caught had to be submitted. Every box of fish had to be labeled by boat, catch location, species, and weight (figure 7.1).

Figure 7.1   Labeled box of fish, Fraserburgh Fish Market

EU inspectors could arrive at the market and demand to see log books that would be scrutinized for errors. Markets were also observed and minimum pricing enforced. If a box of fish failed to reach its minimum price set by the EU, it would be marked as 'withdrawn' and sprayed with a red dye (figure 7.2) to prevent illegal resale. I was told with disgust by friends at the auction that these fish would later be ground up to make cat food.

EU rules also impacted life and work on the boats themselves. The well known 'quota system' (where boats had to purchase the rights to land certain quantities of certain species) caused significant problems of wastage. I can remember two occasions when trawling out at sea, we brought up an entire haul of herring—a fish the boat did not have a license for. The hopper was, as a result, full of huge quantities of fresh but drowned fish that had to be dumped back into the sea. Rules stating that nets had to be of a certain size of mesh to avoid the unsustainable catching of overly young fish had little effect on this problem of 'throwbacks.' During my fieldwork, another highly controversial EU restriction was introduced—the 'days at sea' scheme. This meant that as well as regulating catches by quota, fishermen could only be out at sea for a set number of days. This was problematic for those fishing a long distance from shore because it financially incentivized staying out to fish in bad weather over spending an

Figure 7.2 Withdrawing boxes of hake that have not made their minimum market price set by the EU

allotted day unproductively returning to shelter in the harbor. For the two Sabbatarian skippers I went to sea with, short six-day trips at sea (to ensure being onshore for Sunday worship) already meant significant time and fuel was spent steaming to and from fishing grounds. Where this inefficiency was compounded by new 'days at sea' legislation, my friends' suspicions that the EU was anti-Christian were very much confirmed.

As Carol's comment about cattle shows, there were concerns with the way that the EU functioned that went beyond the confines of Scottish fisheries. Rhoda, a key informant, said that she had been watching a television program about how the vast majority of grain sold to Britain 'came from the third world.' She suggested that this increasing concentration of grain production into the hands of so few could be a demonic plot to enslave the human race during the end times via the imposition of famine. Where the eschatology of God concerned—among other things—settlement construction, pine trees, and drinking water, the eschatology of the devil was an equally material manifestation of what local people (very appropriately) referred to as 'spiritual things.' Net mesh, log sheets, dumped hauls of herring, withdrawn boxes of hake sprayed with red dye, not to mention marked cattle, and the production of grain; all of these existed as material markers of the imminence of the devil. While these indexes were solidly material, they were not marked by any strong degree of ideational fixity. As above, it is the fluidity of politics and the malleability of the signs they produce that brings the devil (and his objects) into Gamrics' lived temporal experience of the near future.

While many of Gamrie's Brethren fishermen told me that the quota system was demonic first and foremost because it represented the creeping 'end times' advance of the Kingdom of satan, some of the Northern Irish members of the FPCU in the village had quite a different perspective on the issue. For them, the EU was not primarily running an evil shadow dictatorship of the fishing industry, but rather existed as the malevolent political wing of the Roman Catholic Church. I remember a particular conversation I had with two Northern Irish men in the FPCU, William and Alan, who told me (only half jokingly) that the Pope's visit to Britain was probably to crown Tony Blair the new president of the EU. When I asked William if he thought the EU was the Antichrist, he explained in a more serious tone that in the Bible, 'the Beast'[4] represented an earthly political order and 'the Harlot'[5] an evil demonic religion. 'So,' William told me, '"the harlot who rides the beast" refers to the fact that the Roman Catholic Church controls the European Union.' 'You believe that the EU is controlled by the Catholic Church?!' I asked, forgetting to hide my growing disbelief. '*It is!*' William insisted 'you can see that in the way that the EU pushes the social policy of Rome!' 'Do you think that the upcoming appointment of an EU president has something to do with the fact that Tony Blair recently converted to Catholicism?' I responded. 'It can't hurt!' William laughed knowingly, 'it *certainly* can't hurt!'

For the Christians of Gamrie, the devil was brought temporally close—into the soon-to-occur 'near future'—by the efforts of local Christians to establish 'signs of the times,' that rendered the forces of evil as materially imminent. The devil was 'soon' because the fishing industry was being 'crushed' by the 'bear like hug' of the EU and could not survive for much longer; the devil was 'soon' because the Antichrist was gaining control over world grain supplies and was planning an attack via the imposition of famine; the devil was 'soon' because the Roman Pontiff was coming to Britain to crown Tony Blair president of the EU. Unlike Guyer's view of American evangelicalism, for the Christians of Gamrie, these eschatological events—these prophetic certainties—were unfolding neither in the immediate present nor in the distant ('eternal') future, but in the space in-between, that is, in the near future.

Conclusions

In 'The Technology of Enchantment and the Enchantment of Technology,' Alfred Gell (1992) discusses the magical efficacy of Trobriand canoe prows whose brightly colored swirling patterns 'are supposed to dazzle the beholder and weaken his grip on himself' (1992: 44) as he watches the canoe approaching his shores. The intent of the traveler may be to do battle or conduct trade. For Gell, the desired effect is the same—'psychological warfare' (1992: 44). But how do these boards work their magic? Gell's answer, brilliant as it is as a stand-alone interpretation of a single human encounter, also speaks to the enchanted efficacy of prophetic 'signs of the end times.'

> The canoe-board does not interfere seriously...with the intended victim's perceptual processes, but achieves its purpose in a much more roundabout way. [...] Its efficacy is to be attributed to the fact that these disturbances, mild in themselves, are interpreted as evidence of the magical power emanating from the board....[A]n impressive canoe-board is a physical token of magical prowess on the part of the owner of the canoe which is important...That is to say, the canoe-board is not dazzling as a physical object, but as a display of artistry explicable only in magical terms. (Gell 1992: 46)

For Gell, this is true to the extent that 'the enchantment of technology is the power that technical processes have of casting a spell over us so that we see the real world in an enchanted form' (Gell 1992: 44). But how does technology (in Gell's case art) cast a spell over us? The enchantment of technology works its magic, in the language of semiotics, by conflating sign and referent. In speaking of technology (or art) what we are really talking about is how symbols work. The canoe prow invokes fear and awe because its technical difficulty is such that it carries with it a 'halo effect,' that is, it exists 'as a display of artistry explicable only in magical terms' (Gell 1992: 46).

I see the canoe approaching my shores and I look upon the canoe board and I say to myself 'I could never make anything so amazing, nor could anyone for that matter because it's not humanly possible.' Which, for Gell, is exactly the point—'not humanly possible.' Not without the use of magic. As the canoe board comes into full view and the warriors come ashore I am overcome with awe and take leave of my senses. My mind turns from the canoe board to the canoe owner, that is, it turns from the sign to the referent. Any warrior with enough power to enlist and control the magic of the artisan who made such a carving—such an impossible object—is to be feared indeed.

What does this have to do with searching for signs of the end times in Gamrie? It concerns the way that magical symbols work their magic. Remember that 'the enchantment of technology is the power that technical processes have of casting a spell over us so that we see the real world in an enchanted form' (Gell 1992: 46). What Gell says about technology is what I have been arguing for 'signs of the times.' In a sense, 'signs of the times' are just another form of 'technology,' like art is for Gell. So eschatological signs work their magic—cast their spells over us—by conflating 'sign' and 'referent.' When I see a pine tree being planted in the Negev desert or an EU log sheet being submitted to the Scottish Fisheries Protection Agency, I do not just see evidence that points to the material imminence of God and the devil who collectively threaten to bring about the end of the world— I also actually see (and am party to) God and the devil, not only in space, but also in time.

And the world is transformed. No longer disenchanted, the 'technology' of end-times Biblical prophecy, when folded forward onto the present and the near future, works its magic by conflating sign and referent, index and object, cause and effect. The 'real world,' Gell tells us, becomes seen in an enchanted form (Gell 1992: 44). As symbols, the pine tree and the log sheet do not point to an outside agent (God, the devil, the 'saved,' the 'unsaved') but rather point to themselves, obviating the need for symbolic representation of anything but itself (Wagner 1978) as the actual (direct) object of the eschaton.

The world is enchanted, then—it is 'made alive with a kind of magic'—insofar as the social and material relations that constitute the religion of Gamrie are themselves miraculously consubstantiated, via the collapsing of the distance between sign and referent, into objects of both divine immanence and imminence. And the Word became flesh, and dwelt among us (John 1:14). But remember, 'The Word' also became text: 'If you want to know Jesus, here he is!' a friend told me emphatically, as he handed me his Bible. To the extent that his consubstantiation also had demonic implications—satan being existentially present in video cassettes, for example—the same has been shown to occur eschatologically, in the divine materiality of pine trees and the demonic materiality of EU logbooks. Insofar as it has been my aim throughout this book to allow theory to emanate from local experience—it now seems we are at the point where it is possible to theorize with more rigor what is meant by enchantment.

Conclusion

Enchantment

In the religion of Gamrie, belief and experience; ideas and objects; words and language, are all bound together in sets of relationships that cannot easily be separated. Nor should they be separated. Beliefs (about the end of the world, for example) are indistinguishable from the implications they have within the material (economic, demographic, and political) world. Words become objects and objects become words. Not only do people believe things about objects, but they also experience those objects ideationally. Equally, beliefs about boxes of fish are not only implicated within a local theology of eschatology, but those beliefs change the material nature of the objects in question. All this is possible because theological beliefs, material objects, words, language, and the cosmos that contains them are enchanted. Enchantment animates Gamrie religion—it 'makes it alive with a kind of magic.'

Weber and Rational Calculation

Weber, Cannell rightly points out, 'was not an optimist about modernity' (2011: 2). In his famous lecture 'Science as a Vocation' (Weber 1978c), delivered in Munich at the end of the First World War to young aspiring academics, Weber outlined his fears about the ways in which 'ultimate values'—what anthropologists might call 'committed ethical subject positions,' or perhaps 'morality' (cf. Robbins 2007)— were being forced to retreat from public life. This development, he said, was to allow room for the near totalizing force of a modernity that was itself driven by the utterly uncompromising assumption that all things could (and would) be mastered by 'calculation.' The result, in Weber's view, was that sociality was often reduced to means-ends relationships and the impersonal and objectifying forces of bureaucracy and legal formalism. No other forms of relatedness were permissible in such an ideology of modernity, with all behaviors that conducted themselves outside the strictures of empirical calculation—including all religious beliefs and practices—understood as essentially irrational.

The irrationality of non-calculable social relatedness led to a further reduction of the world to pure materiality. The ideal type of the 'value-rationality' of technical means-ends decision making eclipsed normal human contact previously based on the 'ethic of brotherly love' (Weber 1978b: 355; Bellah 1999). All that came into the equation was the potentiality of material gains and losses set against a backdrop of natural causality. Such a view of cause and effect as occurring only within the confines of a 'this-worldly' and 'human-centered' existence reinforced the increasingly uncontested (and incontestable) sense that the cosmos was a purely material and thus utterly banal scientific reality.

For Weber, the effects were multifarious. Most relevant to our discussion here is the reaction of some in 'the Church' who sought to place theodicy within this new framework of natural causality. Suffering, which became an exclusively material reality and not a spiritual one, engendered skepticism about religion, thereby establishing the very thing that theodicy sought to dispel, namely doubt in the metaphysical truth claims of Christianity and religion more generally. The motive behind this failed theodicy—to move into line with the increasing intellectualism of Christian theology as a result of the Protestant Reformation—was itself borne out of the earlier move toward calculation, whereby all phenomena (including the movement of streetcars and the falling of rain) (Weber 1978c: 139) became viewed as potentially learnable and thus entirely without mystery.

The result was not an immediate loss of enchantment (although for Weber this did follow gradually) but rather a loss of transcendence (Weber 1968: 607). Weber's aspiring academics, were, in a very real sense, living in a 'post-metaphysical' world of 'exclusive humanism' (Taylor 2007: 245)—a world that was completely predictable, easily manipulable, fully calculable, and eminently rational. With no mystery, there was no need for magic, and with no need for magic, there was no feeling of transcendence. It was this loss of transcendence that birthed the full effects of modern disenchantment—in all its complexity and contradiction.

Polytheism, Plasticity, and Disenchantment

At the heart of the modern scientific paradigm, for Weber, was the notion of progress *ad infinitum*, that is, the triumphant assertion that humankind was travelling along an upward evolutionary trajectory, which, by definition, would incessantly redefine the successes of past generations as inconsequential footnotes along the path to greater things. All present attainment of knowledge was incomplete, fleeting, and to be rewritten by those who would expose its errors and surpass its limitations. Such a vision, while truthfully describing modernity, was, for Weber, intolerably meaningless.

> Science has created this cosmos of natural causality and has seemed unable to answer with certainty the question of its own ultimate presuppositions. [...] Viewed in this way, all 'culture' appears as man's emancipation from the organically prescribed cycle of natural life. For this very reason culture's every step forward seems condemned to lead to an ever more devastating senselessness. The advancement of cultural values seems to become a senseless hustle in the service of worthless, moreover self-contradictory, and mutually antagonistic ends. (Weber 1978b: 355–357)

Because Weber uses science as a trope for modernity, the 'senselessness' and emptiness of the modern condition springs from the failure of science to apprehend the meaning of its own 'ultimate presuppositions' of rational calculation and 'progress.' Asceticism comes 'to dominate worldly morality' principally through the 'economic conditions of machine production' as detached from 'the highest spiritual and cultural values [of] religious and ethical meaning' leaving only 'purely mundane passions' in its wake (Weber 1977: 181–183). With the metaphysics of religion having been replaced by the triviality and predictability of a purely material world, the world is left bereft of the enchantment of transcendence and becomes disenchanted. As religion becomes increasingly consumed by 'intellectualism,' its original 'charisma' and 'mysticism' are replaced by 'doctrine' and 'book religion,' granting ever more significance to the rationalist supposition that the whole universe is knowable and subject to human learning.

This collapse of the monopoly over metaphysics that 'traditional' (in our context, Christian) religion(s) once held fosters the development of new 'alternative salvations' (Weber 1968: 602–610) and thus new kinds of (re)enchanted polytheisms. In this context, the 'detraditionalization' of the *post*modern era (its experimental, reflexive,

contingent, uncertain, risky, disorganized, and disembedded character) (Heelas, Lash, and Morris 1996: 3) actually comes to look rather
modern. Politics offers me salvation from a meaningless death by my
making the ultimate (self) sacrifice in battle. Aesthetics offers me salvation from everyday routine through a (self) obsession of pure artis-
tic form divorced from content. Eroticism offers me salvation from
reproductive functionality via ecstatic sexual (self) fulfillment. For
Weber, these (modern) 'alternative salvations' and 'old gods' offer
little but empty and selfish promises, detached, as they are, from the
overwhelming, 'world denying love' of the truly enchanting (traditional) world religions. In an ironic twist in the analysis, it is exactly
these (supposedly (re)enchanting) 'alternative salvations' (themselves
arising out of the failure of rational-intellectualist Protestant theodicy)
that brought about the full arrival of disenchantment. I am speaking
here of what Weber calls the 'loss of plasticity' (Weber 1978c: 148)
in modern life.

The alternative salvations of politics, aesthetics, and eroticism,
based as they are on different 'ultimate values' both produce and are
produced by social fragmentation. Gone is the singularity of 'tradi-
tionalist...domination, which rests upon a belief in the sanctity of
everyday routines' (Weber 1978d: 297). The resultant fragmentation
is incompatible (and incommensurable) because these 'salvations' are
based on competing values. Eroticism competes over sexuality and
against Puritan asceticism. The politics of death in battle takes a different view of the value of aesthetic form to that of the artist. Religion
is required to inhabit an independent sphere all on its own, away from
politicians and artists and eroticists, yet forced to conduct its 'business' (for that is what it increasingly becomes) through the same
rationalist framework of all forms of modern calculation, or else set
itself up in direct opposition to the ideology of rationality. However,
a key difference remains for Weber between the old salvationist religions and the modern—essentially reactionary—sources of salvific
'ultimate value.' Where the world religions of old are (or, at least *were*)
inextricably bound to wider happenings in the cosmos, this is not so
for the modern salvations of politics, sex, and art. Weber, discussing
Nietzsche's view on the relationship between beauty and the unholy,
has this to say:

> But all these are only the most elementary cases of struggle that the
> gods of the various orders and values are engaged in....We live as did
> the ancients when their world was not yet disenchanted of its gods
> and demons, only we live in a different sense.... *The bearing of man*

has been disenchanted and denuded of its mystical but inwardly genu-
ine plasticity.... Today the routines of everyday life challenge religion.
Many old gods ascend from their graves; they are disenchanted and
hence take the form of impersonal forces. They strive to gain power
over our lives and again they resume their eternal struggle with one
another. (Weber 1978c: 148–149. Emphasis added)

The most devastating final consequence of this is the loss of the
'inwardly genuine plasticity' for modern subjects (Weber 1978c: 148).
In 'Science as a vocation' (Weber 1978c), this involves a loss of the
physical and metaphysical holism once enjoyed by 'pre-modern' subjects. Physically, where people were once 'sated with life,' they are
now 'wearied' by it (Weber 1978b: 356–357); no longer are moderns held by the meaningfully bounded closure that laboring within
the 'organic life cycle' afforded (cf. Connell 1978: 207–208), left to
the 'senselessness' of unrelenting rational development and the bit-
ter realization that all their accomplishments will be known only for
their inevitable redundancy. Metaphysically, where premoderns lived
with one model of salvation in any given society, moderns live with
several. It is in this sense that the 'gods ascend[ing] from their graves'
(Weber 1978c: 149) have lost their cosmological rootedness, that is,
their sense of being unavoidably implicated in the real functioning
of the universe and its contents. With no felt connection to seed-
time and harvest, 'tradition'—defined as 'a belief in the sanctity of
everyday routines' (Weber 1978d: 297)—undergoes its own (almost
millenarian) disappearance (cf. Connell 1978: 214). For Taylor, here
again echoing Weber, this creates

> a new sense of the self and its place in the cosmos: not open and porous
> and vulnerable to a world of spirits and powers, but... "buffered" [...]
> [that is, a] self which is aware of the possibility of disengagement [...]
> [in] a pluralist world, in which many forms of belief and unbelief jostle,
> and hence fragilize each other. (Taylor 2007: 27, 42, 531)

The world created by rational modernity is not littered with dead
gods but with disconnected and competing gods; it is marked not by
secularization but by segregation and 'disengagement' (Taylor 2007:
42). Disenchantment, then, is the reduction of ultimate *values* to personal *tastes*, with modern subjects divorced from the moral imperative to (collectively) act upon any of their clamorous and seemingly
arbitrary ideals. The very concept of 'ultimate' value becomes increasingly at odds with the sheer relativity of rational action, leaving moderns either incapable or unwilling to take principled moral action.

Out of intellectual paralysis or moral nihilism, Weber's moderns are exposed to the relativity of free floating and competitive polytheism whose fragmented (and fragmenting) impersonal forces provoke careless skepticism by creating their own forms of disenchanted, human-centered, and post-metaphysical sociality.

My friends were left struggling with a dual reality; an enchanted universe lived within an increasingly disenchanted village; enchanted words spoken by a disenchanted language; and enchanted objects held within a disenchanted materiality. This was especially true of the fishing industry. Trawlers were instruments of mechanized labor and sites of divine salvation; EU fishing quotas were rational bureaucracies and a demonic plot to enslave the human race via the imposition of global famine. Even disenchantment was given an enchanted gloss: 'the unsaved' were spiritually blinded by the devil, whose greatest trick was an act of disenchantment, 'to persuade the world he doesn't exist.' While for some in Gamrie, epistemologically, God and the devil had vanished, ontologically—and thus existentially—their presences remained unchanged. The reaction of 'the saved' was to fight the assumption that 'the routines of everyday life challenge religion' (Weber 1978c: 149). Indeed, for Gamrie's Christian fisher families, the reverse was held to be true, that is, their experience of religion challenged the routines of everyday life.

Enchantment as Consubstantiation

Having described Weber's notion of disenchantment, I want to end by theorizing enchantment as a kind of consubstantiation. Consubstantiation normally refers to that view of the Christian Eucharist that attempts to explain the real (material and spiritual) presence of the body and blood of Jesus as existing *alongside* the real material presence of the bread and the wine. This differs from transubstantiation, which suggests that the body and blood (the inner 'substance') literally but invisibly *replace* the bread and wine (the external 'accident'). In consubstantiation, then, what occurs is not replacement but bifurcation: while the 'accident,' as in transubstantiation, remains both singular and unchanged, the 'substance,' contra transubstantiation, miraculously develops a dual nature whereby the body and blood of Christ are physically present alongside the bread and wine. Crucially, as in my analysis of preaching, my use of this theological term emerges not from local understandings of communion ('breaking bread') but from local assertions regarding the divine specialness of scripture. What we see in my Christian informants' view of the

Bible is the same kind of bifurcation that we see in consubstantiation, namely, a book that is *simultaneously* the literal 'living and breathing Word of God,' and, a collection of bound pages, that, over time, gets old and falls apart (cf. Engelke 2007). Taking this local view of scripture as our starting point, I want to apply its logic to the whole experience of religion in Gamrie.

Enchantment works its magic by allowing the material (bound pages) and the spiritual (God's breath) to coexist—co-substantiate—within both words and objects. It is this coexistence that I describe as consubstantiation. Sermons (whether 'preaching' the gospel or 'teaching' the Bible) were delivered and received in such a way that both God and the preacher were speaking subjects. 'Whatever God says to you in the preaching and teaching of the scriptures *do it* and be obedient to what God tells you!' came the shrill cry from the pulpit one Sunday night in the Kirk. So too with testimony and witness; words spoken by men at sea are also words spoken by God. Mark not only spoke about God but for God whenever he sought to share the gospel with Brice and others onboard the *Flourish*. The same was true for Alasdair—'I couldna come out my bedroom this morning without speaking to my Lord. If I didnae have Jesus with me just noo I couldnae speak to you'—a man who would be left silent without the enabling presence of the Lord. So too, finally, for the Bible itself—not just a book, but a 'living,' 'speaking,' 'breathing' book—'if you want to know Jesus, *here he is.*'

Sermons and words of witness; Bibles and Bible reading notes, these things are enchanted—made alive—by the magic of consubstantiation. This magic powerfully unites two kinds of 'substance' (words of man with words of God; printed pages with pages warm with the breath of God) within a single 'accident' (a sermon, a book) and in so doing, allows the material to indwell the spiritual and vice versa. Words are not the only objects implicated in the magic of consubstantiation—material things too, are deployed as objects of enchantment. Hauls of prawns materially index the presence of God, just as Seventh Day Adventist video cassettes materially index the presence of the devil. Objects, far from being neutral materiality in a spiritual cosmos, are 'charged' (Taylor 2007), bringing forth both blessings and curses.

Gamrie religion, enchanted, as it was, by divine and demonic words and objects, challenged the routines of everyday life, thereby inverting Weber's formulation of modern disenchantment. What it challenged, specifically, was the totalizing rationalism of disenchantment that glossed life as pure 'accident,' containing only the surface materiality of, variously, the bread and wine, the haul of prawns, or the video cassette. Enchantment challenges the routines of life not by locating God and the devil outside everyday language and materiality, but precisely by locating these divinities within them. Providence and spiritual attack are amazing yet unsurprising; they inspire awe yet remain part of the everyday to the point of being *eminently expected*. Robert's bookmark was clear: 'As you read, remember to be expectant, God wants to fellowship with you and speak to you every day.' It was here, in the reading and talking and walking and fishing of everyday life that the enchantment of routine—and the routine of enchantment—was experienced. What emerges is a new understanding of disenchantment and its relationship to enchantment. In order to explain this I want to examine one final piece of ethnography.

While helping Sarah, my landlady, on her stall at a craft fair in the village school one spring afternoon, I met a woman called Dorothy Gilmore who had accompanied her husband to the fair to help sell his wood carvings. As we talked, her eyes lit up when I mentioned the name of my brother's minister in Aberdeen, a man known in local Christian circles for his spiritual interest in Israel. What followed was one of the most remarkable conversations I had while on fieldwork. After asking a few careful questions about my own Christian background, Dorothy began to tell me of her belief that she was descended from the Virgin Mary (via the Lost Tribe of Benjamin) and had been personally tasked by God to reveal to the Jews that Jesus was the Messiah. By way of supporting evidence, she explained to me that her own middle name was Mary and her son's name, Derek, meant 'the ruler.' She went on to insinuate that she actually *was* Mary (the mother of Jesus) but stopped just short of claiming that her son was the Christ. 'Do you think it's relevant that your husband is a carpenter?' I asked with a creased brow to indicate my seriousness. '*Yes*,' she nodded knowingly, '*I do*.'

Dorothy continued by telling me that God had revealed this mission to her through her knowledge of Doric that she said was God's chosen language through which Jesus' true identity as the Savior would be made known to the Jews. God had shown her that the Bible (best read in Scots) contained thousands of hidden Doric references only visible when the reader began to divide up the words of scripture according to their phonetic Doric pronunciation. At this point she gave me an example. 'The Bible says "*Jesus rode into Jerusalem on a Donkey.*" If you take the word "donkey" and split it into two you get the words "don" and "key" don't you?' she said. I agreed that this was true, but, to her amazement, I did not see her point. Eventually relenting, she revealed that the true hidden meaning of the word 'donkey' was as follows: The river that runs through Aberdeen is the River Don, and, insofar as 'Don' is also a byname for Aberdeen, when we combine this realization with our second word—'key'—we come to the conclusion that '*Don* is the *key*,' that is, Aberdeen(shire) is the key in revealing Jesus's true identity to the Jews.

Dorothy, beaming at my stunned silence, went on to describe how she had collected an entire file of similar linguistic evidence to support her case. She gave several more examples, one of which helped me to more fully grasp the extent of her claims. 'Just before Jesus ascended into heaven he told his disciples "fear not you will see me in a little while,"' she said. The word 'while' in Doric is pronounced (and spelt) '*file*,' meaning, Dorothy explained earnestly, that Jesus's final words on earth *really* read 'you will see me in a little *file*.' After years of study, this discovery was the key watershed moment for Dorothy who realized that what Jesus was actually talking about was *her file* of Biblical Doric codes. From that moment on, everything else fell into place; the file was nearly complete and she was looking for someone to hand it over to the Jewish religious authorities in Israel.

As we spoke it was clear that she wanted me to take up this quest to deliver the file. My hesitation led Dorothy to suggest I spend some time studying her website that would give me all the answers I would need as long as I read it '*carefully*.' The Internet would be a particularly helpful medium for me, Dorothy explained, because my surname was Webster; I was, quite literally, a 'Web' 'Star,' in the same way, she said, that Benjamin Netanyahu ('Net' 'in' 'Yahoo') was. I asked if others knew of her true identity and recognized the things she spoke of as being true. 'Oh yes,' she assured me, 'there are others,' mentioning in particular that 'thousands of Freemasons' were convinced of the validity of her 'file' but were collectively engaged in a determined and diabolical conspiracy to cover the matter up—for what reasons, she did not elaborate.

Just as I got up to leave, the tone of the conversation became suddenly darker. 'Don't worry if you fall into the hands of the security services,' Dorothy said, 'they won't be able to harm you. I'm trying to *tell* you something without *actually* telling you.' After a pregnant pause she implied that it was very possible that she had put me in grave danger by revealing her secret quest to me—a secret so powerful that government agents might, even at that precise moment, be looking to capture and silence me. Dorothy ended our conversation with the comforting (if further disorientating) suggestion that the reason I would come to no harm was because I, like her, was part of the lost Tribe of Benjamin and thus had special protection from God. She urged me one final time to look at her website and wrote the address down on the back of her husband's business card. And with the card in my hand, I thanked her, returning to my seat beside Sarah's key chains and fridge magnets.

The functioning of enchantment can be observed where symbols, as concrete things in themselves, achieve a conflation of sign and referent, that is, they consubstantiate without one or the other substance ever changing. God is *in* my washing machine and yet my washing machine still functions as before, with neither substance nor 'presence' accorded more importance or agentive power than the other. It is by coexisting that they attain their importance and agentive power: without earthly matter we simply have ethereal metaphysics; without 'spiritual' presence we have only rationally calculable materiality. Thus, the enchanting power of consubstantiation posits a kind of 'incarnation'—God is made, not so much into miraculous flesh or bread, but (locally) into words, texts, and other everyday objects.

Plasticity and the Monotheism of 'The Word'

Where disenchantment is centrally concerned with the modern subject's loss of 'inwardly genuine plasticity' (Weber 1978c: 148) and its replacement with the 'senselessness' of progress *ad infinitum* (Weber 1978c: 137), Gamrie's religion is marked by a cosmological rootedness that makes fishing for prawns, preaching 'The Word,' looking for signs, and witnessing to the 'unsaved' all eminently enchanted. And it is in Gamrie's sense of 'cosmological rootedness' that we see the fragmentation of the irreconcilable values of modernity finally dealt with. Among the Christians of Gamrie, we find six different religious groupings, who, despite sharing a history of denominational schism, remain united by the centrality of 'The Word' and by experiences of the immanence and imminence of transcendence. So central was this 'Word' that Luke, an informant who struggled with learning difficulties, told me of a time in his life where he had been on the verge of abandoning his faith because of his illiteracy. The key moment in Luke's conversion came when a friend taught him to read, opening up to him not only the Bible, but also his salvation.

Divine presence was experienced as being both 'near' and 'soon,' through the preaching and teaching of scripture, through words of testimony and witness, through the 'zero-sum game' of fishing for prawns and men, through the experience of divine providence and demonic attack, and finally, through the anticipation of the eschaton. 'The Word' played the key mediating role not only between human-divine relationships, but also between different religious experiences. Whether I was at a Free Presbyterian prayer meeting, a Kirk 'men's breakfast' or a CB prophecy meeting, 'The Word' remained central. So strongly was this felt, that some of my informants summarized Gamrie religion, in a play on Trinitarian theology, as 'Father, Son and Holy *Bible*.' The religion of Gamrie received its cosmological rooted-ness in and through words of preaching, prayer, testimony, witness, and storytelling, all of which occurred not only in church, but also at home, on the street and at sea. It was 'The Word,' then, that dis-pelled the fragmentary 'meaninglessness' and 'senselessness' of mod-ern disenchantment.

Yet, the 'polytheism' of Gamrie's 'non-Christian' 'others'—variously based on devotion to money, art, wildlife conservation, or motorbikes—is indicative of the wider (and partially disenchanting) 'triple pinch' of economic, demographic, and eschatological pressure that the village is subject to. These 'alternative salvations' created a fragmentary break-away from the ultimate value of 'The Word' by introducing a 'poly-theism' of competing values. This irreconcilable competition for the 'souls' of Gamrics provided an ever-widening range of personhoods in the village—one could be an artist, a 'biker,' a marine conservationist, and so on—and it was these 'identities' that imputed a sense of 'ulti-mate value' (who I *really* am') to both self and other.

Where Gamrie's *Christian* cosmos differs, is in its refusal to enter into any such assignation of multiple identities. For my Christian informants, their internally coherent cosmos, rooted, as it was, to the monotheism of 'The Word,' replaced the socio-spatial fragmentation of the self and other with only two categories of persons that had any 'ultimate value'—the 'saved' and the 'unsaved.' This duality was a cause of tremendous pain and anxiety to my Christian informants, who, particularly in their old age, felt the ever-pressing need to exhort those with whom they had contact (most especially their grandchil-dren) to embrace the singular salvation of 'born-again' faith.

The God of the Christians of Gamrie, and the devil who opposes them, do not lack cosmological roots but are intimately (immanently and imminently) attached to the things of this world. The cosmos of local Christian metaphysics is thoroughly objectified by a whole con-stellation of material objects, both onshore (washing machines, trees, and video cassettes) and at sea (waves, boats, nets, and prawns). This is not to say that Gamrie religion—objectified on land and at sea—is not also implicated in the 'skies above.' Indeed, the 'spiritual work' of prayer, salvation, and worship were clearly described as being directed toward the 'heavenly realms.' For the Christians of Gamrie, then, God and the devil were experienced as present in both this world and the world beyond.

The world my Christian friends inhabited was enchanted because the cosmological rootedness of their devotion to 'The Word' maintained the 'plasticity' of their social and spiritual lives. Their religiosity hinged on a common experience of 'The Word' that defined their personhood, and, in one of two ways, the personhood of all those around them. This 'Word' was implicated not only in the immanence of space (the land, sea, and heavens above), but also in the imminence of time, extending back into Biblical and 'revival' history, and moving forward into the near future of the soon-to-occur apocalypse. The product of this enchanting 'Word' was, simply put, an enchanted world.

The 'Ethical Causality' of a God-Ordained World

For the Christians of Gamrie, the arrival of modernity brought neither purely rational calculation, nor the disenchantment of the world into meaningless banality but a very different experience of everyday life. Fundamental to understanding this contemporary experience is a view of daily routine as directed by 'irresistible divine intention'—a view essential to the maintenance of an enchanted world. Part of the work of *dis*enchantment, then, can be seen in its replacement of ethical causality with natural causality. Where ethical causality states that we live in a God-ordained world within an ethically orientated cosmos, natural causality states that the world is guided by the impersonal and value-free laws of science. 'There's no such thing as coincidence, only Godincidence,' my informants would often tell me. Such was their cosmos.

Given that Godincidence and spiritual attack were occurring within the enchanted timetable of dispensationalist eschatology, the result was that the everyday details of life (both the extraordinary and the routine) were indeed God-ordained and ethically orientated, surrounded, as they were, by events that transcended everyday life without stripping away or denying their quintessentially this-worldly character. Enchantment, then, addresses the ways in which a life of consubstantiation renders sociality as elusively greater than its individual parts.

Think here of Dorothy Gilmore and her 'little file.' Dorothy was also named 'Mary.' Her husband was a carpenter and her son's name meant 'the ruler.' The family, despite appearing quite ordinary, had a 'calling' on their lives of truly cosmological significance. Indeed, Dorothy's family and the original 'Holy Family' were, in important respects, one and the same. The Bible was best read in Scots, but English translations also contained thousands of hidden linguistic codes that could be discovered by splitting words and sounding them with a phonetic Doric pronunciation. Names, likewise, contained hidden meanings. The world could be divided up into those to whom Dorothy's quest had been revealed and those to whom it had not. What's more, the world was governed by the struggle between hidden forces of evil (secret government agents and Freemasons) and equally mysterious forces of good (the Lost Tribe of Benjamin). While the battle would be intense, good would ultimately triumph because of the special protection granted by God to his people. Final victory would be won with the ushering in of the apocalypse; an event that would be triggered by the mass conversion of all of Israel's Jews to Christianity in a single day as a result of the presentation of Dorothy's file that revealed Jesus to be the Messiah.

Such was the enchanted nature of Dorothy's Christian cosmology. While some readers might be inclined to interpret such views as the product of mental illness, I want to offer a different analysis. Specifically, I want to use my encounter with Dorothy to suggest that what she and my other Christians friends experienced as enchantment may be seen as broadly analogous to imaginings of the 'moment of consecration' under consubstantiation. Where I use consubstantiation as a *theological* lens through which to view the anthropological concept of enchantment, it is also explicitly my intention to use enchantment as an *anthropological* lens through which to view folk-theological experience of my Christian informants. This positioning of theology and anthropology alongside each other has a dual purpose. First, it is born out of a desire to see 'beliefs' and 'objects' treated as unavoidably implicated in each others' work. Beliefs have (or 'take') objects while objects are also a kind of belief. Second, this positioning also acts as 'a kind of writing' that seeks to realize Taylor's 'language of perspicuous contrast' (1985: 125) or what I have referred to as a language of mutual give and take. By avoiding both ethnocentric reductionism and pure apology, Taylor advocates constructing a way of looking at (and writing about) the world as a formulation of 'both their way of life and ours as alternative possibilities in relation to some human constants at work in both' (1985: 125). The human constants I have chosen to analyze have been words and objects, or, more generally, language and materiality.

'The Word': Bifurcation, Consecration, and Conflation

But what of Dorothy and her Doric codes? If we are to understand her experience in terms of the enchantment of consubstantiation, what might her (and all my other Christian informants') 'moment of consecration' look like? The answer lies in both bifurcation and conflation. In the Eucharist, the substance of the bread coexists *alongside* the substance of the flesh, but *within the single 'accident.'* Put another way, the 'inner essence' of the substance undergoes bifurcation *within* the single externality of the accident. Externally, the bread is *just* bread; internally it is simultaneously *both* bread and flesh. The same happens to Dorothy, her family, and her 'little file.' Dorothy is both herself and the Virgin Mary, although she looks like herself. The Bible is both the Christian scriptures and a series of hidden Doric codes, although, even under careful scrutiny, it simply looks like an (albeit Holy) book. The British government is not only the primary seat of political and legislative power, but also—in conjunction with Freemasonry—involved in a demonic conspiracy to overthrow the eschaton.

What we see in this example—and in the many other 'ethnographic moments' that make up the core of this book—is that the enchanted religious worldview of Gamrie is constructed from a series of bifurcations of 'substance' and conflations of 'accident.' This is to say, that while the external form remains unchanged—the book, the Government, and Mary herself—the inner essence is experienced as holding a dual reality of the 'not only ... but also.... ' *Not only* did my landlady have a working washing machine *but also* a material index of the presence of God in her life and home. *Not only* does the preacher use his own voice when speaking from the pulpit, *but also* the voice of God.

If bifurcation allows two realities (two real 'substances') to exist within a single 'accident,' then the 'moment of consecration' (when enchantment achieves its magic) is locally experienced whenever 'The Word' is invoked. It is by words and 'The Word' that the religious experiences of Gamrics are 'consecrated' and thereby receive their dual (natural and supernatural) presence. When 'The Word' is deployed, that is, when words containing scripture or scriptural themes are read, spoken, 'preached on,' or 'prayed over', what we see, to return to Weber, is a move from the register of 'rational,' 'natural causality' to the register of 'God-ordained,' 'ethical-causality' (Weber 1978b: 351–354). When a pronouncement of 'providence' or 'attack' is given, when a 'testimony' is shared, when a sermon is preached, when a prayer is offered, when a hymn is sung, or a religious experience related—it is in and through the deployment of words and objects (and words-as-objects) that the ethical causality of 'The Word' enchants the world of my Christian informants.

But what is actually going on within ethical causality? How does it 'work its magic'? How was I to experience a sermon not only as the words of a preacher but also as the words of God? How was it that Jackie Sr. experienced a bountiful haul of prawns not simply as a consequence of his skill and experience as a skipper, but also as divine provision? What Gell (1992) helps us see here is not the enchanting process of bifurcation but of *conflation*; how the sign is conflated with the referent; how the 'something that stands for something' itself becomes the actual object. Crucially, this conflation occurs *within* a single 'accident'—the spoken sermon, the haul of prawns—that remains, in outward form, unchanged by the consecrating and conflating pronouncement of the enchanting 'Word.'

Preaching and testimony, providence and attack, and signs of the end times—these, to echo Gell, are what we might call the 'technologies' of millenarianism and thus the technologies of Gamrie religion. Like the Trobriander who carves a canoe prow so intricate that it casts a spell over me, leading me to conflate owner with prow with carpenter, so too the Gamric who narrates a powerful sermon, a moving testimony, an exciting 'Godincidence,' a terrifying attack. These 'technologies' cast their spells in like manner, causing me to conflate (in my mind's ear) speaker with word with God (or the devil). Wood carved, words spoken, nets cast—all act, when undertaken in a properly 'enskiled' manner, to dissolve the distinction between sign and referent, enchanting the world, and its contents in the process.

Where this ethnography is about the religious experiences of a (relatively) small number of Protestant fishermen in northeast Scotland, it is also an ethnography of a village in dramatic transition. Studying Gamrie at this time of transition has provided us with a window through which to view much bigger social processes. Economic globalization and recession, environmental exploitation, rural depopulation, demographic ageing, modern bureaucracy, technical calculation, social rationalization, liberalization, secularization, disenchantment—all these have been discussed in terms that go well beyond the limits of the village, to, in some cases, the global stage.

Had my ethnography been conducted 20 or 30 years ago, as Knipe's (1984) ethnography of the cultural ecology of Gamrie's fishing industry was, the picture would have been very different, largely because the 'triple pinch' would not have exerted the same pressure over the lives of those in the village as it does today. Fishing was booming in 1980s, and although some depopulation was already being experienced, the churches were still able to attract those in their teens, twenties, and thirties in a way that cannot be said to be the case presently. While it has been 'the last of the last days' eschatologically for many decades now, the same was certainly not the case economically or demographically. Had I waited 20 or 30 years in the future to conduct my ethnography, it is my assertion (and the assertion of many of my informants, and, perhaps not incidentally, the assertion of many supporters of the secularization thesis) that there would be very little religion left in Gamrie to analyze (cf. Bruce 2011: 99). Consequently, the opportunity to examine the relationships between religion and economics, demographics, modernity, or disenchantment would have been be lost to us, at least within this local Scottish context.

Studying this particular village at this particular time affords us some special (if not unique) insights. At this precise moment we see Gamrie located—within the triple pinch—at the center of a convergence of several different anthropological and sociological processes, most specifically with regard to how economics and demographics cut across local deployments of words and objects. The religion of Gamrie helps us see—in preaching, testimony, fishing, providence, attack, and eschatology—that Christianity does not exclusively produce transcendence nor does modernity exclusively produce disenchantment. Thus, the extent to which we are able to see in Gamrie's Christianity not just its transcendence, but also its immanence and imminence, will determine the success of my argument. Likewise, the extent to which we are able to see in Gamrie's modernity, not just rational calculation, but also the enchanting power of words and objects, will determine the wider contribution this argument is able to make. From this perspective, it is within the detail of the local that the import of the global ('bigger picture') resides. Where for Bruce,

> What matters is the trajectory of change. For how long and to what extent does vicarious or popular religion survive the decline of the Christian churches? The answer is not long and not much. (Bruce, 2011: 99)

it seems that my informants, observing the same decline, approach secularization with a different scale in mind, producing different answers as a result. For the Christians of Gamrie, the idea of 'secularization' is important not only as a way of describing the decline of the Christian churches, but as a way of experiencing that decline within an enchanted cosmos. 'Macro' trends (like secularization) only mattered to my Christian friends insofar as they could be appropriated back into the 'micro' religiosity of Gamrie. More than this, 'macro' social trends appeared positively microscopic when placed within the totality of the unfolding of dispensational time—with enchantment looking correspondingly more 'macro' as a result. Young people no longer went to church because they lived in a secular world, yet this world was itself a *product* of demonic trickery and a *prediction* of end-times Biblical prophecy. To (partially) echo Bruce, what mattered for my friends was the trajectory of change. For how long and to what extent would secularization survive the unfolding of the eschaton and the establishment of God's Kingdom on earth? The answer was not long and not at all. It was simply a matter of perspective and a matter of time.

A New Enchantment

But remember how there are many different 'villages' within Gamrie, 'populated' by a range of different people who themselves hold seemingly incommensurable ultimate values (cf. Lambek 2008). Gamrie's Christians appear caught between the local and the global, inhabiting, as they do, a world of black and white within a world of grey. Gamrie's teenagers, by and large, seem more interested in enjoying money, cars, and alcohol than in committing to 'a life of Gospel obedience.' Many of Gamrie's middle aged 'English incomers' devote themselves to the visual arts—to painting, sculpture, and photography—which, given the heavy logocentric bias of the local religion, is a passion not entirely shared by the churches. Gamrie's summer residents appear drawn to the village because of its natural beauty and diverse wildlife, with many valuing a version of environmentalism that sits awkwardly with the (economic and religious) 'calling' of local Christian fishermen. Gamrie's subculture of bikers, influenced by the message and lifestyle of punk rock, is perhaps most at odds with the somewhat puritanical outlook of Gamrie's chaste and (almost entirely) teetotal Christians.

What are we to do with this plurality? Does the lived reality of the 'triple pinch' not take us back to a disenchanted polytheism stripped of its 'inwardly genuine plasticity' (Weber 1978c: 148)? It seems not, especially where we recognize that enchantment and disenchantment are inseparable. What the Christian experience of Gamrie shows us is the 'irreconcilable ultimate values' of modernity pushed—in an apparently dialectical relationship—to its outer extremes. Boats

named after Biblical themes provoke a boat to be named 'Evolution.'
The expectation that Sunday ('the Lord's Day') be kept as a day
of quiet rest encourages groups of bikers to time their thunderous
descent down the village brae to coincide with the start of the morning church services.

Yet there is also convergence. The Christians of Gamrie continue
to enjoy the patterns of 'modern' consumption that their religion
leaves open to them—they eat well, dress well, drive expensive cars,
and take luxury foreign holidays. Insofar as the religion of Gamrie is
undoubtedly a 'book religion' heavily invested in 'doctrine' (Weber
1978b: 351), it is not surprising that it also shares some wider hall-
marks of modernity, especially where these things remain attached
not to the lavish hedonism of 'the sins of the flesh' but to the rather
less sensual (if equally material) 'signs' of success at ones 'calling' to
be a diligent and skilful fisher of prawns and men.

We are left, as in much of the book, with, if not a straightforward oppositional dualism, then certainly a somewhat incommensurable duality—that of an enchanted Christian world shaped by the
immanence and imminence of transcendence, that, in many respects,
is forced to orbit around a larger context of social, economic, and
demographic disenchantment. But it is not only the differing 'worlds'
of enchantment and disenchantment that exist as incommensurable
realities in Gamrie; words too can be incommensurable and so too can
objects. It is their incommensurability—their inability and unwillingness to compromise with their source of ultimate value—that deter-
mines their relations to other worlds with other values.

Where it is 'The Word' that exists as the utterly uncompromising
object of 'ultimate value' for the Christians of Gamrie, all that falls
outside its orbit is demonic and therefore incommensurable. Yet, if
the experience of Luke, my friend who conquered his illiteracy shows
us anything, it is that, for Gamrie's Christians, it is not just familiarity with words, but a certain kind of sincere and committed literacy
that is required. What was needed was a literacy that allowed 'The
Word' to enchant the world so that the signs and referents of Gamrie
religion became everyday indexes of the immanence and imminence
of transcendence.

As with immanence and transcendence, enchantment and disenchantment are inseparable. Importantly, many of my Christian informants themselves recognized this as true of their experience. On one
of my last visits to Gregor and Carol's house before I left the village,
I found both of them to be in as dejected a mood as I ever saw them.
'I sometimes wonder if God has just *abandoned* this village, ken.

I *canna* see nae future for *any* of the fellowships in the village. I do sometimes wonder if God has just *abandoned* us,' Carol told me with a pained expression. Where enchantment was experienced by local Christians in terms of the immanence and imminence of God and the devil through words and objects, that is, it was experienced in terms of divine presence, then perhaps a locally appropriate reformulation of disenchantment would not be that the people have forgotten God, but that God has forgotten—that is, has 'abandoned'—the people. To the extent that such a conflation is anthropologically possible, this might point us toward a new type of enchantment—what we might want to call the re-enchantment of disenchantment.

Notes

Introduction

1. This figure does not take into account the large number of men in Gamrie who are retired fishermen, nor does it include those who were once fishermen but who now work on the oil rigs or supply boats.
2. Greek (noun): *belief.* The word was commonly employed in an economically contractual sense.
3. Greek (verb): *to believe.*
4. 'Witness' was a common but nebulous term in Gamrie, referring to any word or deed that had a positive or negative impact upon the spread of the gospel. Where being a 'good witness' meant living a life befitting one's Christian calling, being a 'bad witness' was the result of sin or hypocrisy.
5. That is, the sharing of spiritual experiences—most especially the story of how one became a 'born again' Christian.
6. 'Divine providence' referred to God's omnipresent and omniscient extension of care, that is, His daily intervention in human affairs by way of intimate protection and provision.
7. 'Demonic attack' referred to the activities of the devil and demons that sought to harm Christians spiritually and/or physically.

1 Situating Gamrie

1. A ritual where the groom, shortly before the wedding, is dressed in women's clothes and covered in 'blackening' (traditionally soot and engine oil) and then paraded around the village. See Knipe (1984: 124) for a more detailed account of a blackening he witnessed in Gamrie in 1981.

2 The Triple Pinch

1. Population 12,500 (SCROL 2001).
2. Population 18,000 (SCROL 2001).

3. Because this 2001 census data is prerecession, some indicators, such as unemployment, may have changed. Data from the Scottish 2011 census had not been released at the time of writing.
4. Several of my informants told me that pelagic fishermen would immediately lose their berth if they were found to be working a second job because the skippers they worked for demanded the crew be available at all times.

3 Preaching

1. Known in North America as the 'Potluck supper.'
2. Following Gamrie practice, I use 'the gospel' and 'the glad tidings' interchangeably.
3. Luke 8:18.
4. 'Kynd' here meaning disposition, nature, sort, that is, 'it depends on the nature of our hearing.'

4 Testimony

1. My use of Foucault here is intentionally limited and specific, and should not be read as indicating broad support for his overarching theoretical paradigm.

5 Fishing

1. Also known as 'discards'; where perfectly fresh and saleable fish come up in the nets dead but must be thrown back to sea because the boat does not have the required license and/or quota.
2. A deckhand. Lowest and worst paid position on the boat.
3. United Christian Broadcasters.
4. New Living Translation.
5. English Standard Version.
6. Supposedly involving binge drinking, eating curry, and engaging in coprophilia.
7. This is my own summary produced by synthesizing Prattis's (1973) interest in 'incongruence' and Stiles's (1972) interest in 'solidarity' and 'equivalence.'
8. The local dialect in Northeast Scotland.

6 Providence and Attack

1. This term was common among Gamrie Christians, asserting that all things appearing to be coincidence were actually authored by God and His providence.
2. The 'Harry Potter' books were held by many in Gamrie to be demonic literature used by the Devil to desensitize children to the evils of witchcraft.

3. This idea is drawn from Wagner's work on symbolic obviation, defined as 'the collapsing of one existential modality...to produce another' (Wagner 1978: 34). In the context of semiotics, the sign becomes the signified.
4. Keane defines indexicality as that which 'signifies by virtue of a real relationship of causation or contiguity to its object' (Keane 1997b: 19) The 'realness' of such a relationship is said to be existential.
5. By 'cosmological rootedness' I refer to my informants' sense that their Christian lives were unavoidably implicated in the real functioning of the universe and its contents.
6. The similarities here with La Fontaine's (1998) analysis of tales of satanic child abuse, and beliefs in the literal existence of a cult of satanists, are striking.

7 Eschatology

1. Hebrew: 'together.'
2. Isaiah 35 and 41.
3. See also Harding's discussion of evangelicals hiding copies of the New Testament in the caves of Petra, in the hope of them being discovered by—and thereby triggering the conversion of—Jewish survivors fleeing the horrors of the Tribulation (2000: 229).
4. Revelation 13.
5. Revelation 17.

Bibliography

Almeida, Miguel Vale de. 1996. *The Hegemonic Male: Masculinity in a Portugese Town.* Oxford: Berghahn Books.

Anson, Peter. 1930. *Fishing Boats and Fisher Folk on the East Coast of Scotland.* London: Dent.

Asad, Talal. 1993. *Genealogies of Religion: Disciplines and Reasons of Power in Christianity and Islam.* Baltimore: Johns Hopkins University Press.

———. 2003. *Formations of the Secular: Christianity, Islam, Modernity.* Stanford: Stanford University Press.

Austin, John Langshaw. 1962. *How to Do Things with Words.* Oxford: Oxford University Press.

Bauman, Richard. 1983. *Let Your Words Be Few.* Cambridge: Cambridge University Press.

Bellah, Robert. 1999. 'Max Weber and World-Denying Love: A Look at the Historical Sociology of Religion.' *Journal of the American Academy of Religion* 67 (2): 277–304.

Bialecki, Jon. 2009. 'Disjuncture, Continental Philosophy's New "Political Paul", and the Question of Progressive Christianity in a Southern California Third Wave Church.' *American Ethnologist* 36 (1): 35–48.

———. 2011. 'No Caller ID for the Soul: Demonization, Charisms, and the Unstable Subject of Protestant Language Ideology.' *Anthropological Quarterly* 84 (3): 679–703.

Bielo, James. 2009. *Words Upon the Word: An Ethnography of Evangelical Group Bible Study.* New York: New York University Press.

———. 2011. *Emerging Evangelicals: Faith, Modernity and the Desire for Authenticity.* New York: New York University Press.

Bloch. Maurice. 1986. *From Blessing to Violence.* Cambridge: Cambridge University Press.

———. 1992. *Prey into Hunter: The Politics of Religious Experience.* Cambridge: Cambridge University Press.

Braverman, Irus. 2009. *Planted Flags: Trees, Land, and Law in Israel/Palestine.* Cambridge: Cambridge University Press.

Brierley, Peter. 2000. *The Tide Is Running Out.* London: Christian Research Association.

Brown, Callum. G. 1997. *Religion and Society in Scotland Since 1707.* Edinburgh: Edinburgh University Press.

Bruce, Steve. 2001. 'Christianity in Britain R. I. P.' *Sociology of Religion* 62 (2): 191–203.

———. 2002. 'Praying Alone? Church-Going in Britain and the Putnam Book.' *Journal of Contemporary Religion* 17 (3): 317–328.

———. 2011. *Secularization: In Defense of an Unfashionable Theory.* Oxford: Oxford University Press.

Brusco, Elizabeth. 1995. *The Reformation of Machismo: Evangelical Conversion and Gender in Colombia.* Austin: University of Texas Press.

Bynum, Caroline Walker. 1987. *Holy Feast, Holy Fast.* Berkeley: University of California Press.

Cahn, Peter. 2006. 'Building Down and Dreaming Up: Finding Faith in a Mexican Multilevel Marketer.' *American Ethnologist* 33 (1): 126–142.

Calvin, John. (2007) 1559. *Institutes of the Christian Religion.* Peabody: Hendrickson Publishers.

Campbell, John Kennedy. 1979. *Honour, Family and Patronage.* Oxford: Oxford University Press.

Cannell, Fenella. 1999. *Power and Intimacy in the Christian Philippines.* Cambridge: Cambridge University Press.

———. 2005. 'The Christianity of Anthropology.' *Journal of the Royal Anthropological Institute* 11:335–356.

———, ed. 2006. *The Anthropology of Christianity.* London: Duke University Press.

———. 2007. 'How Does Ritual Matter?' In *Questions of Anthropology*, edited by R. Astuti, J. Parry, and C. Stafford. Oxford: Berg.

———. 2010. 'Anthropology of Secularism.' *Annual Review of Anthropology* 39:85–100.

———. 2011. 'On Science as a Vocation: Placing Value Beyond the Fiscal'. Unpublished paper given at 'The Arts and Humanities: Endangered Species?' workshop, CRASSH, University of Cambridge: 1–3.

Carsten, Janet. 1997. *The Heat of the Hearth: The Process of Kinship in a Malay Fishing Community.* Oxford: Clarendon Press.

Christian, William. 1972. *Person and God in a Spanish Valley.* Princeton: Princeton University Press.

Coad, F. Roy. 1968. *History of the Brethren Movement.* Milton Keynes: Paternoster Press.

Cohen, Anthony. 1987. *Whalsay: Symbol, Segment and Boundary in a Shetland Island Community.* Manchester: Manchester University Press.

Coleman, Simon. 2000. *The Globalisation of Charismatic Christianity: Spreading the Gospel of Prosperity.* Cambridge: Cambridge University Press.

———. 2006. 'Materializing the Self: Words and Gifts in the Construction of Charismatic Protestant Identity.' In *The Anthropology of Christianity*, edited by F. Cannell, pp.163–184. London: Duke University Press.

———. 2010. 'An Anthropological Apologetics.' *South Atlantic Quarterly* 109 (4): 791–810.

Connell, John. 1978. *The End of Tradition: Country Life in Central Surrey.* London: Routledge and Kegan Paul.

Crapanzano, Vincent. 2000. *Serving the Word: Literalism in America from the Pulpit to the Bench.* New York: New Press.

———. 2007. 'Co-futures.' *American Ethnologist* 34 (3): 422–425.

Csordas, Thomas. 1994. *The Sacred Self: A Cultural Phenomenology of Charismatic Healing.* Berkeley: University of California Press.

———. 1996. 'Imaginal Performance and Memory in Ritual Healing.' In *The Performance of Healing*, edited by C. Laderman and M. Roseman. New York: Routledge.

Darwin, Charles. (2008) 1859. *On the Origin of Species.* Oxford: Oxford University Press.

Davie, Grace. 1994. *Religion in Britain Since 1945: Believing without Belonging.* Oxford: Wiley-Blackwell.

Dickson, Neil. 1997. 'Open and Closed: Brethren and Their Origins in the North East.' In *After Columba, after Calvin: Religious Community in North-East Scotland*, edited by J. Porter, pp. 151–170. Aberdeen: Aberdeen University Press.

Douglas, Mary. 1966. *Purity and Danger: An Analysis of the Concepts of Pollution and Taboo.* London: Routledge.

Durkheim, Émile. (2008) 1912. *The Elementary Forms of Religious Life.* Oxford: Oxford University Press.

Emerson, Edwin. 1960. *Comet Lore: Halley's Comet in History and Astronomy.* New York: Schilling Press.

Engelhardt, Jeffers. 2010. 'The Acoustics and Geopolitics of Orthodox Practices in the Estonian-Russian Border Region.' In *Eastern Christians in Anthropological Perspective*, edited by C. Hann and G. Hermann, pp. 101–123. Berkeley: University of California Press.

Engelke, Matthew. 2004. 'Discontinuity and the Discourse of Conversion.' *Journal of Religion in Africa* 34 (nos. 1–2): 82–109.

———. 2007. *A Problem of Presence: Beyond Scripture in an African Church.* London: University of California Press.

Etter, Roberta, and Stuart Schnelder. 1985. *Halley's Comet: Memories of 1910.* New York: Abbeville Press.

Evans-Pritchard, Edward Evan. 1976. *Witchcraft, Oracles and Magic among the Azande.* Oxford: Oxford University Press.

Faubion, James. 2001. *The Shadows and Lights of Waco: Millennialism Today.* Oxford: Princeton University Press.

Festinger, Leon. 1956. *When Prophecy Fails: A Social and Psychological Study of a Modern Group that Predicted the Destruction of the World.* New York: Harper-Torchbooks.

Foucault, Michel. 1993. 'About the Beginning of the Hermeneutics of the Self: Two Lectures at Dartmouth.' *Political Theory* 21 (2): 198–227.

Feeley-Harnik, Gillian. 1994. *The Lords Table: The Meaning of Food in Early Judaism and Christianity.* Washington, DC: Smithsonian Books.

Freud, Sigmund. (2001) 1913. *Totem and Taboo.* London: Routledge.

Geertz, Clifford. 1973. *The Interpretation of Cultures*. London: Fontana Press.

———. 2001. *Available Light: Anthropological Reflections on Philosophical Topics*. Princeton: Princeton University Press.

Gell, Alfred. 1992. 'The Technology of Enchantment and the Enchantment of Technology.' In *Anthropology, Art and Aesthetics*, edited by Jeremy Coote and Anthony Shelton, pp. 40–63. Oxford: Clarendon.

Glendinning. Tony. 2006. 'Religious Involvement, Conventional Christian and Unconventional Nonmaterialist Beliefs.' *Journal for the Scientific Study of Religion* 45 (4): 585–595.

Goethe, Johann Wolfgang von. (1807) 2008. *Elective Affinities: A Novel*. Oxford: Oxford University Press.

Guyer, Jane. 2007. 'Prophecy and the Near Future: Thought on Macroeconomic, Evangelical, and Punctuated Time.' *American Ethnologists* 34 (4): 409–450.

Handler, Richard. 1986. 'Authenticity.' *Anthropology Today* 2 (1): 2–4.

Hanganu, Gabriel. 2010. 'Eastern Christians and Religious Objects: Personal and Material Biographies Entangled.' In *Eastern Christians in Anthropological Perspective*, edited by Chris Hann and Goltz Hermann, pp. 33–55. Berkeley: University of California Press.

Hann, Chris. 2007. 'The Anthropology of Christianity per se.' *European Journal of Sociology* 48:383–410.

Harding, Susan Friend. 1991. 'Representing Fundamentalism: The Problem of the Repugnant Cultural Other.' *Social Research* 58 (2): 373–393.

———. 1994. 'Imagining the Last Days: The Politics of Apocalyptic Language.' In *Accounting for Fundamentalisms: The Dynamic Character of Movements*, edited by M. Marty and R. Appleby, pp. 57–78. Chicago: Chicago University Press.

———. 2000. *The Book of Jerry Falwell: Fundamentalist Language and Politics*. Princeton: Princeton University Press.

Heelas, Paul, Scott Lash, and Paul Morris. 1996. *Detraditionalization: Critical Reflections on Authority and Identity*. Oxford: Blackwell.

Hillis, Peter. 2002. 'Church and Society in Aberdeen and Glasgow, c. 1800–c. 2000.' *Journal of Ecclesiastical History* 53 (4): 707–734.

Hirschkind, Charles. 2001. 'The Ethics of Listening: Cassette-Sermon Audition in Contemporary Egypt.' *American Ethnologist* 28 (3): 623–649.

Howe, Richard Herbert. 1978. 'Max Weber's Elective Affinities: Sociology within the Bounds of Pure Reason.' *American Journal of Sociology* 84 (2): 366–385.

Howell, Brian. 2007. 'The Repugnant Cultural Other Speaks Back: Christian Identity as Ethnographic 'Standpoint.' *Anthropological Theory* 7 (4): 371–391.

Hubert, Henri, and Marcel Mauss. 1968. *Sacrifice: Its Nature and Function*. London: Cohen and West.

Jedrej, Charles, and Mark Nuttall. 1995. *White Settlers: The Impact of Rural Repopulation in Scotland*. London: Harwood Academic Publishers.

Jenkins, Timothy. 1999. *Religion in English Everyday Life*. Oxford: Berghahn Books.

Johnson, Twig. 1979. 'Work Together, Eat Together: Conflict and Conflict Management in a Portuguese Fishing Village.' In *North Atlantic Maritime Cultures*, edited by Raoul Andersen, pp. 241–252. London: Mouton Publishers.

Jorion, Paul. 1982. 'The Priest and the Fishermen: Sundays and Weekdays in a Former "Theocracy."' *Man*, n. s., 17 (2): 275–286.

Just, Roger. 1988. 'Anti-Clericalism and National Identity: Attitudes towards the Orthodox Church in Greece.' In *Vernacular Christianity: Essays in the Social Anthropology of Religion*, edited by Wendy James and Douglas Johnson, pp. 15–30. Oxford: JASO.

Keane, Webb. 1997a. 'From Fetishism to Sincerity: On Agency, the Speaking Subject, and Their Historicity in the Context of Religious Conversion.' *Comparative Studies in Society and History* 39 (4): 674–693.

———. 1997b. *Signs of Recognition: Powers and Hazards of Representation in an Indonesian Society*. Los Angeles: University of California Press.

———. 2002. 'Sincerity, "Modernity" and the Protestants.' *Cultural Anthropology* 17 (1): 65–92.

———. 2004. 'Language and Religion.' In *A Companion to Linguistic Anthropology*, edited by A. Duranti. Oxford: Blackwell.

———. 2006. 'Anxious Transcendence.' In *The Anthropology of Christianity*, edited by F. Cannell. London: Duke University Press.

———. 2007. *Christian Moderns: Freedom & Fetish in the Mission Encounter*. London: University of California Press.

———. 2008. 'The Evidence of the Senses and the Materiality of Religion.' *Journal of the Royal Anthropological Institute*, n. s. (14):110–127.

Keller, Eva. 2004. 'Towards Complete Clarity: Bible Study among Seventh-Day Adventists in Madagascar.' *Ethnos* 69 (1): 89–112.

———. 2005. *The Road to Clarity: Seventh-Day Adventism in Madagascar*. London: Palgrave Macmillan.

———. 2007. [Untitled reply] in Robbins, Joel. 2007. 'Continuity Thinking and the Problem of Christian Culture: Belief, Time, and the Anthropology of Christianity.' *Current Anthropology* 47 (6): 5–38.

Knipe, Ed. 1984. *Gamrie: An Exploration in Cultural Ecology*. London: University Press of America.

La Fontaine, Jean. 1998. *Speak of the Devil*. Cambridge: Cambridge University Press.

Laderman, Carol. 1996. 'The Poetics of Healing in Malay Shamanistic Performances.' In *The Performance of Healing*, edited by Carol Laderman and Marina Roseman. New York: Routledge.

Lambek, Michael. 2008. 'Value and Virtue.' *Anthropological Theory* 8 (2): 133–157.

Lima, Diana. 2012. 'Prosperity and Masculinity: Neopentecostal Men in Rio de Janerio.' *Ethnos.* 77 (3): 372–399.

Luhrmann, Tanya. 1989. *Persuasions of the Witch's Craft: Ritual Magic in Modem Culture.* Cambridge: Harvard University Press.

———. 2004. 'Metakinesis: How God Becomes Intimate in Contemporary US Christianity.' *American Anthropologist* 106 (3): 518–528.

———. 2010. 'The Absorption Hypothesis: Learning to Hear God in Evangelical Christianity.' *American Anthropologist* 112 (1): 66–78.

———. 2012. *When God Talks Back: Understanding the American Evangelical Relationship with God.* New York: Alfred A. Knopf.

Malinowski, Bronisław. 1926. *Crime and Custom in Savage Society.* London: Routledge.

———. 1927. *Sex and Repression in Savage Society.* London: Routledge.

Marty, Martin, and Scott Appleby. 1994. *Accounting for Fundamentalisms: The Dynamic Character of Movements.* Chicago: University of Chicago Press.

Marx, Karl. (1977) 1843. *Critique of Hegel's 'Philosophy of Right.'* Cambridge: Cambridge University Press.

———. (1971) 1867. *Capital: Volume One.* London: Lawrence & Wishart.

Mayblin, Maya. 2010. *Gender, Catholicism, and Morality in Brazil: Virtuous Husbands, Powerful Wives.* New York: Palgrave Macmillan.

McCrone, David. 1992. *Understanding Scotland: The Sociology of a Nation.* London: Routledge.

McDannell, Colleen. 1995. *Material Christianity: Religion and Popular Culture in America.* London: Yale University Press.

Meek, Donald. 1999. '"Fishers of Men": The 1921 Religious Revival, Its Cause, Context and Transmission.' In *After Columba, after Calvin: Religious Community in North-East Scotland,* edited by James Porter, pp. 135–142. Aberdeen: Aberdeen University Press.

Meyer, Birgit. 1999. *Translating the Devil: Religion and Modernity among the Ewe in Ghana.* Edinburgh: Edinburgh University Press.

Nadel-Klein, Jane. 2003. *Fishing for Heritage: Modernity and Loss along the Scottish Coast.* Oxford: Berg.

Needham, Rodney. 1973. *Belief, Language and Experience.* Oxford: Basil Blackwell.

Pálsson, Gísli. 1994. 'Enskilment at Sea.' *Man,* n. s., 24 (4): 901–927.

Pina-Cabral, João de. 1986. *Sons of Adam, Daughters of Eve: The Peasant World View of the Alto Minho.* Oxford: Clarendon Press.

Prattis, Ian. 1973. 'A Model of Shipboard Interaction on a Hebridean Fishing Vessel.' *Journal of the Royal Anthropological Institute* 29 (3): 210–219.

Robbins, Joel. 2003. 'What Is a Christian? Notes towards an Anthropology of Christianity.' *Religion* 33:191–199.

———. 2004. *Becoming Sinners: Christianity and Moral Torment in a Papua New Guinea Society.* Berkeley: University of California Press.

———. 2006. 'Anthropology and Theology: An Awkward Relationship?' *Anthropological Quarterly* 79 (2): 285–294.

———. 2007. 'Continuity Thinking and the Problem of Christian Culture: Belief, Time, and the Anthropology of Christianity.' *Current Anthropology* 47 (6): 5–38.

Robbins, Joel, and Matthew Engelke. 2010. 'Introduction.' *South Atlantic Quarterly* 109 (4): 623–631.

Robertson Smith, William. (1889) 1972. *The Religion of the Semites: The Fundamental Institutions.* New York: Schocken Books.

Ruel, Malcolm. 2001. 'Christians as Believers.' In *A Reader in the Anthropology of Religion*, edited by M. Lambek. Oxford: Blackwell Publishers.

Sahlins, Marshall. 1996. 'The Sadness of Sweetness: The Native Anthropology of Western Cosmology.' *Current Anthropology* 37 (3): 395–428.

Schweitzer, Albert. 2009. *The Quest of the Historical Jesus.* Memphis: General Books.

Scott, Michael. 2005. '"I Was Like Abraham": Notes on the Anthropology of Christianity from the Solomon Islands.' *Ethnos* 70 (1): 101–125.

Smilde, David. 2007. *Reason to Believe: Cultural Agency in Latin American Evangelicalism.* Berkeley: University of California Press.

Smith, Robert. 1988. *One Foot in the Sea: Fishing Villages of North East Scotland.* Edinburgh: John Donald Publishers.

Spinoza, Baruch. (2007) 1670. *Theologico-Political Treatise.* Cambridge: Cambridge University Press.

Stark, Rodney. 1999. 'Secularization, RIP.' *Sociology of Religion* 60 (3): 249–273.

Stiles, Geoffrey 1972. 'Fishermen, Wives and Radios: Aspects of Communication in a Newfoundland Fishing Community.' In *North Atlantic Fishermen: Anthropological Essays on Modern Fishing*, edited by Raoul Anderson and Cato Wadel, pp. 35–60. St John's: Memorial University of Newfoundland.

Stromberg, Peter. 1993. *Language and Self-transformation: A Study of Christian Conversion Narrative.* Cambridge: Cambridge University Press.

Tambiah, Stanley Jeyaraja. 1968. 'The Magical Power of Words.' *Man*, n. s., 3 (2): 175–208.

Taylor, Charles. 1985. 'Understanding and Ethnocentricity.' In *Philosophy and the Human Sciences: Philosophical Papers vol. 2.* Cambridge: Cambridge University Press.

———. 2007. *A Secular Age.* Cambridge: Harvard University Press.

Taylor, Lawrence. 1995. *Occasions of Faith: An Anthropology of Irish Catholics.* Philadelphia: University of Pennsylvania Press.

Thompson, Damian. 2005. *Waiting for Antichrist: Charisma and Apocalypse in a Pentecostal Church.* Oxford: Oxford University Press.

Thomson, James. 1849. *The Value and Importance of the Scottish Fisheries.* London: Smith, Elder.

Tomlinson, Matt. 2006. 'The Limits of Meaning in Fijian Methodist Sermons.' In *The Limits of Meaning: Case Studies in the Anthropology of Christianity*, edited by Matthew Engelke and Matt Tomlinson, pp. 129–146. Oxford: Berghahn Books.

Tomlinson, Matt. 2009. *In God's Image: The Metaculture of Fijian Christianity.* London: University of California Press.

Tsintjilonis, Dimitri, 2007. 'The Death Bearing Senses in Tana Toraja.' *Ethnos* 72 (2): 173–194.

Tumminia, Diana. 2005. *When Prophecy Never Fails: Myth and Reality in a Flying-Saucer Group.* Oxford: Oxford University Press.

Turner, Edith. 1996. *The Hands Feel It: Healing and Spirit Presence among a North Alaskan People.* DeKalb: Northern Illinois University Press.

Tylor, Edward Burnett. (1871) 2010. *Primitive Culture.* Cambridge: Cambridge University Press.

Voas, David. 2006. 'Religious Decline in Scotland: New Evidence on Timing and Spatial Patterns.' *Journal for the Scientific Study of Religion* 45 (1): 107–118.

Wagner, Roy. 1978. *Lethal Speech: Daribi Myth as Symbolic Obviation.* New York: Cornell University Press.

———. 1986. *Symbols That Stand for Themselves.* Chicago: University of Chicago Press.

Weber, Max. 1968. *Economy and Society.* New York: Bedminster Press.

———. 1977. *The Protestant Ethic and the Spirit of Capitalism.* London: Harper Collins.

———. 1978a. 'Bureaucracy.' In *From Max Weber: Essays in Sociology,* edited by H. H. Gerth and C. Wright Mills pp. 196–244. New York: Oxford University Press.

———. 1978b. 'Religious Rejections of the World and Their Directions.' In *From Max Weber: Essays in Sociology,* edited by H. H. Gerth and C. Wright Mills pp. 323–361. New York: Oxford University Press.

———. 1978c. 'Science as a Vocation.' In *From Max Weber: Essays in Sociology,* edited by H. H. Gerth and C. Wright Mills pp. 129–157. New York: Oxford University Press.

———. 1978d. 'The Social Psychology of the World Religions.' In *From Max Weber: Essays in Sociology,* edited by H. H. Gerth and C. Wright Mills pp. 267–301. New York: Oxford University Press.

Webster, Joseph. 2012. 'The Immanence of Transcendence: God and the Devil on the Aberdeenshire Coast.' *Ethnos.* DOI:10.1080/00141844.2 012.688762.

———. 2013. 'The Eschatology of Global Warming in a Scottish Fishing Village.' *Cambridge Anthropology* 31 (1): 68–84.

Žižek, Slavoj. 2006. 'Notes towards a Politics of Bartleby: The Ignorance of Chicken.' *Comparative American Studies* 4 (4): 375–394.

Websites

FIS. 2009. Fish Information and Services: World News. http://fis.com/fis /worldnews/worldnews.asp?l=e&ndb=1&id=38405 [Accessed December 9, 2010].

GENUKI. 2011. Aberdeenshire. http://www.genuki.org.uk/big/sct/ABD/ [Accessed January 6, 2011].

God TV. 2011. Israel Trees. http://www.god.tv/israeltrees [Accessed January 7, 2011].

SCROL. 2001. Comparative Population Profile: Gardenstown Locality Scotland. http://www.scrol.gov.uk/scrol/browser/profile.jsp?profile= Population&mainArea=gardenstown&mainLevel=Locality [Accessed June 3, 2010].

Index

CPSIA information can be obtained at www.ICGtesting.com
Printed in the USA
LVOW10s2238140716

496339LV00008B/31/P